THE METHOD AND THEORY
OF ETHNOLOGY

THE
METHOD AND
THEORY OF
ETHNOLOGY

An Essay in Criticism

By PAUL RADIN

With an Introduction by
ARTHUR J. VIDICH

BERGIN & GARVEY PUBLISHERS, INC.
MASSACHUSETTS

First published in 1987 by
Bergin & Garvey Publishers, Inc.
670 Amherst Road
South Hadley, Massachusetts 01075

789   987654321

Printed in the United States of America

Library of Congress Cataloging-in-Publication Data

Radin, Paul, 1883–1959.
   The method and theory of ethnology.

   Reprint. Originally published: New York: Basic
Books, 1966. With new chapter.
   Includes indexes.
   1. Ethnology—Methodology.   2. Ethnology—Philosophy.
3. Boas, Franz, 1858–1942.   I. Title.
GN345.R33   1987   306'.01'8   86-29921
ISBN 0-89789-117-1
ISBN 0-89789-118-X (pbk.)

Contents

Introduction

ARTHUR J. VIDICH

Paul Radin is known primarily as a substantive ethnographer who devoted his major efforts to a lifetime study of the Winnebago Indians, and he would have preferred to be known as such. This book, *The Method and Theory of Ethnology,* represents an unwilling commentary on issues with which he did not wish to preoccupy himself but which he was driven to discuss because he thought that anthropology was drifting in the wrong direction. However, because he was so thoroughly identified with the urgency of the historical task of describing and comprehending the primitive world as it was while he was alive, he felt a responsibility to state explicitly, rather than only through the example of his own studies, wherein anthropology had made its theoretical and practical errors. That he was eminently qualified to perform this task is attested by the fact that no one else has so clearly and with such breadth of vision subjected anthropological studies to a critical appraisal.

Yet in spite of the breadth and wisdom of *The Method and Theory of Ethnology*, there is little evidence that Radin's insights had any effect on redirecting the course of ethnological studies. Social anthropologists remain committed to the same values and erroneous methods they held to thirty years ago when this study was published. One might have expected that ethnology would have responded to such an insightful dissection of its theoretical weaknesses with a critical re-examination of itself. That it would not do so was quite adequately explained by Radin in his ethnologic reply to R. R. Marrett's review of this book:

I would indeed be a Don Quixote if I thought the windmills would cease revolving merely because I tilted against them. But at times it is of value to tilt against them simply in order to call the attention of the world to the fact that they are present and revolving "in their own sweet way" and that they will continue to do so "as long as the spirit of Man bloweth where it listeth."[1]

Radin was too much a realist to think that the professional ways of anthropologists would change simply because they had been described and ana-

[1] *American Anthropologist*, vol. 36, no. 2, p. 316, April–June 1934.

lyzed. Certainly none of the ethnologists' primitives changed as a result of the monographs that were written about them. Man's wondrous immunity to criticism is a hard-won first principle of ethnological science, and it can be expected to hold as true for the primitives as for ourselves, even those among us who are hallowed by the prestigious symbols of science and professionalism.

It would, therefore, be as bootless today as it would have been quixotic for Radin to try to explain why the windmills have continued to revolve. Yet thirty years *have* passed and some changes have taken place; many new tribes have been studied, many new techniques have been introduced, fewer references are made to primitives and many more to underdeveloped societies. There are now base-line constructs, cross-cultural files, and linguistic models. Many practitioners now expertly apply the findings of anthropology, and finally there are many more anthropologists to remind us of the progress of their science.

Though Radin's strictures apply today as much as before, it is less clear how his model of criticism applies to the New Anthropology. In this brief essay I will try to explain the critical perspective Radin applied and to suggest with a few key illustrations how this perspective is still valid for a criticism of the New Anthropology.

Radin's Conception of Anthropology

Radin's perspective was that of the humanist historian who attempts to understand society from the point of view of its meaning to its participants. When one approaches primitive society with this attitude, it is clear that there is no way to keep the individual and his actions from being the central datum of social science investigation. To the outsider unversed in technical anthropology, this does not seem to be a particularly novel or startling point of departure; just the reverse, from a common-sense point of view it seems to be the natural beginning and ending point for the study of men. But it is much easier for the novice to see and, ironically, for the professional to forget that anthropology begins and ends with the study of *men* (not Man in general) than it is actually to conduct one's studies with this in mind. The assumption of this common-sense attitude raised some harrowing problems for the student of primitive men because the presuppositions and conceptions of the primitive view of the world are so alien to Westerners, who, nevertheless, have appointed themselves the examiners and interpreters of the history, psychology, and organization of non-Western traditions. This simple proposition, which contains so many hidden problems, was Radin's beginning point.

First, one has to ask if it is humanly possible to understand and explain the primitive world when as Western observers we are so inevitably bound to our own vision historically determined by Western styles of thought, prejudices, and intellectual traditions. It is apparent that anyone who could write a book like *The Method and Theory of Ethnology* had contemplated all the inner complexities of this problem only to discover such deep differences in initial presuppositions between ourselves and the primitives as to make impossible a full inner understanding of them. However, having seen the deep gap between his own and his subjects' systems of comprehension, Radin used this observation as the foundation on which to build all his work. In effect his answer to the impossibility of the anthropologist's task was that "although it couldn't be done, you have to do it anyway." His life work constituted an attempt to refute his own initial observation, and because he saw the contradiction so clearly and consistently he was able to face squarely all of the methodological and theoretical issues peculiar to the ethnological craft.

Realizing that there was no easy way to study primitive society on its own terms, Radin was forced to confront some exceedingly difficult prac-

tical problems. He felt he could not rely on a then
current practice of training and employing natives
to write reports on themselves and their own customs. While he thought that such documents could
be extremely useful, in that they also added to the
record, this shifting of the burden of observation
onto the native did not absolve the anthropologist
from his own obligation as interpreter. Even the
native reporter was biased and provided no more
basis for placid acceptance of his biases than those
of the anthropological observer. If one was to be an
anthropologist, there was no way to accept any data
at face value, since all data are valid only in the full
awareness of the time and place they are collected
and the quality of their source.

This did not mean that there was anything wrong
with a native's being an anthropologist, but it did
mean that his work would inevitably be different
from that of the alien anthropologist. This is not a
question of validity or reliability but rather the
more fundamental question of a difference in two
worlds of understanding. Radin was much too
aware of the work of classical historians to fail to
see the validity of an inside perspective, but it was
one thing for Herodotus to write history and quite
another thing for a primitive to engage in similar
activities under the guidance of a Western anthropologist, since this merely permitted the an-

thropologist to screen himself behind the native whom he had trained and engaged to make observations.

It was equally illegitimate for the anthropologist to comprehend primitive life wholly from the perspective of Western values. This is easy enough to agree with when one considers the reports of Christian missionaries and Western traders, explorers, and administrators who have left us with such images as pagan savagery, primitive childishness, victims of unquestioned custom, or simple-minded, irrational, nonlogical souls incapable of individuality. However, it is more difficult to see that the point applies equally to any social science point of view used to study and evaluate primitive life on the basis of scientific categories which are themselves peculiar to the Western world. This is not to say that one must work without categories but that the categories that one employs and the problems they imply must have some heuristic relation to the data, in this case the world of the primitives. One of the risks of being both a social scientist and a Westerner is that one brings with him the burden of current social scientific intellectual thought styles, which are made all the more onerous when they are legitimized by a tradition of professional thought rather than by the world of experience of his subjects.

To know the primitive world requires that the anthropologist be wholly aware of the historical context and the personal factors relevant to every observation he makes before he can be sure of its significance. We know from studies of Western society made by observers who have spent a lifetime imbedded in their own culture that to reach this level of sophistication is at best extremely difficult, and moreover that any two highly intelligent and educated observers, because of differences in personal and intellectual experience, may see the same things differently. When one remembers that the anthropologist enters native society as a stranger unversed in its history and language, it is apparent that his problem is much more difficult than that of the social scientist who studies his own society. It was probably Margaret Mead's supreme self-assurance that led Radin to criticize her so sharply on this point. He says:

. . . it is the amazing assumption that any outsider can obtain the type of information she specifies except after an intensive study of a lifetime. Indeed, I seriously doubt whether an outsider can ever obtain it. And yet . . . she . . . claim[s] to have accomplished all this in investigations that never lasted longer than a year and generally were of shorter duration. That she carefully organized her method of approach does not give her the qualifications which only a long and protracted residence and a complete command of the language can possibly bestow. Of what avail is it that she says,

> Behind every general statement about the behavior of children in Manus and Samoa lies a long line of observations, which are not made at random and recorded casually, but are made systematically about a selected group of children, on points which preliminary investigation has shown to be most significant. . . . In Manus I studied the effect of the personality of fathers upon the personality of the sons whom they have reared.

Any adequate study of this kind, even under the most favorable conditions, can be done only after many years of intensive application. What one gets within a year, or for that matter within five years, even if endowed with unusual penetration into the personality of others, is bound to be superficial. . . . And that is precisely what her published work demonstrates.[2]

What Radin is objecting to is not Mead's ethnologic project or the fact that her work, like all ethnological investigation, has ultimately a subjective dimension. He regards her work as essentially unhistorical in that she does not deal over a period of time with "real and specific" men and women who live in a historical tradition. Short-term field studies

[2] *The Method and Theory of Ethnology* (hereafter cited as *MTE*), pp. 178–179. The quote from Mead is from her essay "More Comprehensive Field Methods," *American Anthropologist*, vol. 35, pp. 11–12, 1933.

pose formidable historical limitations on the investigator, who by the measure of his length of stay
must be all the more historically conscious and
humble in the face of his data.

It becomes a patent impossibility and an illusion
to think that an observer can study an alien world
over a period of a year or two and feel any assurance in what he says about it: he faces so many
subtleties and nuances of meaning of which he is
not aware, that any understandings must necessarily
be crude and proximate. One can gain a measure of
assurance about his data only when he knows it
from as many angles and over as long a time as possible, and even then his results remain proximate.

Radin committed himself to this type of depth
study, and as he became successively more involved
in the Winnebago Indians he learned that each new
level of comprehension and insight gave him a different understanding of and posed further problems for interpreting Winnebago society. The
meaning of this is concretely illustrated in Chapter
VII of this book, where, through a vast range of
different levels of knowledge collected at different
times, Radin interprets Rave's account of the introduction of the Peyote cult into his tribe. In this
masterful methodological exercise he shows how
each increase in depth of perception gained over
time evokes a more total awareness of the complex-

ity of the material. The complexity is given both by Radin's experience and by the events as they evolve, and each is accounted for in carrying out the analysis.

Lest the reader think that Radin did not carry his approach beyond a methodological exercise, it is worth mentioning here his study *The Trickster*,[3] in which he shows in detail what he means by working from detailed protocols to interpretations of data. In *The Trickster* we see who said what, when, and in what context, how it is related to what others said, and how the myth as expressed by the Winnebago being studied is related to its manifestations elsewhere. Moreover, the reporting is so complete and sensitive to the classic themes of mythology that it is possible for Karl Kerenyi in his commentary in the same book to co-ordinate Radin's treatment of the trickster theme with the classical studies of Hermes as well as Goethe's *Reynard the Fox* and Thomas Mann's Felix Krull: "The bourgeois trickster of the last surviving social order." In *The Trickster* Radin provides much more than an illustration; he shows what, under the care of a practiced hand and a keen awareness, anthropology could become. Given his awareness of ethnological data, it is understandable why Radin continuously returned to the Winnebago for further insights and

[3] New York: Philosophical Library, 1956.

why at the time of his death he was still working
with informants whom he had known fifty years
earlier.

Radin's response to his data made his work a
daring and risky venture unlike the work of many
ethnologists. Since there were so many groups to
study and so few anthropologists to study them, the
established professional procedure was to make a
one- or two-year field trip to a tribe, write a monograph, and then turn to another group. In this way
anthropologists hoped to learn a little about many
different groups on the assumption that, given the
rapid disappearance of primitive life, broad cover-
age was a worthy ground on which to concede investigation in depth. In choosing the alternative
enterprise of attempting to describe and understand
a specified group over a long period of time, Radin
appeared to isolate himself in the peculiarities of
Winnebago history and society to the point of
standing alone in both his ethnological understanding and in the specific problems he posed. The more
deeply he engaged himself in Winnebago life, the
more he developed a distinct perspective on primitive society and on anthropology in general.

However, out of what appeared to be a unique
attitude and a specific commitment to a particular
group, Radin achieved two major and singular ac-
complishments. First, he has left us with what is

perhaps the most complete and detailed long-term record in monographs and field notes that we have of a priimtive society as seen by a single observer through all the stages of his own intellectual history. And second, he developed an extraordinarily subtle awareness of what the world of an alien primitive society was like. It was this latter viewpoint that gave him the capacity to project himself into and interpret primitive societies which he knew only through the work of others. This, in fact, is the significance of Radin's last opus as embodied in *The World of Primitive Man,* that great synthetic work which could only have been written after a lifetime of study and reflection informed by a deep familiarity with concrete detail.

Claude Lévi-Strauss seems to misunderstand the value of long-term depth studies when he says, "When one confines oneself to the study of a single society, one may do valuable work. Experience shows that the best monographs are generally produced by investigators who have lived and worked in one particular region. But they must forego conclusions about other regions." [4] On the contrary, Radin could become an interpreter of primitive society in the four corners of the globe specifically because his initial yardstick was built out of an intimate familiarity with the primitive indivdual and

[4] *Structural Anthropology* (New York: Basic Books, 1963), p. 12.

xx   Introduction

the deeper tone of his historical and social life.
Radin had learned to see primitive men as people
on their own terms and because of this trained understanding could project himself even through the
work of others into the social world of societies he
had not personally encountered in the field.
There is no implication here that Radin worked
from the assumption that all primitives are similar,
though he did not exclude the possibility of a qualitative distinctness of primitive life and mind. He
held this view in spite of the other implication
throughout his work of the existence of universal
dimensions of human psychology which exist outside the framework of history. It was in fact one of
the historian's problems to discover what in human
psychology might be universal, the better to be able
to distinguish the primitive from the civilized.[5] In
other words, Radin took the radical historicist point
of view in order to be able to arrive at his generalizations out of historically specific instances rather
than *ad hoc* predetermined categories.

This unique perspective resulted not simply because of Radin's particular exposure to primitive
life—other anthropologists have been exposed without producing simliar results—but also because of

[5] The most fully developed statement of this theme is to be found
in the work of Stanley Diamond. See especially his "The Search for
the Primitive," in *Man's Image in Medicine and Anthropology* (New
York: International Universities Press, 1963).

his particular attitudes to Western society. He saw the Western world as a conquest-civilization which had managed to incorporate its intellectual strata into the task of providing justifying ideologies for conquest and domination. It appeared to him that the values of social science itself were frequently only reflections of the dominant social, political, and economic currents peculiar to the civilization in which they existed. To the extent that this was the case he saw that studies of primitive life continuously face the risk of reflecting ourselves and the established framework of Western thought more than the inner dimensions of primitive society.

As a student of society, the anthropologist has the special problem of being imbued not only with his professional perceptual baggage but also with his own culture's perceptual blinders. For example, what does it mean to use the TAT or Rorschach as a way of understanding primitive psychology unless these devices are standardized to the meaning categories of the primitives? Any results stemming from the application to primitives of tests developed by Westerners are as interesting as projective data on Westerners as they are clues to primitive personality. In Radin's view, the task of understanding the primitive could not be accomplished without alienating oneself from the dominant and accepted values of contemporary Western civilization. Seen in this light, the fact that anthropology was a legitimate part of Western institutions and an academic discipline as well was a disadvantage for which one had to make allowances in his work.

The first task was to become aware that such a disadvantage exists, for without this knowledge one could not know his own sources of identification and hence his observations would willy-nilly be subject to unrecognized value predispositions which, though they might be currently acceptable, merely reflected a particular stage of Western expansion. A condition for achieving this deeper awareness would be an inner knowledge of Western history, its values, and the role of Western society in the evolution of the world. In other words, personal alienation is a professional requirement for the ethnological observer, and the alienation that is achieved must be based on a full intellectual awareness of that from which one is alienated.[6] It is very important to emphasize this because alienation has not been an atypical psychology for anthropologists. In fact, in the past, anthropology has provided an outlet similar to the role of the frontier in American history for those within American academic

[6] This theme was originally developed in my review essay of Radin's *Festschrift, Culture and History,* edited by Stanley Diamond (New York: Columbia University Press, 1960), in the Brandeis University *Justice,* June 19, 1961.

life who have been personally disaffected from and uncommitted to the established order. The point is that one must distinguish the shallow escapist forms of "alienation" from a fully aware intellectual alienation which has been the anthropological heritage. The latter can only arise in one who has personally and intellectually confronted his role in his own society. It is in this that Radin achieved what is perhaps his greatest accomplishment, for through his studies of Western history, philosophy, economics, politics, and psychology he gained a personal perspective that enabled him intellectually to comprehend his own history and his own immediate experience, thus freeing himself from any narrowly restricting viewpoints governed by *ad hoc* acceptance of Western values or by personal disaffection from them. His commitment was to classical scholarship, to an understanding of human history in the broadest meaning of the phrase, and to the task of understanding the range of human nature in both its specific manifestations in particular cultures and on a higher universal plane. In Radin there is the quality of the deeply liberated intellect, a man who saw that the anthropologist like other social scientists was engaged in a lifelong dialogue with his own society and that there is no way to escape this problem. To avoid this confrontation is to turn what should be a conversation into a soliloquy, whose results are only a projection of the investigator himself.

In *The Method and Theory of Ethnology* Radin applied his perspective to the work of other anthropologists as well as to anthropologists themselves. Thus, for example, what caught his attention in Boas's work was that Boas employed the attitude of a nineteenth-century biologist-geographer-naturalist in his study of men. Out of this observation Radin was able to show how Boas's personal background, intellectual development, and theoretical attitude colored his vision of the primitive world. In making this observation Radin was much too sensitive a critic to imply that it vitiated Boas's work: he showed only how it influenced Boas's work, granting always that valuable observations and results could emerge because of or in spite of his theoretical presuppositions and personal inclinations.

Radin's analysis of Boas took account of the fact that the way in which he viewed primitive life changed in accordance with changes in himself; just as there is no way to understand primitive life except by understanding the role of the individual, so there is no way of understanding the role of the ethnographic record without also understanding the ethnographer. What was unique about Boas was that he was always willing to be influenced by his own experience, so that in the course of his career he admitted a multiplicity of theoretical perspectives. Although Radin was very sympathetic to this aspect of Boas's greatness, he also saw that since Boas occupied such a towering position in the development of anthropology, his changes in perspective had a decisive effect on the evolution of American ethnology. Radin used this insight as a basis for examining the rest of post-Boasian anthropology in the United States.

Boas was personally a powerful figure who did not tolerate theoretical or ideological differences in his students. In this as well as in other respects, as has been observed by Stanley Edgar Hyman,[7] he was similar to Freud. He expected his students to take his advice as to the problems they should study and where they should study them, and he took an intellectual and personal dislike to students who acted independently. Boas asked for and received a strong sense of identification from his successful students, so much so that some of them affectionately referred to him as "Papa." Through this mechanism of intense personal involvement and loyalty, Boas was able to make a generation of students an extension of himself and his ideas.

Boas had the added quality of being quite dog-

[7] Stanley Edgar Hyman, "Freud and Boas: Secular Rabbis?" *Commentary*, pp. 264–267, March 1954.

matic about his position, but the position did not remain constant over a period of time. This had far-reaching effects, for it meant that any particular group of students who encountered him in a given phase of his work became identified with that particular portion of Boas's viewpoint which was then current. Depending on a particular student's capacity to maintain some flexibility and his ability later in his career to disidentify from Boas, this meant that the work of Boas's former students tended to reflect the particular phase of Boas's thinking with which they had come into contact while they were his students. Any particular student then took as his intellectual point of departure that point of view to which he was exposed. Insofar as Boas's students dominated the field, American anthropology became an elaboration of different phases of Boas's career, each phase being represented by a different age and sex grouping of his students. Though he does not say so explicitly, Radin saw these interpersonal mechanisms at play and he used this observation as the co-ordinating principle for his evaluation of the American ethnologists' work which he saw as limited by the theoretical boundaries Boas had set. The assignment of a key place to Boas is evidenced in the organization of *The Method and Theory of Ethnology,* in which Radin first establishes the origin of American ethnology's central problems in Boas and then proceeds to trace out how subsequent workers began with his presuppositions and elaborated ethnology within his framework.

What this meant for ethnology was that it continued in a tradition that did not take account of the major discoveries and theoretical viewpoints of late nineteenth-century European social science, which Boas either rejected or did not know and which as a consequence were not responded to by his students. One result was that his students continued to study culture traits, culture items, trait complexes, and native and natural areas on the model of physical particles and biological processes even after Boas had dropped these concepts himself. In fact some students carried these concepts to their logical extreme by quantifying abstracted cultural traits to such a point that primitive society was presented in mathematical terms. In the meantime, however, the great nineteenth-century historical researches had been written, Marx had completed his analysis of Western institutions, Weber's historical sociology was in print, and psychoanalysis had come into the world. That Boas did not incorporate these developments into his work does not constitute grounds for criticizing him, but the fact that his students were so deeply committed to him that they also, with few exceptions, failed to incorporate them was of prime importance, for it meant that anthropology did not respond to the currents of Western thought that most explicitly tried to comprehend the role of Western society in world history. Any anthropologist who failed to participate in his own intellectual history would by the degree of his nonparticipation also fail in his anthropological enterprise, since he could not come to conscious intellectual terms with the reasons for doing what he was doing. How much of anthropology is only a glorification, direct or indirect, of Western world dominance is a question that has not yet been analyzed or discussed by anyone.

What was unique about Boas's student, Radin, is that while also enormously impressed by teacher and master, he responded to the master's most radical lesson—namely, the *example* of intellectual independence. He learned that to try to identify with Boas as a totality was to identify with a complex set of biological and physical models adequate for Boas but not for himself, and to identify with one segment of Boas was unnecessarily restricting. Radin elected to discover his own problems in relation to his own personal experience and intellectual development. In this fundamental sense he emulated Boas, though in Radin's case he identified with a quite different set of intellectual developments which he thought were more relevant to understanding his data and to his conception of what ethnology should be. As the reader will see, the writing of *The Method and Theory of Ethnology* was at once an act of disidentification from Boas and an evaluation of ethnology as a whole from the point of view of the social and psychological methods and theories Radin had discovered himself.

Radin was extraordinarily sensitive to the specificity of history and to the historically determined role of the individual in determining its course. He saw men as imaginative and creative actors, always capable of exceeding the bounds of their own history in ways that made it difficult, if not impossible, to know on the basis of past events what future they would create. One could only know what men might become by knowing what men have been in the past. Because of this, Radin felt with Maitland that anthropology had the choice "between being history or nothing."

Radin's conception of history was very much like that of R. G. Collingwood, who argued that the study of human nature was not only distorted but broke down when conducted by analogy to the natural sciences: ". . . the science of human nature was a false attempt—falsified by the analogy of science—to understand the mind itself, and . . .

whereas the right way of investigating nature is by
the methods called scientific, the right way of investigating the mind is by the methods of history." [8]
What is individually human is revealed by the
actions men enact. Nowadays it is not even fashion-
able to talk about "human nature" because everything we observe is already culture and a pattern of
culture and the individual is seen simply as social-
ized, acculturated, and highly plastic and malle-
able to the demands of culture and society. In this
perspective individuals readily become abstracted
into a generalized conception of Man. Thus it becomes possible to talk about the Superorganic or
Man and His Works as if there were no specific
men involved. In this attitude the quality of being
human gets lost and Man becomes reified, just as at
other times Human Nature and Culture have taken
on a similar aspect.

Radin is very specific about what he means by
history, even though the simplicity of his definition
may leave disappointed the reader who feels that
complexity, rigorousness, and scientic apparatus
are signs of intellectual respectability.

The [historical] task, let me insist, is always the same:
a description of a specific period, and as much of the

[8] R. G. Collingwood, *The Idea of History* (New York: Oxford University Press, 1956), p. 209.

past and as much of the contacts with other cultures as is necessary for the elucidation of the particular period.

. . . This can be done only by an intensive and continuous study of a particular tribe, a thorough knowledge of the language, and an adequate body of texts; and this can be accomplished only if we realize, once and for all, that we are dealing with specific, not generalized, men and women, and with specific, not generalized, events. But the recognition of specific men and women should bring with it the realization that there are all types of individuals and that it is not, for instance, a Crow Indian who has made such and such a statement, uttered such and such a prayer, but a particular Crow Indian. It is this particularity that is the essence of all history. . . .[9] In addition, even if we realize that the history of a culture is unprocurable, no description ever carries conviction unless its recorder is convinced that it has had a history." [10]

It is from this vantage point that Radin criticizes as pseudo-history the work of Kroeber, Wissler, Sapir, Benedict, Mead, Rivers, Tylor, and the so-called German Historical School of anthropologists. His argument against these authors' conceptions of history is best illustrated by his critique of Sapir, whose essay "Time Perspective in Aborigi-

[9] *MTE*, pp. 184–185.
[10] *MTE*, p. 177.

nal American Culture" [11] has since been treated as a
classic of ingenuity in historical reconstruction. It
is worth repeating Radin's criticism of Sapir's essay
at some length because it is fundamental to an understanding of both the present volume and
Radin's work as a whole.

Sapir prefaces his study with the significant remarks
that

> . . . one of the characteristic traits of history is its emphasis
> on the individual and personal. . . . The historical recon-
> struction of the cultural anthropologist can only deal with
> generalized events and individualities. . . . This limitation
> . . . need not in the least obscure the application of historical
> methods to the field of anthropology.[12]

I must insist that if this really were so, if the reconstruction of aboriginal cultures were actually limited in
this manner, then it would most definitely preclude the
application of historical methods to the field. Even if
we were to grant the justification of substituting conceptualized events and conceptualized individuals for
real events and real individuals, which no historian
would conceivably do because it is at bottom quite meaningless, one might pertinently ask how Sapir arrived at
his notion of the generalized event or generalized individual. He nowhere vouchsafes us this information. But
to continue: "These generalized events and individu-

[11] *Geological Survey of Canada,* Anthropological Series, No. 13.
[12] E. Sapir, "Time Perspective . . .," p. 4.

alities introduce a purely quantitative, not qualitative, correction into our initial ideal of historical treatment." [13] If I follow Sapir's argument here, he first admits that history deals with specific individuals and events, that in the reconstruction of the history of aboriginal culture it is impossible to obtain the requisite information with regard to these individuals and events, and that therefore we must operate with generalized events and individualities! Since, however, the latter do not properly exist, we must, so to speak, re-endow them with as much reality as we can; and since we cannot give them a qualitative correction, we must give them a quantitative one! In other words, we are asked to devitalize something which we have never known and then to endow this unknown something with a new life and assume that what we have breathed into it is the life it originally possessed. This is certainly a most amazing type of procedure.[14]

It is clear from the above analysis that Radin has cut through the unexamined magical substructure of Sapir's analysis: he specifically points to Sapir the magician when he characterizes him as "breathing life" into something which originally did not possess it. This level of criticism, which cuts through the fundamental metaphors of a discipline, reveals the measure of historical conscious-

[13] *Ibid.*
[14] *MTE*, pp. 55–57.

ness which Radin brought to his work. As a culture historian he was therefore able to see that ethnology could not aspire to the exactness of the natural and physical sciences as far as logical methods were concerned and that ethnology "need properly have no purpose, any more than a description of the civilization of Greece or England has a purpose, over and above that of being a specific account of a given culture" and that the lack of a scientific method does not interfere with "the correctness of the pictures Thucydides drew of Greece, Gibbon of Rome, and Burckhardt of the Italian Renaissance." [15]

When one combines this historical attitude with the knowledge that the ethnological observer is himself a historical creature subject to new planes of understanding as his intellectual vision grows, it is apparent that the ethnologist can never be sure that he has exhausted all the possibilities of his data at any particular stage of his research. One is forced continuously to entertain provisional attitudes toward one's "conclusions" since one cannot know in advance that later work and further information will not lead to different planes of understanding. Radin "solved" this problem in the only way possible for a historically minded ethnologist. On the

---

[15] It was in this sense that in spite of Sapir's and Mead's strictures on history, Radin could not accept their work as he could that of Gibbon or Burckhardt.

one hand he never stopped studying the Winnebago, and on the other hand he never assumed a
final attitude toward his data. As a consequence he
never produced a "definitive" study or a closed
system of analysis that might interfere with his ob-
servational freedom. Everything must remain provisional, not only because of the obvious factor of
social change, but also because of the constant am-
biguity of the human condition. Yet this did not
make Radin an eclectic. Quite the contrary, a willingness to admit the empirical world in all its complexity made it all the more necessary to begin one's
work with an explicit point of view and with a
problem, no matter how provisional these might be.

It was the openness of Radin's system that enabled him to incorporate such vast amounts of
empirical data into his substantive work. What he
could do is best illustrated in his books *Primitive
Religion* and *Primitive Man as a Philosopher*. In
these books he examines the origins of religion in
relation to individual psychology, the social and
economic functions of religion, the relation between religion and authority, the distinctions between primitive and Western religions, and the
role of the thinker as contrasted with that of the
man of action. Because of his world-wide grasp of
ethnological researches and his ability to select and
reject on systematic rather than personal grounds,

he was able to present in *The World of Primitive Man* a comprehensive and systematic analysis of primitive life and a typology of culture history without at the same time devitalizing primitive men as persons. Having arrived at a way of handling empirical material that was true to the meaning categories of the primitives and yet which allowed him to make general statements about primitive psychology, society, and history, he was in a unique position to evaluate the ethnological researches of others.

For example, he was able to assess the work of E. B. Tylor without falling into the trap of being mystified at his being the "father" of anthropology. While professional academic anthropology was venerating Tylor as its culture hero, Radin treated him in the context of his time and place. Tylor, after all, worked at a time when the empirical data of anthropology were not only exceedingly limited but also quite primitive. However, he had worked out a conception of culture that allowed him to order the data he had available. Radin saw that such a gross conception of culture as Tylor had formulated was not serviceable for an analysis of the data of later ethnological researchers. To make the concept of culture the key concept and the supreme ordering device for all ethnological data prevented the development of more refined categories of social analysis, eliminated the existence of individuals, and insofar as culture *per se* was studied, destroyed history. Tylor, merely out of necessity, had used culture as a kind of grab-bag concept. To the extent that later anthropologists fixated on culture as an object of study, they were left in a position from which their only focus of investigation was the study of everything; and as the data accumulated—as literally mountains of monographs were published—the task of synthesis came more and more to focus on the relating of disembodied facts or the *ad hoc* collection of culture inventories. Ultimately this led to a formless eclecticism of facts in which culture itself was reified to such a point that at present it seems to be and do everything and anything. At the stage when this occurred, anthropology was left without a basis for formulating specific problems derived from the empirical worlds of the observed and the observer. In this view, the pre-eminence of the culture concept represents the defeat of any anthropology that would attempt to remain true to values other than those of Western scientific and academic professionalism.[16]

Radin astutely saw that whenever a science lacks

[16] Best exemplified in the work of A. Kroeber and C. Kluckhohn, *Culture: A Critical Review of Concepts and Definitions*, Papers of the Peabody Museum of Archeology and Ethnology, Cambridge, Harvard University, Vol. 47, No. 1, 1952.

problems, its practitioners tend to become obsessed with methods, forgetting that "a method, after all, is a varying procedure changing with the nature of the facts studied and the problems posited." It was in the light of these observations that Radin analyzed the trend to quantification in both American and European ethnology. When Radin talked about the quantification of anthropology, he meant "the equating of the data of culture with those of the natural sciences, the analysis of a culture into its constituent elements, and the attempt to establish time sequences." To approach ethnology from any of these perspectives usually meant that the ethnologist reduced his cultural data to unit characters and then proceeded to treat his selected unit characters as the objects of analysis. Out of this came evolutionary studies, trait constructs, distributional analyses, and eventually cross-cultural trait comparisons. It is Radin's contention that the attempt to quantify data not only destroys the specific validity of ethnological observations but also leads to the scientific cul-de-sac of making methodological rather than substantive problems the primary concern. Radin was not alone in reacting against quantitative methods, for Radcliffe-Brown, Malinowski, Benedict, and Mead did too. However, as the reader will see in the pages that follow, the reactions of these ethnologists led to alternative approaches that remained equally nonhistorical and antithetical to the role of the individual in historical analysis.

Radin and Lowie

In a field so important as anthropology, it is surprising that so few attempts have been made to analyze critically its ideological and perspectivistic presuppositions.[17] There is no doubt that the vastness and eclecticism of the field have made this a particularly difficult task. It is perhaps also true that those who are most deeply committed are least likely to step aside to view themselves and their work from a vantage point other than the one to which they owe allegiance. Radin, who was cer-

[17] In a recent essay, "Objectivity in Anthropology," *Current Anthropology*, vol. 5, no. I, pp. 47–55, 1964, Jacques J. Maquet analyzes the colonial social and political factors which in the past have conditioned the quality, scope, and bias of African ethnology. To my knowledge this is the first serious effort to do a sociology of ethonological knowledge since Radin wrote his book. Maquet's essay is significant because he has reopened the lines of internal criticism which Radin took as his point of departure in Chapter IV, "The Factors in the Determination of the Ethnological Record." In writing the pages that follow, the greatest help I have received has been from students who over the past four years have participated in my anthropological theory seminar at the Graduate Faculty of the New School for Social Research. I wish especially to take this occasion to acknowledge my indebtedness to Dr. Philippa Strum, Peter Ries, and Benjamin Klienberg, whose work on Lowie and DuBois I have drawn upon freely.

tainly on the professional margins of the field, having for one thing never been committed to a school or an institution of higher learning, never suffered the disadvantages of being an insider. However, as is well known, the great advances in science have frequently been made by academic outsiders who have been able to bring fresh and novel perspectives to a body of data. Neither Darwin nor Morgan ever held academic chairs, and Tylor was not academically trained. As anthropology over the course of time has become more and more accepted in accredited and established institutions of higher learning, so, in direct ratio, has its accumulated "knowledge" become more sacred and immune to criticism. Under these conditions criticism finds little acceptance except insofar as it stays within the framework of the unexamined presuppositions of investigation.[18]

But it is also true that it is not wholly possible to ignore criticism. From a careful reading, it would appear that one effect of Radin's book was to provoke a response from R. H. Lowie in the form of the latter's *The History of Ethnological Theory*.[19] In his book Lowie seems to set as his task a refuta-

[18] One of Radin's more ambivalent academic friends has gone so far as to impugn his work on the ground that Radin never became a loyal member of a department of anthropology; see H. Hoijer's obituary of Paul Radin in the *American Anthropologist*.

[19] New York: Rinehart, 1937.

tion of the major critical themes embodied in *The Method and Theory of Ethnology*. It is instructive to compare the works of these two authors because of the differences in the portrait and methods of anthropology which they represent.[20]

Reading Radin one is struck by the clarity of his characterization of the different schools in ethnology and the subtlety of his explanations of how these schools have arrived at their positions. One is left without any doubt as to where Radin stands on the issues he poses. While Lowie's book is a history of ethnological theory and thereby ostensibly not a vehicle of criticism *per se,* he does take a position and reviews his subject from a critical standpoint. Yet Lowie, for all his grasp of the factual elements of successive theories and for all the relevance of his comparisons of these elements with later, better information, fails to formulate a well-defined position toward his subject and leaves us with a sense of formlessness in his efforts.

Where Radin was thoroughly consistent in the pursuit of his argument and perspective, wherever it led him, no matter whose toes were stepped upon on the way, Lowie more clearly set out to defend anthropology and the particular school of which

[20] Cora DuBois has noted the close connection between these two books in "Paul Radin: An Appreciation," in the Radin Festschrift, *Culture and History,* p. xiv.

he was a representative. It is for this reason, perhaps, that the tone and theoretical point of view expressed by Lowie in *The History of Ethnological Theory* is not consistent with his other work and with himself. The substantive work of Lowie, who was a highly cultivated and educated man, highly trained in historical scholarship, always went beyond the theoretical framework he postulated for ethnology. Radin had a deep appreciation for Lowie's substantive work, even though he disagreed with his formal statement of what anthropology should be.

For Lowie, the development of anthropological knowledge has been gradual and cumulative and, while there have been occasional false starts and dead ends, anthropologists have been successful, largely through the gift of providence and the good fortune of Boas's existence, in phrasing the correct problems and in finding solutions to them. Being true to his school's tradition, Lowie has a quarrel with the evolutionists, but for him the issue has been substantially resolved against them. There is also in his book an underlying but persistent quarrel with the functionalists, Radcliffe-Brown and Malinowski, who had then recently appeared on the scene, but they are easily dispensed with by showing, quite rightly in this writer's view, that there was nothing new in the idea of functionalism since the work of most anthropologists had been functionalist all along. Insofar as Radcliffe-Brown and Malinowski asserted that the functionalist approach showed the interrelationships between different parts of society, they were merely making explicit—that is, creating a methodology of—what had been practiced by their predecessors. This was nothing new, and Lowie is to be credited for pointing it out.

But the most provocative sections of Lowie's book are not those dealing with the chronological development of ethnology or with the claims of the functionalists but are the glimpses he gives us of his opinions concerning anthropology as a science, which stand in such sharp contrast to Radin's views.

Perhaps we can trace the differences between these two men to the difference in their conceptions of ethnology and of the proper concerns of the ethnographer. For Radin, ethnology is simply the study of specific aboriginal cultures; for Lowie, it is the "science of Culture." Lowie sets before us an all-embracing definition of culture as "the sum total of what an individual acquires from his society—those beliefs, customs, artistic norms, food-habits, and crafts which come to him not by his own creative activity but as a legacy from the past. . . ." This view of culture as a congeries of elements passively received by the individual, and separated from his creative activity, which can be itemized and "totaled," provides a key to much of Lowie's methodology; for the moment it is enough to identify the perspective as essentially that of Tylor and Boas.

Out of these definitions of ethnology come distinguishable differences in the conception of the ethnologist's task. Lowie, committed to the totaling up of all the elements of culture, decided that "the ethnographer's duty lies in depicting the whole of cultural reality. . . . The ethnographer must ignore nothing that belongs to the social tradition." It is crucial to note just what Lowie means by "the whole of cultural reality." Is this literally all of culture everywhere, or simply the total culture of some specific group or community? Only later in his book, in discussing Radin's position, as it happens, does Lowie provide us with unambiguous indications of his own position. Radin, on the other hand, makes it quite clear that he sees the ethnologist's responsibility as the provision of the fullest possible account of the specific culture under study ("our primary duty is to the specific tribe we are describing") and that this includes its specific historical development, wherever possible. Hence he prescribes for study only such part of the data "as bears directly upon the culture as a whole." Commenting on this, Lowie objects that it constitutes an arbitrary restriction on the scope of investigation, since the life of any given tribe is "merely a segment . . . of human culture, and correlations are permissible in all directions with associated intratribal traits, with neighboring cultures, with physical environment." For Lowie, any one culture is but an artificial unit segregated for purposes of expediency, and not a functionally co-ordinated set of activities (what Lowie takes for a "natural" unit), since social tradition can be shown to vary from village to village, and even from family to family. Thus he concludes that "there is only one natural unit for the ethnologist—the culture of all humanity at all periods and in all places." As a theoretical orientation this position leaves us at precisely the same starting point prescribed by Tylor in his definition of culture, from which one is left only with the possibility of examining units, traits, adhesions, and their correlations, all disembodied from the living reality of culture.

Lowie is quite sure that ethnology cannot be a science, *if* we take science to mean a systematized body of knowledge organized into laws and propositions which allow for the accurate prediction of future events. For Lowie, it is the element of laws of prediction that ethnology lacks. In referring to Durkheim, whom he takes to be the source of this error in anthropology, Lowie writes: ". . . the

writer cannot rid himself of the prejudice that the
new science, like its predecessors, must aim at general laws." [21]

Similarly he criticizes Morgan for crediting
"himself with possessing a generally valid scheme
of sequence by which unknown events could be
safely deduced." [22] He is also dubious about Tylor's
use of the word "laws":

At times, to be sure, Tylor's reference to "laws" in
civilization seems to imply no more than a recognition
that its phenomena are causally determined; but he obviously has more in mind when he compares these principles with the law of magnetic attraction.

Now, this position requires much modification in
order to retain any validity. The attraction of iron
filings by a magnet is a predictable phenomenon, but
the savage tendency to explain fossil remains by myths
of giants is not similarly predictable. We are merely
wise *after* the fact . . .[23]

To these scholars who insist that ethnology must
possess laws or be relegated to the status of an "inferior" science, Lowie offers an alternative view of
the scientific basis of anthropology:

[21] *The History of Ethnological Theory*, pp. 202–203.
[22] *Ibid.*, p. 59.
[23] *Ibid.*, p. 77. Emphasis in the original.

We have repeatedly mentioned correlations. They are, in our opinion, the closest approximation ethnology is likely to achieve to the ideals of exact science. Some scholars, indeed, postulate "laws," feeling that otherwise ethnology would lapse into an inferior status. This is aping ideals applicable only to a part of physics and in no way incumbent on other branches of learning. Every science formulates its data according to their nature and may even differ in its procedure and results from problem to problem. Biology uses mathematics sparingly and for limited purposes; astronomers predict eclipses but are unable to calculate the gravitational pull exerted by all bodies on all others. The ethnologist, correspondingly, may never discover laws; yet his scientific respectability remains unimpaired so long as he co-ordinates, with a maximum of attainable efficiency, the particular phenomena he studies.[24]

Apart for the moment from Lowie's strictures on correlations, which we have already indicated was one of Radin's central foci of criticism, this is a description of a neatly subdivided universe of sciences, each pursuing its own objectives in its own way. In this rather stable and complacently accepted universe, the anthropologist need have no fears for his scientific respectability, even if he should lack "laws." There is in this statement a slight tone of defensiveness—he protesteth too much

[24] *Ibid.,* p. 288.

—which seems to be a plea for admission into the hallowed portals of science.

If ethnology is not to postulate laws but find correlations, one must ask of Lowie to what material he will address himself in order to find the correlations. His answer to this question is that the ethnologist must concern himself with the formulation and solution of individual and necessarily disparate problems. Surely it is difficult to disagree with this attitude, but it is reasonable to ask: Which problems? And, if they are disparate, why have they taken the particular forms of disparateness which they have taken? Here Lowie offers us what Radin has already criticized, for he tells us that we must deal with units of culture.

For Lowie, there are subdivisions of culture or cultural units and at the same time there are interrelations between these subdivisions. Hence it is not possible to speak of "closed cultural systems." But granting this, does it follow that the ethnologist is enjoined from studying, in their own right, "cultural systems" defined as such by their own participants; that is, should he ignore the definitions of cultural boundaries given by the participants themselves? This is the point which Lowie is apparently unwilling to concede, since he is unwilling to take the natives at their own word as to what is the constitution of their own world. Since for Lowie the family, the clan, the tribe, are not "natural units," they are not cultural units. In this conclusion Lowie is imitating the approach of the natural scientist, and he is led as far afield as Boas whom he also emulates and who had by this time already abandoned this line of inquiry. He continues to labor under the misapprehension that "natural units"—for example, living things—are functionally closed systems, then applies the concept of "unit" (as he uses it, synonymous with "closed system"), and is thus able to ignore the fact that nonetheless real cultural systems do exist and not merely those established by the artificial lines of demarcation set by the ethnologist.

What is involved here is the tendency on the part of the social scientists impressed with the methods of natural scientists to confuse cultural facts with physical facts, and to import notions of classification prevalent in physics and biology into their own fields. In denying or ignoring, which comes to the same thing, the existence of co-ordinated sets of activities because they are not closed off one from another and in claiming that the cultural system is but the artifice of the ethonologist, Lowie is in effect declaring that there is no order in the world of phenomena other than that established by the (natural) scientist. All this implies what C. Wright Mills in *The Sociological Imagination* calls the fetishism of the concept. That is, the concept is seen as the device for ordering reality and is the property of the scientist, to be applied at his discretion. Unfortunately, however, at some point in this procedure the fictions of scientific analysis tend to become transformed into the realities of social existence, and reality is overwhelmed by the concept. Lowie fails to see this issue and as a result falls back on stating the need for concepts:

> The student of culture, then, will be unable to predict what he may need, let alone what his colleagues may require for their purposes; but his inescapable duty is to define his concepts and arrange them in a spatial, temporal, and causal context.
> Concepts must be clear and rigid, rising above the fluidity and vagueness of the raw phenomena. . . .[25]
> The clarification of concepts, then, directly gauges scientific progress. . . .[26] Apt concepts, then, are a primary goal. Without them even a simple charting of distributions is invalidated.[27]

One might well ask as Radin did of Sapir how it is possible to move from fluid and vague raw phenomena to rigid and clear concepts and, if this is a legitimate style of investigation, what is the

[25] *Ibid.*, p. 280.
[26] *Ibid.*, p. 281.
[27] *Ibid.*, p. 283.

validity of the conclusions which are reached by it. In Lowie there is no clear answer to this question. We are simply presented with the concepts which the investigator chooses to concoct and are asked to overlook the data because of their intractability. This rather casual abdication of the data leaves the ethnologist free to pursue his goal of defining and clarifying apt concepts in the interests of scientific progress.

But remember here Lowie's reminder that he has "repeatedly mentioned correlations," for the role of the anthropologist is also to "co-ordinate, with a maximum of attainable efficiency, the particular phenomena he studies." With this dictum Lowie completes his circle, having started with intractable data, which are then converted into precise concepts, which are then available for scientific analysis by the relational method. It is not for nothing that Lowie is at pains to argue for his style of anthropology.

The one anthropologist above all others who receives Lowie's praise is Boas, whom he distinguishes from lesser figures by his "capacity for defining problems so as to prepare a clear-cut solution. . . ." [28] In referring back to Boas as the crucial figure in anthropology, Lowie accomplishes two purposes: he adds legitimacy to his position

[28] Ibid., p. 148.

against "laws," and he reaffirms Boas in the face of Radin's earlier criticism. In view of the role that Lowie assigns to Boas in the history of ethnological theory, there can be no doubt that he is upholding the master in the face of the "disaffected" pupil. The stakes, after all, were high. Radin's critique of Boas was inevitably, by extension, also a critique of all those who remained loyal, so that beneath the surface of Lowie's apparently academic treatment of his subject there lurks a much deeper interpersonal drama in which the stakes are no less than betrayal of the master, with all that implies for introducing self-doubt and consternation in the ranks of the loyal. A retrospective perusal of Lowie's book leaves the reader with the distinct impression that he is witness to an academically courteous form of clique warfare.

What is much more important than this thinly disguised warfare, however, is Lowie's positive contribution. In this writer's view this contribution is essentially a methodological one which derives from his observation that culture cannot be reduced to laws.[29]

Lowie implies throughout his book that the reason for the inability of ethnology to discover unfailing laws is the complexity of the material involved. Culture, he maintains, is too varied a phenomenon

[29] *Ibid.*, p. 145.

to be ruled by any consistent laws. The nonapplicability of laws to ethnology, then, is a function of the heterogeneous subject matter rather than of the would-be theoreticians.

It is here that Lowie displays his own deficiencies. He is apparently unaware that he has insisted on the possibility—indeed the necessity—of procedural as distinguished from substantive laws. Two of these we have mentioned : the need for concepts, and the ethnologist's deliberately confining himself to a particular, limited problem. This is the positive aspect of the negation of ethnological laws. In discussing especially the earlier writers, Lowie is extremely critical of what he considers to be faulty methodology. He scores Sir John Lubbock for "subjective judgments," naïvely passed on the basis of resemblance to or deviation from European standards.[30] He praises Boas for the techniques he developed.[31] He assumes that with the chronological development of ethnology there will be a concomitant refinement of procedures unavailable to previous workers. However, he seems oblivious to the contingency that the discovery and improvement of techniques as yet unknown may lead to the formulation of valid substantive laws. It is not claimed that this stage is inevitable or even, from

[30] *Ibid.*, p. 24.
[31] *Ibid.*, pp. 131–136.

any past or present indications, likely in the foreseeable future. It must be noted, however, that just as early ethnographers could not predict the growth of methods which are today considered to be minimal, so their modern counterparts cannot anticipate developments which are yet to come. Lowie leaves himself open to the criticism that substantive predictions cannot be made at this moment because we do not know enough to be able to formulate them, and by this measure his argument against the laws is essentially a weak one compared to the criticism against substantive laws, as advanced by Radin, which has the historical perspective as its point of departure.

There is another sense in which Lowie has perhaps given too much credit to the current practitioners of his art. In speaking further of Lubbock, he writes:

This last sentence illustrates another major error—the complete abandonment of objective criteria. . . .
The modern scientific procedure is to refrain from *all* subjective pronouncements; to recognize that while material objects and rationalistic schemes are "higher" or "lower"—better or less suited to their purpose—this does not hold for art, religion, and morals, where no universally recognized standards exist.[32]

[32] *Ibid.*, pp. 24–25.

If ever a believer in scientific objectivity hoisted himself with his own petard, Lowie did so when he penned these sentences. According to what sacred pronouncements are material objects to be judged —or even catalogued—on the basis of their suitability for their purpose?[33] Why should the prime factor not be their beauty, or their age, or the pedigree of their maker? Evaluation dependent upon their relative practicality is surely no more than an indication of modern Western standards of judgment and bias. For all the talk about "objectivity" or the elimination of ethnocentricism in one's work, it seems to be difficult to achieve in practice.

The theoretical attitude leading to the fetishization of the concept is related to the methodological attitude of objectivity. Thus the scientific field worker aims at objectivity: this means that because particular cultural items are looked upon as objects, the culture itself, of which these are supposedly the constituent elements, is itself regarded as an object, from the outside. Radin makes the point that the ethnologist faithful to this approach denies himself involvement in his subject for the sake of objectivity, only to separate himself from his data.

In spite of his protestations to the contrary,[34] the

---

[33] Just as with functionalism in general, this appears as a form of technical rationality.

[34] *The History of Ethnological Theory*, p. 291.

problems inherent in Lowie's praise of modern objectivity remain. It is not necessary here to invoke Weber's earlier strictures or to recite the ideological commitments apparent in the work of all ethnology in order to support the now commonplace observation that man, whether scientist or layman, cannot be "objective." Lowie still could not admit that any ethnographer's investigation of any problem is inevitably colored by ideological and perspectivistic frameworks from which he cannot escape, just as he cannot exist without them. There may well be limitations imposed upon the anthropologist by his subject matter, but surely a far more serious hindrance is to be found in the very nature of those who undertake its practice.

Radin and Lévi-Strauss

Lowie's book is essentially a reaffirmation of the ethnology which Radin had found deficient. Since that time two other theoreticians have attempted to plot a different course for ethnological research: Lévi-Strauss and Clyde Kluckhohn, whose respective books *Structural Anthropology* and *Anthropology and the Classics* may serve as cases in point, have set forth alternative styles for the anthropological investigator. Since Lévi-Strauss presents us with a more comprehensive and systematic style, let us start with him.

Anyone undertaking a discussion of Lévi-Strauss would commit a grave injustice if he did not at the outset call to the reader's attention Susan Sontag's magnificent assessment of his work in her review of *Structural Anthropology*.[35] In that brief sketch informed by her familiarity with modern French intellectual life and Lévi-Strauss's relation to it, Professor Sontag succeeds in demonstrating the relation between Lévi-Strauss's anthropological style and its intellectual and political sources within the Western world. Lévi-Strauss, she notes, is caught in the middle of several contradictions, which stem on the one hand from his desire to make anthropology scientific (especially as defined by American social scientists) and on the other by his conception of anthropology "as a total occupation, involving a spiritual commitment like that of the creative artist, or the adventurer or the psychoanalyst." In order to convey fully Professor Sontag's insights, let me quote at length from her statement:

Tristes Tropiques is one of the great books of our century. It is rigorous, subtle and bold in thought. It is

[35] *The New York Review of Books*, vol. 1, no. 7, pp. 6–8, 1963. Reprinted in *Against Interpretation*, © 1963, 1966 by Susan Sontag. Used here by permission of Farrar, Straus & Giroux, Inc.

beautifully written. And, like all great books, it bears an absolutely personal stamp; it speaks with a human voice. . . .

The profoundly intelligent sympathy which informs *Tristes Tropiques* makes all other memoirs about life among preliterate peoples seem ill-at-ease, defensive, provincial. Yet sympathy is modulated by a hardwon impassivity. In her autobiography Simone de Beauvoir recalls Lévi-Strauss as a young philosophy student-teacher expounding, "in his detached voice, and with a deadpan expression . . . the folly of the passions. . . ."

Anthropology has always struggled with an intense, fascinated repulsion towards its subject. The horror of the primitive is never far from the anthropologist's consciousness. Lévi-Strauss marks the farthest reaches of the conquering of the aversion. The anthropologist in the manner of Lévi-Strauss is a new breed altogether. He is not like recent generations of American anthropologists, simply a modest data-collecting "observer." Nor does he have any axe—Christian, rationalist, Freudian or otherwise—to grind. By means of experience in the field, the anthropologist undergoes a "psychological revolution." Like psychoanalysis, anthropology cannot be taught "purely theoretically," Lévi-Strauss insists in several essays on the profession and teaching of his subject in *Structural Anthropology*. A spell in the field is the equivalent of the training analysis undergone by the psychoanalysts. Not written tests, but the judgment of "experienced members of the profession" who have undergone the same psychological ordeal, can determine "if and when" a candidate anthropologist "has, as a result of his field work, accomplished that inner revolution that will really make him into a new man." However, it must be emphasized that this literary-sounding conception of the anthropologist's calling—the twice-born spiritual adventurer, pledged to a systematic *déracinement*—is complemented in most of Lévi-Strauss's writings by an insistence on the most unliterary techniques of research. His important essay on myth in *Structural Anthropology* outlines a technique for analyzing the elements of myths so that these can be recorded on IBM cards. European contributions to what in America are called the "social sciences" are in exceedingly low repute in this country, for their insufficient empirical documentation, for their "humanist" weakness for covert cultural criticism, for their refusal to embrace the techniques of quantification as an essential tool of research. Lévi-Strauss's essays in *Structural Anthropology* certainly escape these strictures. Indeed, far from disdaining the American fondness for precise quantitative measurement of all traditional problems, Lévi-Strauss finds it not sophisticated or methodologically rigorous enough. At the expense of the French school (Durkheim, Mauss, and their followers), to whom one would expect him to be allied, Lévi-Strauss pays lavish tribute throughout the essays in *Structural Anthropology* to the work of American anthropologists —particularly Lowie, Boas and Kroeber. But his real affinity is clearly to the more avant-garde methodol-

ogies of economics, neurology, linguistics, and game
theory. For Lévi-Strauss, there is no doubt that anthropology must be a science, rather than a humanistic study.
The question is only how. "For centuries," he writes,
"the humanities and the social sciences have resigned
themselves to contemplate the world of the natural and
exact sciences as a kind of paradise where they will
never enter." But recently, a doorway to paradise has
been opened by linguists, like Roman Jakobson and his
school. Linguists are now able to reformulate their
problems so that they can "have a machine built by an
engineer and make a kind of experiment completely similar to a natural-science experiment," which will tell
them "if the hypothesis is worthwhile or not." Linguists
—as well as economists and game theorists—have
shown the anthropologists "a way to get out of the
confusion resulting from too much acquaintance and
familiarity with concrete data."

Thus the man who submits himself to the exotic to
confirm his own inner alienation as an urban intellectual ends by aiming to vanquish his subject by translat-
ing it into a purely formal code. The ambivalence
toward the exotic, the primitive, is not overcome after
all, but only given a complex restatement.[36]

Anyone who has read the work of Lévi-Strauss,
especially *Tristes Tropiques* and *Structural Anthropology,* cannot fail to see the disparity in tone,

[36] *Ibid.,* pp. 6–7.

style, and feeling between his personal and scientific statements. For present purposes let us examine how Lévi-Strauss manages to "vanquish his subject" and how his style of inquiry differs from Radin's. To start with, Radin and Lévi-Strauss would appear to agree in their conceptions of history, for Lévi-Strauss states:

The issue can . . . be reduced to the relationship between history and ethnology in the strict sense. We propose to show that the fundamental difference between the two disciplines is not one of subject, of goal, or of method. They share the same subject, which is social life; the same goal, which is a better understanding of man; and, in fact, the same method, in which only the proportion of research techniques varies.[37]

The crucial phrase here is the variation in the "proportion of research techniques." To understand what Lévi-Strauss means by this it is necessary to point out the differences he sees between the ethnographer, the ethnologist, and the historian:

The ethnographer is someone who collects data and . . . presents them in conformity with requirements that are the same as those of the historian. The

[37] Lévi-Strauss, *Structural Anthropology*, Chapter I.

historian's role is to utilize these studies when the observations extend over a *sufficient period of time.* The
ethnologist also draws upon the ethnographers' observation when they include a *sufficient number of different
regions.* At any rate, the ethnographer furnishes documents which the historian can use. And, if documents
already exist and the ethnographer chooses to integrate
their contents into his study, should not the historian
. . . envy him the privilege of writing the history of a
society which he has experienced as a living reality? [38]

One is surprised to hear from Lévi-Strauss this
simpliste distinction between the ethnographer and
the ethnologist; it is as if it is straight out of a textbook by an American anthropologist, and it is
equally unsatisfactory. By what stretch of the
imagination is one to separate the work of the ethnographer from that of the ethnologist when in all
the recent history of anthropology the cardinal dictum has been that the ethnologist must pursue
studies in the field? But by postulating the ethnographer as the faithful recorder of history in one
place and at a given time and distinguishing him
from the ethnologist whose observations extend
over a sufficient period of time and include a sufficient number of different regions, Lévi-Strauss
opens the way to a purely synchronic ethnography,

[38] *Ibid.,* pp. 17–18. Emphasis supplied.

if such a thing is possible in light of the fact that all observations must necessarily take place over a period of time. The postulated ethnographer is clearly doing more dirty work than would appear to be the case at first glance.

If one grants that the preliterates have a past, then it is certainly the ethnographer's obligation to take note of it in whatever form it may exist since this past bears on all that he observes. It does not matter if this past exists only in the memories of those who have lived it, but in any event it is not likely to be the case that it will exist only in personal memories. We have, after all, lived through four hundred years of Western contact with preliterate societies; and documents, reports, and observations have accumulated, including those contributed by the anthropologists. It is, in short, precisely the ethnographer who must be the historian. In the light of Radin's clarification of this issue, it is all the more surprising that Lévi-Strauss continues to make this error.

However, this hypothetical textbook ethnographer serves a deeper purpose in the methodology of Lévi-Strauss. Apart from placing the historian in the role of envying the ethnographer ("the privilege of writing the history of a society which he has experienced as a living reality") it allows him to distinguish the ethnologist from the historian in the "proportion of research techniques" which they employ. Immediately following the quote given above, Lévi-Strauss tells us how they differ: "They differ, principally, in their choice of complementary perspectives: History organizes its data in relation to *conscious expressions* of social life, while anthropology proceeds by examining its unconscious foundations." [39]

Now the terms conscious and unconscious have been given many formulations, but still one might expect that in modern usage they would bear some relationship to the Freudian lexicon. But in Lévi-Strauss's usage nothing could be further from the expected. For him the term unconscious is used as his prime connecting link to a formal anthropology which would find its ultimate resting place in linguistic models. [40] It is instructive to show how he accomplishes this maneuver.

As is typical of the anthropologists, Lévi-Strauss characteristically begins by paying his respects to Tylor, whom he credits, after duly repeating that famous definition of culture as all things, as having been the first to observe the "unconscious nature of collective phenomena." He then goes on:

[39] *Ibid.*, p. 18. Emphasis supplied.

[40] In the logics of his system, the term "unconscious" for Lévi-Strauss comes close to current sociological usage of the phrase "latent function."

We know that among most primitive peoples it is very difficult to obtain a moral justification or a rational explanation for any custom or institution. . . . Even when interpretations are offered, they always have the character of rationalizations or secondary elaborations. There is rarely any doubt that the unconscious reasons for practicing a custom or sharing a belief are remote from the reasons given to justify them.[41]

With this and without further ceremony we are assured that it is a fruitless effort to pay attention to what the natives themselves say, for indeed they know not what they do. One might even infer that it is unnecessary to record what they say, which is indeed a strange procedure for one who maintains that the ethnologists and the historians share the same subject, goals, and methods.

In warming up to the elucidation of his approach, Lévi-Strauss gives to Boas "credit for defining the unconscious nature of cultural phenomena with admirable lucidity [because] by comparing cultural phenomena to language . . . he anticipated both the subsequent development of linguistic theory and a future for anthropology whose rich promise we are just beginning to perceive. He showed that the structure of language remains unknown to the speaker until the introduction of a scientific gram-

---

[41] *Structural Anthropology*, p. 18.

mar." [42] Thus enamored of the linguistic method, Lévi-Strauss proceeds to inform us that:

> From words the linguist extracts the phonetic reality of the phoneme; and from the phoneme he extracts the logical reality of distinctive features. And when he has found in several languages the same phonemes or the use of the same pairs of oppositions, he does not compare individually distinct entities. It is the same phoneme, the same element, which will show at this new level the basic identity of empirically different entities. We are not dealing with two similar phenomena, but with one and the same. The transition from conscious to unconscious is associated with progression from the specific toward the general. [43]

As a basic methodology, then, we start with the phonetic reality of the phoneme as extracted by the linguist. Once the linguist has found the same

[42] *Ibid.*, p. 19. At this point in Lévi-Strauss's work it is clear that by focusing on the phoneme he is reaching back to the early Boas to find a mechanism for handling "units" of culture. It would appear that Lévi-Strauss's structural approach has its roots in the older trait-listing of the Boasian school insofar as the conception of cultural traits arises out of the linguistic metaphor. In this respect Lévi-Strauss accommodated to the tradition of scientistic anthropology in the United States in a way that Radin never did. It appears also that Lévi-Strauss played the role of incorporating American structural anthropology into French thought. Maurice Merleau-Ponty seems to confirm this in his essay, "From Mauss to Claude Lévi-Strauss," in *Signs* (Evanston, Ill.: Northwestern University Press, 1964), pp. 114–125.

[43] *Structural Anthropology*, pp. 20–21.

phonemes, he has found the basic identity of empirically different identities and he has solved his problem. It is clear that the reality here is the reality of the linguist and not the reality of the informant, but of course the problem of the informant has already been solved by the convenient device of eliminating him. In the sleight-of-hand of the linguistic metaphor, words and their meanings, literally the essence of all social life as historically lived, simply lack a place and the "progression from the conscious to unconscious" is the progression in the analyst's work from the phoneme to the construction of his logical realities. The historical individual, wayward in his ways, has been put safely in his place and can be ignored because, as Lévi-Strauss contends, "the unconscious activity of the mind consists in imposing forms upon the content." Simone de Beauvoir makes a strong point when she recalls Lévi-Strauss expounding "in his detached voice, and with a deadpan expression . . . the folly of the passions," but as Professor Sontag has pointed out, Lévi-Strauss's style has two sides. *Tristes Tropiques* is a richly personal and emotional report which will stand as a classic statement for the time and place in history which it describes. Lévi-Strauss separates his personal and his scientific worlds in order to be able to retain the purity of his scientific approach.

Lévi-Strauss's monumental resistance to the unconscious as a form of inner psychic life serves
other purposes as well, for it turns out, unnoticed
by Professor Sontag, that he has an axe to grind
against psychoanalysis. He goes on to say:

And even today, secondary elaborations (i.e., rationalizations) tend to acquire the same unconscious quality as
soon as they are formulated. With surprising rapidity
—which shows that one is dealing with an intrinsic
property of certain modes of thinking and action—
collective thought assimilates what would seem the most
daring concepts, such as the priority of *mother-right,*
animism, or, more recently, *psychoanalysis,* in order to
resolve automatically problems which by their nature
seem forever to elude action as well as thought.[44]

The almost casual insertion of psychoanalysis,
seemingly as an afterthought without further
adumbration, dispenses with too much too easily to
be taken as a remark without a point. Lévi-Strauss
is here attempting to assimilate the corpus of psychoanalytic insights into intrinsic properties of
modes of thinking. He is arguing that all mental
processes can be reduced to forms which are ultimately knowable as collective rather than individual manifestations. Under the practiced hand of

[44] *Ibid.,* p. 19. Emphasis supplied.

the scientistic anthropologist who has discovered
the irreducible categories, all psychic mystique can
be reduced to structural form. There is here a failure to understand that the psychoanalysts in their
analyses recognize and work with the unresolved
tensions and conflicts (the essential ambivalence in
human psychology) and attempt to comprehend
human nature in these terms. They apply their
rationality to the contradictions which cannot
have a resolution and which can be scientifically resolved only at the cost of eliminating the subject
matter.

Apart from their results, can we dismiss the psychoanalysts so easily? The logics of Lévi-Strauss's
position demand just such a dismissal, because to
admit that the natives have an unconscious, Freudian or otherwise, would destroy the architectonics
of the phoneme. Mother-right is another question.
Freud at least tried. To begin with the phoneme is
not to try at all, and such is the position, I am
afraid, Lévi-Strauss leaves us in while dispensing
out of hand with those who would take words
seriously.

It is precisely the conception of the unconscious
that brings us back to Radin, for he tried to find a
way to legitimately treat this dimension of the
human mind. In the concluding chapter of *The
Method and Theory of Ethnology*, Radin lays

great stress on the effects of the invention of writing
on the nature of men's mentality.

Radin states as he had earlier in *Primitive Man
as a Philosopher* that "the whole tendency of writing has been to elevate thought and thinking to the
rank of the exclusive proof of the verities, to differentiate the subjective from the objective in a
fashion unknown until then." He goes on to note
that problems of great importance which have so
far been barely touched are inherent in this transition to writing: "It is here where the psychoanalysts
have been illuminating, although it is difficult to
escape the conviction that, with the possible exception of Jung, they have blundered upon this field
rather than come upon it properly, with a true
realization of what it contains." True, Radin did
not develop this theme, but in his later, much neg-
lected book, *The Trickster,* he tried to analyze with
the accumulated wealth of his own collected histories the psychic significance of the trickster myth
in human history. What is significant in this study
is Radin's faithfulness to the words and word
meanings of his informants. Nowhere can it be
said that he disembodies his analysis from the word
by an easy resort to the reduction to "basic identities
of empirically different phenomena." Here it need
only be said that his quest in his study of the trickster remained consistent with his concluding re-

marks in the present book: "I doubt whether the
picture of essential human nature that eventually
emerges will be flattering to our understanding,
although possibly there may be some solace in the
fact that the history of civilization is largely the
history of the diminution of the rôle played by our
compulsive activities, the record of the enlargement
of the sphere of awareness of the nature of our
actions." Seen in this light, Lévi-Strauss has succumbed to the exclusive proof of the verities, to the
fixed and rigid meaning categories of Western science as adumbrated in the metaphor of the linguistic mode. Perhaps the method of Lévi-Strauss
succeeds in ordering the universe, but the order
that is achieved is the ethnologist's, not the order
or disorder of the world.

Radin and Kluckhohn

Clyde Kluckhohn was another of the modern
anthropologists who attempted to work out a
method for anthropology, a fact which a glance at
his last book, *Anthropology and the Classics* [45] will
attest to. His learning and his familiarity with
classical scholarship are impressive to anyone in the
modern generation who has had to arrive at a his-

[45] Providence, R.I.: Brown University Press, 1961.

torical perspective without the benefit of a classical education. In Kluckhohn one feels there is a link between the nineteenth and the twentieth centuries and for this reason he is not only a significant but a disappointing figure, for he not only fails to make the link but, what is worse, ends by tipping his hat to the scientistic anthropology of the modern epoch. Hard as he tried, he failed to resolve the discrepancy between his humanism and his desire to be scientific.

Much to his credit, Kluckhohn never attempted to divine a total system for anthropology. In this he was true to the complexity and historical specificity of the material. His Navaho materials collected over the period of a lifetime are enough to dispel any implication of premature foreclosure by arbitrarily imposed schemes. Unfortunately, large parts of this vast collection of data were collected under his supervision by several generations of students and hence were not part of his direct experience. This is not meant to minimize Kluckhohn's intimate familiarity with Navaho life, which he studied for many years. It is rather to say that the vastness of the material collected by dozens and dozens of observers posed special problems of codification, classification, and control. The use of a system of classificational categories, coders, and a filing system (the Navaho files) inevitably places

some distance between the material and the ethnologist, introducing a measure of alienation not present when the investigator himself is solely responsible for his own data collection. This alone created
special problems for Kluckhohn, and there would
seem to be little doubt that, in the final analysis, it
affected his method of ethnology.

In *Anthropology and the Classics,* Kluckhohn
deliberately turns away from his Navaho studies,
which had served as the original source for the development of his theories, and instead applies his
perspective to Greek civilization. To the extent
that his method is successful, this approach gives
us an opportunity to see his work in a highly distilled
form, for in the very brevity of *Anthropology and
the Classics* the central features of his mode of work
are highlighted.

Kluckhohn tells us that it is his desire to

focus upon the relation between anthropology and the
humanities of which classical studies are the oldest and
the outstanding example. Anthropology, properly speaking, is not a social science, though it is often called one
today. It does contain social science elements, now alike
as regards viewpoint, method, and content. Historically,
however, it derives from the natural sciences on the one
hand and the humanities on the other.[46]

[46] *Anthropology and the Classics,* p. 23.

On the face of it, this statement would seem to be clear enough in indicating the starting point for anthropological studies. However, two pages later Kluckhohn quickly qualifies his statement in order the better to give anthropology a special place. He quotes Kroeber, who he says "suggests that 'anthropology largely represents an unconscious effort of total natural science to extend itself over an area traditionally held by the humanities.'" By way of comment Kluckhohn adds: "This may seem like an imperialistic claim of anthropology, and the statement should doubtless be qualified in various respects, but it strikes me that Kroeber is basically right.[47]

Here Kluckhohn seems to be stating, without further elaborating in what various respects he would make his qualifications, that the science of anthropology does have a possibility for vanquishing its humanistic foundations. The key to his position on the relation between anthropology and the humanities appears on the same page as the above statement from Kroeber:

In an epoch when, for better or worse, science is dominant on the intellectual horizon, it is not surprising that students of the oldest humanity [classical studies] find something in that science [anthropology] which has—

[47] *Ibid.*, p. 25.

along with its scientific aspect—deep humanistic roots. In our days many Hellenists are men in search of a theory. They find some theoretical framework and some ideas suitable to their purposes in anthropology . . .[48]

Here the humanism in anthropology has been relegated to its historical origins, its roots, and its scientific dimensions have come to the fore as a source of ideas and frameworks for the classical scholars, no doubt deficient in their own methods, who lack theories for comprehending their own material. In spite of the earlier bow to the humanities, anthropology does after all hold the key to the hallowed portals of science. Kluckhohn proceeds to turn this key and to open the portals, which is to say to apply his method of anthropology to the classicists' data.

It is in the chapter, "A Brief Grammar of Greek Culture," that Kluckhohn states his approach explicitly, and it comes as a surprise that he takes as his irreducible starting point the linguistic model:

Students of culture must do as the linguists have done and identify the significant structure points which define the essential character of each culture. . . .[49]

Linguists in their elegant analyses of one aspect of culture have found it extremely useful to set up a series

[48] *Ibid.*
[49] *Ibid.*, p. 44.

of distinctive contrasts or oppositions, usually binary,
which serve to identify each separate phoneme (sound
class distinctive in that language). A "lump" or "bundle" of such "distinctive features" defines a phoneme.
In its simplest form the process is like a specialized version of the "twenty quesions" game. Thus one may ask,
"Is the phoneme vocalic? Yes or No?" In Russian,
eleven such questions will identify each phoneme
uniquely. . . . There are grounds for supposing that a
similar approach will yield good results with other aspects of culture, including cultural values.[50]

These words sound remarkably similar to Lévi-
Strauss's insofar as the phonemic model is the basic
point of departure in constructing the essential
framework of a culture. But Kluckhohn's application is different. Where Lévi-Strauss is concerned
with extracting the "unconscious" drift of culture
form, Kluckhohn is concerned with defining the
"essential character of each culture" as expressed
in cultural values. This latter part of his project
reminds us more of Ruth Benedict's *Patterns of
Culture* and *The Chrysanthemum and the Sword,*
in which she attempts to distill the essential themes
of the societies she analyzes. The only difference
between Benedict and Kluckhohn is that Benedict,
explicitly working as a poet, never states her meth-

[50] *Ibid.*, pp. 47–48.

odology, while Kluckhohn works from an explicit linguistic analogy. Kluckhohn's enterprise is an amalgam of Lévi-Strauss's method and Ruth Benedict's themal analysis. However, the amalgamation, like many others, is achieved with some difficulty. Kluckhohn is concerned with values and through these values to arrive at the essential character of each culture. It is Kluckhohn's first task to find out what the values of a culture are by the method of phonemic analysis. Now the term "value" in the social sciences, in spite of Kluckhohn's brave efforts to the contrary, has always been a great sponge, with a tendency to absorb too much. Kluckhohn, who sets out with the definition: "A value is a selective orientation toward experience, implying a deep commitment or repudiation, which influences the ordering of 'choices' between possible alternatives in action," [51] is quickly overwhelmed by the spongy qualities of the concept, at the cost of sacrificing his phonemic method: "The entities of value-culture do not have the all-or-none character of a simple physical event like the phonemes found in language culture. Rather they seem to have the character of weightings or emphases that are, on the whole, dominant in the culture." [52]

[51] *Ibid.*, p. 46.
[52] *Ibid.*, pp. 48–49.

It is not difficult to see this statement as an escape clause, for in it Kluckhohn has sacrificed the tangible and returned to Benedict's poetry; but the return is not complete, because to locate his cultural values Kluckhohn introduces the device of a panel of poets whose collective average judgment defines a culture's profile. Thus:

In recent years my students and I have done a number of trial runs in constructing cultural profiles according to a set of binary oppositions. . . . The particular contrasts used were obtained in the first instance from the study of the philosophical and anthropological literature and then modified through a series of successive approximations as a consequence of our empirical experience. The ontological status of these pairs is not that of true dichotomies but rather that of bi-polar dimensions. The two-feature oppositions are not so constituted that one empirically excludes the presence of the other. It is rather a question of dominance of emphasis. This is a system of priorities—not of all-or-none categories.[53]

The procedure, then, is to find contrasting pairs from the "study of the philosophical and anthropological literature" and subsequently modify them by "successive approximations as a consequence of . . . empirical experience." It is not too much to say that this process of collective judgments, with

[53] *Ibid.,* p. 46.

their reference back to some vague empirical experience, is not only fuzzy but bears little resemblance to rigorous linguistic analysis. It is in fact so far removed that it is possible for Kluckhohn to make his analysis without any reference at all to empirical data, except insofar as he uses them to fill in his binary oppositions.

Kluckhohn and his collaborators worked with thirteen pairs of binary oppositions, of which he applied eight to the Greek data to illustrate how his method works. The oppositions consist of the following word pairs: Determinate vs. Indeterminate, Unitary vs. Pluralistic, the Human vs. the Supernatural, Evil vs. Good, Individual vs. Group, Self vs. Other, Free vs. Bound, Discipline vs. Fulfillment. It is not possible to examine critically the reasons why these particular pairs have been selected because Kluckhohn tells us nothing about why he selected them rather than some others. However, in elaborating on the meanings of these pairs, Kluckhohn does tell us what each one means. Thus, Self vs. Other refers to "the relative emphasis placed upon egoism and altruism," and he has "no hesitation" in placing the Greeks on the "self" dimension. Or again, Discipline vs. Fulfillment is "roughly . . . the 'Apollonian-Dionysian' contrast of Ruth Benedict," and he finds that the Greek position "was about an equal weighting or a balance" between these two value-qualities. In each case he supports his choice of dominant emphasis between the pairs by presenting vignettes of supporting data. Once all the dominant emphases in the pairs of words have been located, the task of analysis is considered completed and the culture in question has been typified by its particular pattern of value phonemes. It should be noted that Kluckhohn's oppositions are Western academic oppositions and not those found in human nature.

It is clear that in following this procedure Kluckhohn is doing much more and much less than the work of an ethnologist. He has presupposed that once he has his system of binary opposites he will be able to make linkages between his model and the open systems of the empirical world. He suggests that his model has been abstracted from the empirical world, but that is all he tells us about the particular empirical world that was his starting point. In fact, so high is the level of abstraction on which he deals with Greek civilization that almost the whole of this civilization disappears from view. Social theory has by this method of inquiry not only lost its connection to the real world but triumphs over it.[54] Of what use is a complicated methodology, no matter how ingeniously evolved out of modern linguistics, when there are no data out of which it

[54] For a similar critique of systematic sociological theorizing, see J. Bensman and A. Vidich, "Social Theory and Field Research," in *Sociology on Trial,* ed. M. Stein and A. Vidich (Englewood Cliffs, N.J.: Pentice-Hall, 1963), pp. 162–172.

derives? If this is the end result of modern ethnography, we could well do with less of it.

There is in Kluckhohn as in Lévi-Strauss a suggestion of the work of the game theorists—"a specialized version of the twenty questions game"—which leaves me with the uneasy feeling that the investigator has been overwhelmed by the complexity of the world. The game theorists fix the parameters of their world in advance, leaving nothing to discover. But in confronting the real world, no amount of advance fixing of the parameters of a given game will make reality bend to the requirements of the game. The outlines of the real "game" of life and of culture, and even the actors who are playing the scene, are always changing. Human beings, as the historians have known, do not fit the rational formats of the social scientists; and the systematic models of the social scientists do not fit the living, evolving, changing realities of human action. Simply to be on the side of prudence, the ethnologist would do well to work with the data at hand, forgetting those "systems of priorities" which stand in the way of even universal historical documentation, not to mention "explanations" which cannot be traced back to a concrete empirical observation.

The earlier anthropology, as adumbrated by Lowie and criticized by Radin, was concerned with cultural traits and their interrelations. The operat-

ing metaphors of the earlier theorists were borrowed from the natural sciences, especially zoology,
biology, and physics.[55] To the extent that they re-
lied on these borrowed metaphors, they remained
in the trap of treating their data on terms other than
their own. Lévi-Strauss and Kluckhohn, as modern
writers, have borrowed their metaphors from linguistics, and their results have been equally disappointing for similar reasons because phonemic
analysis, while perhaps adequate for phonemic
analysis, cannot be expected to provide a key to the
rest of "cultural reality." [56]

Radin's Historicism and
Psychological Anthropology

I cannot conclude this essay without making a
few comments concerning the relevance of *The*

[55] Stanley Edgar Hyman has traced some of the implications for
anthropology of these metaphorical borrowings in his book, *The
Tangled Bank: Darwin, Marx, Frazer and Freud as Imaginative
Writers* (New York: Atheneum, 1962).

[56] Oddly enough the efforts of these men to find in linguistics the key
to cultural anthropology now seem to be spurned by some of the linguists themselves. In the recent special issue of the *American Anthropologist* entitled *The Ethnography of Communication* and edited by John
J. Gumpers and Dell Hymes, which can be taken as an official voice,
a call is made for an ethnography of communication which would
study all "communicative acts characteristic of a group" wherein the
"elements and relations of phonology appear partly in a new light
when viewed from the higher stratum of grammar. . . ." *American
Anthropologist*, vol. 66, no. 6, pt. 2, pp. 1–3, December 1964.

Method and Theory of Ethnology for the substance of contemporary ethnology. If there were any indication that the general lines of Radin's criticism referred only to methods and styles of inquiry that have since died, this would be unnecessary. But that does not seem to be the case. Though the world and its inhabitants have changed, ethnology and its practitioners, though they may now call themselves social anthropologists, still seem to be committed to the same practices Radin criticized thirty-five years ago. For present purposes I will take psychological anthropology as a major illustration of the implications of Radin's historical approach for modern anthropology.

It is in the "field" of "culture and personality" that the ethnologists have most clearly responded to intellectual currents outside their own traditions —namely, Freud and psychoanalysis in general. What attracted the ethnologists to the Freudian psychology was its attempt to go outside of Western character to locate the universal dimensions of the psychology of men. With the publication of *Totem and Taboo,* in which Freud postulated the universality of the Oedipal situation and the centrality of the primal horde in the emergence of conscience, the ethnologists were challenged on their own territory and, moreover, were provoked to respond. But ironically Freud, who was not an ethnologist, had got his ideas from reading some of the ethnologists,

yet only then did the ethnologists respond to him
and by *their* response gave a new direction to ethnology. The admixture of theory and research in
this bit of Western intellectual history is too complicated to decipher here, but it is clear that the
Freudian imagination has been a potent force in
giving us our image of primitive society, no matter
how weighty the treatises of the objective scholars.

Not that all ethnologists responded equally or for
that matter at all. Even into the twentieth century,
it is possible to be an ethnologist and remain unaware of the major intellectual currents in Western
society. Boas was secure enough to ignore Freud
and even to dismiss him as irrelevant, but it became
increasingly difficult for others to do so as Freudian
ideas gained general acceptance. So, for example,
both Malinowski and especially Sapir, not to mention a host of others who followed later, took account of Freud's existence. That it took Freud, who
had never visited a primitive society, to make
ethnology aware of personality is itself ironic,
for it reveals how much the image of the primitive derives from projecting our theories onto
him. Odd as it now may seem, it was Freud
who showed the ethnologists that primitives had
psyches.

What is more strange, however, is that once hav-

ing discovered the individual and his psyche, ethnology had almost no way of coping with them. At
the present time, with the exception of a few men
such as Hallowell, LaBarre, Erikson, and Homer
Barnett, who are concerned with problems of social
psychology and the psychology of the self, ethnology gives the impression of appearing to accept
Freud while denying the specific roles of individuals and their inner psychic life.

A genuine response to the implications of psychoanalysis would have meant an acknowledgment
of the enormous complexity and idiosyncrasy of
human motivation and a willingness to penetrate as
deeply into primitive life and its meaning categories as depth psychology has done for Western
men. This would call for intensive examination of
primitive myths, symbols, dramatic rites, tales, history, social relations, and interpersonal psychology
as these appear at specific times and places, and the
relationship of these to the institutional life of
primitive society. One can point to Kardiner's and
DuBois's work as attempts to be faithful to this
tradition and we will say more about them later,
but the point is that the psychoanalytic tradition
has been largely ignored if one tries to find other
examples of similar work carried out by field investigators. The conclusions of Margaret Mead's ethnological personality studies were addressed to

problems of Western femininity and adolescence,[57] and the work of Ruth Benedict in *Patterns of Culture* and *The Chrysanthemum and the Sword* set out in the beginning to show the harmonic integration of personality and culture patterns according to personality images derived mainly from Western scholarship, so that in both cases perceptual selection tended to be set in advance.[58] Thus, although one does not find the meaning categories of primitives in their work, they have nevertheless managed to attack much of the smug ethnocentrism of provincial America. Theirs was at least a criticism and rejection of Western values and institutions. Much less can be said for those students of primitive personality who have adopted psychological tests as their major technique for study.

The use of standardized personality "variables," the Rorschach, the TAT, the Draw a Person Test, etc., particularly where standardized scoring procedures are employed, has the effect not only of imposing a pre-established framework of evaluation on the data but reduces the data to index rather

[57] For a full-scale analysis of Mead's work as an expression of her interests primarily in Western rather than primitive society, see Karen Gaylord, "Mead, Freud, and an American Dream: Speculations on the Source, Significance, and Market Value of a 'Scientific' World View," unpublished, 1963.

[58] Benedict's *The Chrysanthemum and the Sword,* which was done partly under the impetus of the military enthusiasm of World War II, is especially revealing of how vulnerable an investigator can be when his perspective is not informed by a historic sense.

than person units. Once personality data are reduced to code categories or indices, it is difficult if
not impossible to re-establish meaningful relationships between psychological data and social or cultural data in a way that takes account of the historical specificity of particular responses. In this style
of investigation, all the unverbalized assumptions
which frame an action are ignored as irrevelant or,
what is worse, as "unscientific." The reduction of
personality to indices has left the ethnologist in the
same theoretical position he was in when he studied
abstracted cultural traits. There is only one final
analytical step left open to him: that is to compare
indices or personality traits cross-culturally (the
so-called Cross-Cultural Personality Studies), in a
way which ignores the historical person and the experience which forms and creates the actor. Instead
of adopting the psychoanalytic emphasis on the individual and attempting to comprehend him in
terms of the particular empirical data of ethnology, some ethnologists found a way to devitalize
the individual, in the same way that others, in
studying culture traits, had devitalized his society.

Personality trait studies and cross-cultural personality trait comparisons are methodologically on
a par with the earlier cultural trait studies and are
open to the same criticism Radin makes of the latter
in *The Method and Theory of Ethnology*. The

point is not that ethnology should become psychoanalytic in Freudian terms. This it obviously could
not do since ethnology had as a first obligation to
be true to its own empirical world. The issue as
Radin very clearly perceived it and stated it in his
book *Primitive Religion* was to link the social and
psychological dimensions of primitive life to a historically valid society.

As I have already indicated, Radin, in the last
chapter of the present volume, tried to point to a
way of utilizing modern depth psychology in ethnology. He extended this effort with the assistance
of Karl Kerenyi and C. J. Jung in his book, *The
Trickster,* which does not have a fully closed structure of analysis because there was no easy way to
solve the problem of linking depth psychology to
concrete historical data. The lack of a solution in
this book, it should be made clear, is due to the difficulty of the problem and not an unwillingness to
face the complexity of the issues. Radin further
developed his viewpoint vis-à-vis psychological
studies in a short review he did in the *Kenyon Review* of Kluckhohn's work. The books of Kluckhohn that he considered are *Mirror for Man* [59] and
Personality in Nature, Society and Culture, [60] the
latter being a collection of essays by students in the

[59] New York: Whittlesey House, 1949.
[60] Edited with Henry A. Murray (New York: Knopf, 1948).

field of "culture and personality." Even granted
that Radin's is not a fully developed statement, he
gives us a clear enough portrait of his objections to
psychological studies as represented in the work of
Kluckhohn:

Some two generations ago the great English legal historian, F. W. Maitland, declared that anthropology
would, very shortly, have to choose between being history or nothing. He was not alone among non-anthro-
pological thinkers in feeling that its data were in no
sense separate and distinct from history.

Maitland was wrong. Anthropology did not become
history nor did it ostensibly become nothing. In fact it
became everything and seemed to have taken its etymo-
logical meaning literally. If students of mankind in
1900 felt that the new discipline had, in its youthful
enthusiasm, taken on too much, that what it needed,
above all, was discipline, critical control of its sources
and some humility in the face of the questions it posed
and sought to answer, what would they have said had
they glanced through the two volumes to be discussed
here? In the first of them, an anthology entitled *Personality in Nature, Society, and Culture,* practically
every fundamental problem connected with man has
been broached and answers suggested. In the second,
Mirror for Man, dealing with anthropology proper,
the field is broadened still more and the relevance of its
data, its methods and its conclusions for the solution of

the practical problems of today and of the future is
stressed and elaborated.

If the new anthropology has come to include so much,
and if it feels itself competent to fruitfully reformulate
the basic problems of man, we have the right to demand
what credentials it possesses. What new knowledge has
it at its disposal which was denied to its predecessors?
What new techniques has it developed to justify such
intrepid optimism and such heroic self-assurance . . . ?

What Kluckhohn and the members of the school to
which he belongs (Benedict, Mead, etc.) actually wish
to imply is that they can give a truer and more adequate
meaning because they possess new facts obtained
through techniques developed within recent years by
psychologists, psychiatrists and psychoanalysts and because they have freed themselves from the presuppositions inherent in the older approach.

What are these new facts? They are, we know, all of
a psychological order and they are all concerned with
personality. Murray and Kluckhohn seem, indeed, to
recognize that psychological facts differ from cultural
ones, but insist that the two are inextricably interwoven,
that one defines the other, and that only by abstraction
can one be dealt with apart from the other. However,
concealed in their whole line of reasoning and their
whole approach lies the assumption that the psychological, not the cultural fact, is fundamental and that
the latter must be transformed into a psychological fact
before it acquires a true meaning. It is not strange then
to find those who take this view of culture attaching

little value to descriptions that seek to present a civilization fully and concretely, in all its multitudinous detail
as it can be directly observed. In their obsession for
knowing why a people as a whole have built up a given
civilization and why an individual behaves as we assume
he is behaving, Kluckhohn et al have completely forgotten what it is that man has built. They have rejected
the study of the content of a civilization in favor of
an attempt to investigate the content of the human
psyche. . . .

Despite the numerous and purely verbal disclaimers
to the contrary, history to them is the unfolding of the
human psyche, a psyche whose essential structure has
been given once and for all. Hence, their complete
unconcern for history and for developmental sequences. . . .

Presumably we must . . . attribute the failure to
analyze the nature of a "psychological fact" to the
idealistic presuppositions of these anthropologists. Assuredly it requires no great insight to realize, first, that
psychologists and psychiatrists are dealing with configurations and constellations of facts, not with individual
facts, and secondly, that these configurations are given
meaning by a specific approach and specific techniques
and that their meaning changes as the approach changes.
Since these anthropologists have failed to understand
this and since they have, in addition, thrown the historical record into the discard, it is small wonder that the
conglomerate they label anthropology turns out to be a
bewildering combination and juxtaposition of observed

cultural facts, inferred cultural facts, personally interpreted cultural facts, psychological "facts," psychological constructs and unanalyzed philosophical assumptions. . . .[61]

We can use this criticism as a point of departure
for a more specific examination of another branch
of culture and personality studies. Over the past
thirty years the students of culture and personality
have produced many studies [62] and with the aid of
more refined technologies of investigation now
available they continue to produce them.[63] However, because the works of Kardiner,[64] especially
his analysis of Cora DuBois's study of the Alorese,
have been the seminal studies for the entire culture

[61] *Kenyon Review*, vol. xi, no. 3, pp. 523–526, Summer 1949.

[62] See especially the works cited by Cora DuBois in her preface,
"Two Decades Later," to the republication of *The People of Alor*
(New York: Harper Torchbook, Harper & Bros., 1961), pp. xxviii–xxx.

[63] The most recent of these are: Paul Parin *et al., Die Weissen-
denken zuviel. Psychoanalytiche Untersuchungen bei den Dogon in
Westafrica* (Zurich: Atlantis Verlag, 1963) ; and Alexander H. Leighton *et al., Psychiatric Disorder among the Yoruba:* A Report from the
Cornell Area Mental Health Research Project in the Western Region,
Nigeria (Ithaca, N.Y.: Cornell University Press, 1963). For a critical
appraisal and a statement of the limitations of these studies, which
are based on the most advanced technology of the Rorschach, the TAT,
and team research, see "African Minds," *The Times Literary Supplement*, pp. 77–79, Jan. 30, 1964.

[64] *The Psychological Frontiers of Society* (New York: Columbia
University Press, 1945) and *The Individual and His Society* (New
York: Columbia University Press, 1939).

and personality "approach," I would like to take
DuBois's analysis in *The People of Alor* to explain
the limits of this style of investigation when seen in
the light of a historical attitude.

Alor is a small island in what was at the time of
DuBois's study the Netherlands East Indies. It is
fifty miles long and thirty miles wide and has a population of about seventy thousand. About ten thousand people living along the coast are Mohamme-
dans; the remainder of the population is pagan and
lives in the interior. DuBois's report is concerned
with a very small village located in Alor and is thus
not actually a study of the people of Alor as a whole
but rather a study of a minute fraction of this population which lives in Atimelang. The "people of
Alor" are really only the people of Atimelang.

When the Dutch arrived in this area in 1908,
they divided the interior into "radjahships," and
the "radjahs" appointed to hold these positions
were drawn from the coastal regions. Prior to this,
there had been only trading relations between the
pagan and Mohammedan populations, with neither
group exerting any dominance over the other.

Under the "radjahs," still holding sway at the
time of DuBois's study, are "kapitans" who with a
handful of field police collect taxes and litigate dis-
putes. This they do through a "kepala" who is appointed to head each village. Groups of friendly

villages are unified under a head man called a
"tumukum." "This hierarchy is a Dutch innovation, but it has been quite heartily accepted by the
native population. . . . The system of litigation,
however, has been far more completely accepted
than the system of taxation." [65]
It was the native custom to locate villages on
mountain spurs and crests, but since the "war of
pacification" in 1918 the Dutch have put "pressure" on the people to move into villages where they
are more accessible to the field police. The Atimelang complex DuBois studied is one of these trans-
posed groups. It consists of five villages with a total
population of about six hundred, the village of
Atimelang and its two hamlets supporting about
180 people. The villages are organized around from
one to seven "dance places" of which each contains
a large lineage house. Each individual member of
a family belongs to several lineage groups. The
people of Atimelang are enmeshed in a complex
system of creditor-debtor relationships, which operate through their membership in these various
lineage groups as well as through the family. Marriage and death entail a complex financial procedure in which an individual may spend his whole
life paying various debts and receiving his outstanding credits. Thus, for instance, the death feast

[65] DuBois, *The People of Alor*, p. 16.

to which each individual is entitled may take place fifteen or twenty years after the time of death, and marriage payments may not be completely liquidated at the time of an individual's death. The several lineage groups of each individual are responsible in various degrees for their debts, and men of the village who perform little productive labor spend most of their lives bargaining over such matters.

The subsistence economy consists mainly of agricultural products which are the property of the women who work the fields. The fields are individually owned by men and women, as well as by children who inherit them. The prestige economy is in the hands of the men and consists of various prized objects, and pigs and fowl. These animals are consumed only on feast days and mainly by the men. Few of the objects of the prestige economy are individually owned; most are held in various forms of partnership and interlocking systems of ownership. All of the various forms of barter are motivated by an attempt to obtain high profits· or interest.

There is no highly formalized religion or mythology in Alor. In fact, one of the salient features of this society is the complete absence of formalization in most aspects of the life of the community. This according to Kardiner and DuBois is due mainly to the child-rearing practices of the people, and the major part of DuBois's book is taken up with the description of these practices and with biographies of individuals whose childhood experiences are emphasized.

The sketch just presented summarizes DuBois's second chapter, called "The Setting," which comprises 12 of the 640 pages of the book. The rest of the book concerns itself with matters which center around the life history of the individual members of the society; about a third is devoted to the process of socialization, while the rest is devoted to individual biographies and psychological tests. This distribution of data might be acceptable if there existed for Atimelang a substantial descriptive literature, but neither Alor nor Atimelang had ever before been seriously studied. This leaves us in the anomalous position of having a vast amount of detailed biographical and test materials along with almost no information about the setting in which they occur. What grounds does a reader have for assessing Kardiner's and DuBois's interpretations except within the framework they themselves have erected? The objection is not that these authors have set a specific problem for themselves. On the contrary, this is much to be admired for it gives their analysis a focus which allows us to see clearly what they are doing, no matter how inadequate the supporting data. However, we might expect such a specific study only after a fairly complete record has been assembled. For example, in a study of the character of Americans such as Riesman's, *The Lonely Crowd,* we are willing to excuse the lack of a full description of American society because such descriptions abound in the existing literature and because the reader himself has a personal knowledge of the society which provides him with a framework for making his own assessments and evaluations. In short, as in the case of Greek civilization, which has been described in some depth, critical opinion must have independent sources from which to work; thus in reading Bruno Snell's study of the Greek mind,[66] anyone who wishes to take the trouble can go back to the sources to satisfy himself concerning the interpretations. It is in this that DuBois is deficient, a fact of which she herself seems to be aware when she says, "Obviously details must await separate publication, since it is not the purpose of this account to give a thorough ethnographic description, but only to include such material as is pertinent to the general problem described in Chapter I."[67]

DuBois is aware that there is more to report even

[66] *The Discovery of the Greek Mind: The Greek Origins of European Thought* (New York: Harper, 1960).
[67] DuBois, *The People of Alor,* p. 27.

though she does not explicitly tell us how what is not reported might bear on her interpretations. She tells us, for example, that

Remarks on religion in this volume, either here or later, do not exhaust the range of spirits recognized or the variety of observances connected with them. An indication of the diversity, as well as the amorphism, of spirit relationships is that in twenty-one households of Dikimpe and its associated hamlets there were at least fifty-six known spirits, altars, carvings, and the like.[68]

Surely a remark such as this reveals that these Alorese inhabit a rich spiritual world which must be of central importance to their psychic and character structure. If that is the world they inhabit, then that is the world we must necessarily know about if we are studying the basic character structure of a people. Kardiner, on the other hand, who approaches his material as a psychologist, is much more carefree with the ethnographic record. In his introduction to *The People of Alor,* he dispenses with the ethnographic historical record with this statement:

Here the orientation is that of an ego psychology in which the operational concept is not the instinctive drive but the integrational units or action systems through

[68] *Ibid.,* p. 37.

which the drive is consummated. Furthermore, the orientation is systematic rather than historical. This does not mean the exclusion of a historical orientation because the study of all integrational systems must be genetic and therefore historically oriented. The present study, although it supplies us with very scant historical background, is almost complete in that it fills the gaps left in other studies by the absence of biographies. These biographies, moreover, not only give us opportunity to check on the reliability of the conclusions drawn from the previous studies, but also furnish us with new orientations for the study of culture and personality.[69]

Kardiner's conception of history is equated with the genetic approach, by which he means biographies. When he talks about a historical orientation, he is referring to the personal biographies of DuBois's informants. There is not any question that biographies constitute an important part of historical data; but insofar as they are individual character sketches, they do not constitute a history of a society. There is really no significant sense in which Kardiner can claim that his studies have a historical orientation. But he compounds his error by claiming that he can "check the reliability of the conclusions drawn from previous studies" by reference to the case histories of the Atimelang. By this proce-

[69] *Ibid.*, p. 7.

dure he assigns the Atimelang case histories, which are the most historically specific material one can imagine, the role of universal referent point for other studies in other societies. This is not historical at all, and the rest of Kardiner's work reveals that he is working exclusively as a clinical psychologist. The objection here is not to Kardiner's use of biographies but rather to his clinical attitude toward his subjects. For him the biographies are not a device for learning and appreciating the historical evolution of the Alorese people but formal structures which lend themselves to the psychologist's clinical examination. By restricting his scope to psychological themes he reveals not only a lack of humanistic cultivation but also a lack of a cultural historical sense. Though it is true that in his analyses of the Comanche and Tanala he assigns a cultural historical causal role to the introduction of the horse and rice technology in shaping the characteristic structures of these societies, these explanations only play the role of allowing him to clean the edges of his psychological analysis. That is, he uses historical factors to start the motor of his psychological machine.

Since so much of DuBois's ethnological material and its interpretation is concerned with the childhood of the Alorese, it is not possible to present a summary which would do justice to her data. Be it sufficient to say that the Alorese child has a very difficult time growing up. The mother's economic responsibility prevents her from devoting enough time to the child, whose care is thus left to older siblings and any male adult who happens to be in the vicinity. Little attention is paid to "affirmative" training, the major emphasis being on keeping the child out of trouble. On the whole the child tends to rear himself and is not guided by a system of punishments and rewards within the context of a love relationship with the mother. Kardiner then summarizes the basic personality of the Alorese in the following way:

In Alor we derived the following features as being of projective origin:

  a. folk tales
  b. religious dogmas and practices which were noteworthy for the absence of idealization, no expectation of good from supernatural, but freedom from persecution
  c. the special attitude of procrastination and action only under threat
  d. absence of conscience and generally low tenacity of superego
  e. lack of interest in conquering the outer world
  f. lack of confidence
  g. easy abandonment of enterprise

h. low aspiration level

i. anxiousness, mistrustfulness

j. poor affectionate fixations

k. ill-defined agression patterns and fixation of life goals on derivatives of breast fetishism through financial transaction. This takes in the most distinctive features of Alorese culture.

. . . They have no "interest" in permanence or durability. . . . Strength does not rate very high; neither does skill; nor are these qualities greatly admired. . . . Honesty is not an admired trait. . . . Their aesthetic sense is limited. . . . They have little investigative drive. . . . The chief positive values are those associated with food and power over others, here closely related to wealth. . . . The values can all be easily derived from the projective systems we have described. The key to the value systems is to be found in the low emotional character of the interpersonal relations of the Alorese, and their deep lack of self confidence and enterprise, which we traced to the poor parental care.[70]

This, of course, is to ascribe a great deal to poor parental care, considering the scope and breadth of the personality characteristics which are enumerated. While it is true that the quality of parental care is important, other factors cannot be ignored.

[70] *The Psychological Frontiers of Society* (New York: Columbia University Press, 1945), p. 22.

However unpleasant it may be to make the acknowledgment, the fact that DuBois studied a captured society living under the threat of extreme forms of sanction by their overlords forces its way through the screen of the projective mechanisms. It would be as oversimplified an approach to try to analyze the personalities of these people without taking into account their personal biographies as it would be to derive their basic personality from their colonial status. Inadequate as these two alternatives are, one can only say that if the man's voice betrays the child's wish, then let us listen to his voice as well and hear both speak at once.

It is possible from the scatter of information that emerges from the biographies to suggest some of the additional factors which may be of importance in understanding the behavior of the Atimelang.

Here is the picture of the influence of Dutch colonization which can be sketched from a few hints and pertinent fragments of dreams found in the several biographies. When the Dutch arrived in 1908, the coastal people were Mohammedan; since they spoke Malay they were used by the Dutch to gain control over the people of the interior. These people lived in the mountainous regions where head-hunting and intertribal wars were prevalent, so that the presence of the Dutch probably offered them a degree of protective security.

The women performed the dull, repetitive tasks such as rearing the children, preparing the meals, and raising the crops. The men were primarily engaged in the predatory and honorific tasks of fighting and gathering wealth through financial manipulation. The word "killer" was still considered a high compliment at the time DuBois did her field work, although predatory activities had already been curtailed by the Dutch for twenty years.

In 1918 the people of the Atimelang complex killed their "radjah," apparently because of his extreme taxation measures. This occurred near the end of the First World War and there is reason to believe that there were some objective grounds for the dissatisfaction which led to the murder. The murder was followed by the "war of pacification," which was not restricted to Atimelang alone but was general throughout the interior, since it is probable that pressure was being exerted for more taxes all over the island. When DuBois was doing her field study, the Dutch considered the operation of pacification to be still in process. It is not clear from the report when taxation had been imposed on the people, but from references in the biographies there is no question that many of the men were taken to prison at the time.

As a result of the "war of pacification" the people of the Atimelang complex were forced to move into the valley in order to be accessible to the field police who began to patrol the interior. *Corvée* labor was imposed and the work consisted mainly of building government structures and keeping the trails open to facilitate the movements of the field police. The men were forced to pay the equivalent of two months' labor for taxes and they were obligated to spend one month a year doing *corvée* labor. However, in practice it seems that when the Dutch had a pressing task they enlisted a whole village, regardless of sex or "legal" restrictions concerning the amount of labor that could be extracted. It is difficult to characterize the general treatment of the people with any precision since it receives no formal recognition in DuBois's work. But again, from the unsolicited fragments of the biographies, one gathers that these people were beaten with rattan switches, herded into jails, stabbed with bayonets, and so forth. All of the usual methods of pacification and control were used.

In the light of this, what does it mean to attribute a lack of initiative to these people? Nowhere does it seem to occur to these analysts that the "special attitude of procrastination and action only under threat . . . absence of conscience . . . lack of interest in conquering the outer world . . . lack of confidence . . . easy abandonment of enterprise . . . low aspiration level" could be "explained" by

anything other than the breast. No doubt the Alorese experienced poor parental care, but this cannot
be explained in terms of psychological patterns; it
can only be explained by their history.

For example, one of DuBois's informants describes his image of his father:

At our house people saw the soldiers coming and slipped
out through the floor of the house and went to hide in
the fields. Some people hadn't yet finished paying their
taxes, but my father had. The present Radjah was clerk
then. He said my father had paid his taxes and let him
go. I got home. My father had a big body, but when I
got home he was sitting there small and all shrunken
together.[71]

The Atimelang "do not idealize their fathers."
Formal methodologies always act as perceptual
blinders and this, of course, is only an extreme example of the process.

One of the interesting subjects whom Kardiner
discusses is Malelaka, the prophet, of whom we are
told:

The subject of this biography, taken at the age of forty-
five, is the most obscure of the four men. He is indirect,
shifty, insinuating, cowardly, grandiose, distinctly para-
noid, circumstantial, internally deeply insecure, hypo-

[71] *The People of Alor*, p. 352.

critical, unconsciously cruel and destructive, but actually timid and pretentious. In other words, a pious fraud. . . . He tells the story of his life with ulterior motives and . . . takes little interest in the narrative of his life which is our paramount interest.[72]

This poor fellow has been imprisoned, tortured, and beaten at the hands of the Dutch, and yet he has still not been transformed into either a good native or a pliable subject! DuBois interrupts the text of the biography to tell us that she is trying to get him to talk about important things, namely his early training ("I tried again to get him talking about human issues"). Malelaka still seems to have retained a perspective of his own and he refuses to talk about the problems which "ought" to concern him. This scene can only be seen as a tragicomedy in which both parties to the transaction refuse to admit defeat and neither can wholly defeat the other.

Malelaka is a much more complicated person than his analysts are willing to grant. Like a true prophet, he was not born in the land of his prophecy. He was born in the village in which the "radjah" who had been in control of Atimelang resided. It was the murder of this "radjah" which had precipitated the "war of pacification" in 1918.

---

[72] *The Psychological Frontiers of Society,* p. 185.

Malelaka dates his career as a prophet to the time
of puberty when he first encountered spirits. In
1928 he prophesied the imminent arrival of Good
Beings who would relieve the people of their misery. These Beings seem to have been a traditional
part of the mythology of the people of Alor. The
people began to build guest houses for these Beings
and in general responded to the prophecy. The
Dutch, however, sent soldiers to destroy the houses
and to arrest Malelaka. He spent either one and a
half or six years in prison—it is not clear from the
information given which figure is correct. At the
time his biography is taken he is still predicting the
arrival of Good Beings. But there is little danger
of trouble this time since, as DuBois informs us, the
war of pacification and the events of 1928 have
helped to give a "nonfanatical and realistic temperament" to the people of Atimelang.

The innumerable and continual references to
Malelaka's hardships at the hands of the Dutch,
his bitter experiences while doing *corvée* labor, his
concern with the affliction that has befallen his people, and his many images of Atimelang being
"raised into the sky and turned over," all of these
can be ignored only at the risk of turning Malelaka
into a prop upon which to hang some preconceived
notions. But it is not just that this man was reduced
to a mere source of data; for, in Malelaka, Kar-

diner had under his eyes one of the most interesting characters of Atimelang without even recognizing it. Even DuBois's methodological screening does not hide the underlying drama in the life of this man. But in the end the theory overwhelms the subject, and Malelaka's rebelliousness and hypocrisy make him "a poor subject." Malelaka is fighting his analysts with the only weapons he has at hand: deceit, negativism, and a somewhat concealed obstinacy, those techniques classically employed by a subjected, but not wholly defeated, people.

Thus while there is something immediately appealing about Kardiner's original project to combine the results of psychological analysis with concrete cultural historical data and to explain institutional interaction in its relation to personality formation, the end product fails for lack of a response to the real complexities of the historical materials. The synthesis Kardiner achieves is the synthesis of his system, and we are left with the systematic formulas of the theory. Kardiner's interest in these primitives is to study and clarify his *concept* of the basic personality of "simpler" cultures so that he can lay bare the structure of the basic personality of Western society. The unwillingness to acknowledge the specific validity of the specific actions of specific persons inevitably results first in premature abstraction, and then to a search for finding all encompassing schemes for handling the lack of closure in the data. In due course the structure of the theory itself captures the observer's fascination and then is transformed into the object of his work. But this exercise from the beginning tells us more about Western men than it does about the Alorese. A clinical approach uninformed by a sense of history forces the analyst to make his interpretations and judgments on the basis of sets of unanalyzed assumptions which possess the legitimacy only of acceptance by other Western students.

I have deliberately focused my critical attention on the formal and methodological dimensions of the work of Lowie, Lévi-Strauss, Kluckhohn, Benedict, Mead, Kardiner, and DuBois in order the better to illustrate what Radin meant by a fully committed historical anthropology. For present purposes it has been convenient to evaluate this selected range of essays and books, not because they represent the exclusive viewpoint of the authors I have considered, but because they represent a side of their work which is not reconcilable with a genuinely historical attitude. It should be noted that each of these authors has been much more ambivalent toward history than is revealed in those of their works that I have treated here. In fact, a characteristic feature of the work of these authors has been an inability to resolve the contradiction between scientistic anthropology and humanistic history.[73] Lowie, Lévi-Strauss, Kluckhohn, Benedict, Mead, Kardiner, and DuBois and, insofar as they are typical representatives, modern anthropology in general have attempted to straddle the fence of science and history. Hoping to have it both ways, they have left anthropology with a split image.

Even while Lowie was arguing passionately for an anthropological science of correlations he was sensitively describing the way of life and the world view of the Crow Indians. No amount of stretching or bending would allow even Lowie to fit his Crow ethnology into his own methodological strictures. Lévi-Strauss, as Susan Sontag has noted, has dis-

[73] Stanley Diamond, in his introduction to *Primitive Views of the World* (New York: Columbia University Press, 1964), is the first to have pointed out the underlying ambivalence of anthropological theory. In that essay he suggests a total re-examination of anthropology by tracing its origins and its major intellectual commitments to the Enlightenment, which produced the ancestors of modern anthropology: Rousseau on the one hand and "Condorcet and company" on the other. Using the contradictions in the thought of the Enlightenment as his point of departure, Diamond boldly sketches a genealogy of anthropological theory and theorists which with remarkable success "places" the major schools of anthropological thought within his organizing principle (see pp. xvii–xxix). Looked at in the light of the fundamental ambivalence of the anthropological enterprise, it is not by chance that a document such as *The Ethnography of Communication* reflects the wish of some anthropologists to retreat from a scientistic linguistics and to readdress themselves to the "problem" of communication and human understanding.

played his ambivalence toward his subject simply by being at once the author of both *Tristes Tropiques* and *Structural Anthropology*, two books so alien from each other in tone and spirit as to appear not to be written by the same author. In Kluckhohn there is the discordance between the lack of feeling and personal involvement in his writings on the Navaho and the deep and personally regenerative human involvement he displayed when he was with the Navaho and when he talked about them. In Benedict's *Patterns of Culture*, but not in *The Chrysanthemum and the Sword*, one's attention is continuously called to her profound rejection of Western institutions and values and her personal involvement with the rhythm and poetry of primitive life as illustrated especially by her treatment of the Zuñi. Margaret Mead in returning to Manus in 1953 to do a follow-up study of *Growing Up in New Guinea* as reported in *New Lives for Old* wanted to provide historical continuity for her subjects in Manus; though the time gap was too large and the historical material too thin, she nevertheless suggests by her intention her desire to be genuinely historical. So too Kardiner and DuBois, in bringing to bear their psychological sophistication, had hoped, as we have shown, to remain faithful to the historical world of the Alorese. All of these authors have spoken with a human voice and have left their personal stamp on some of their work. Yet all have also been caught in an ambivalence which has prevented them from fully pursuing their humanistic and historical impulses to the limits that Radin early in his career had chosen as his goal.

It is perhaps understandable that the choice Radin made is not made more frequently since the price for making it is high, no less than professional ostracism and exclusion from unconscious participation in the dominant ethos of the Western world. Radin possessed that rare courage of remaining true to his convictions in a world in which this quality is not highly rewarded.

In making the choice to become a culture historian, Radin stuck with the logics that choice imposed, irrespective of personal and professional considerations. It removed him more and more from the anthropology that eventually emerged as university subject matter, the anthropology that is taught in graduated sequences of courses and presented as time-honored truth. As his life progressed he found himself at the margins of the profession, alienated from his earlier colleagues who had become "successful" and largely unnoticed by a new generation of students. He came to be thought of as an irascible old man who pursued his own problems. At times his academic superiors patronized him and at other times treated him as a comic figure. If Radin suffered in this role, he did so privately without an outward projection of his feelings. His capacity to suffer neither annoyance nor ridicule from his critics derived from the strength of character he had developed through his work. His alienation was a personal choice as well as a personal style of life and became the basis of living with himself through his work.

The example of Radin is the example of a style in which intellectual pursuits and personal objectives come to be fused into an integrated character and an integrated mode of action. In his quest to find the person in history, Radin discovered and became himself as a person. Thus his work was the source both of his motivation and of his self-creation as a civilized man.

In the last several decades anthropology has seen the development of new methodologies and refined techniques of research. It has developed new theoretical terminologies and totally embracing frameworks for studying primitive societies. In the meantime, anthropologists have witnessed the almost full-scale incorporation of the primitive world into the institutional apparatus of the dominant industrial states of the Western world. Almost before their eyes they have seen even remote, isolated societies penetrated by modern agencies which have inexorably contributed to the destruction of primitive societies and their institutions. The anthropologists along with their primitive cohorts have been witness to the disintegration and re-creation of a world-historical epoch. The future will judge anthropology neither by the systematic coherence of its theories nor by its capacity to be all-embracing. If it will be worth judging at all, anthropology will be judged by its capacity to respond to the complexity of the history whose unfolding it has witnessed. A respect for history presupposes a sense of humility in the face of the human condition and an absence of the pretentiousness which claims to codify that which demands other modes of understanding, if it is to be understood at all.

New York
June 1966

Author's Introduction

It is generally a significant symptom when scholars become too articulate about their methods. A method, after all, is a varying procedure, changing with the nature of the facts studied and the problems posited. Most good investigators are hardly aware of the precise manner in which they gather their data. It may rise into their consciousness on specific occasions but, in the main, they wisely concentrate their energies upon the obvious task of procuring as full and complete a record as possible. Certainly for ethnology, any individual who has received the requisite training and who possesses, in a moderate degree, the attributes of honesty, intelligence, and humility has all that is necessary.

If, then, there has been a notable increase in essays and articles on the method of ethnology within the last ten years, it is well to pause and take cognizance of the fact. The generous view would be to assume that this is a sign of approaching maturity, that we are prepared now to look back upon our work with critical objectivity and devise methods to guard us more efficiently than ever against error. But I am afraid there is no warrant for such optimism. On the contrary, this increase in theoretical and methodological treatises indicates mischief ahead. Discussions on theory and methodology, so a very acute English art critic has recently observed, caused the chatter on the scaffolding of the Tower of Babel. They are only too frequently a substitute for real work. I am somewhat inclined to subscribe to this very unkind sentiment, only I should like to word it differently. Where theory and methodology loom important, it is usually a sign that an *impasse* has been reached; either this, or scholars have exhausted their methods for arranging or understanding their data.

Now, to my mind, this is precisely what has occurred in ethnology and the following essay is an attempt to point out what has happened and why it has happened.

Ethnology is the study of aboriginal cultures. No adequate description of any culture is possible that does not include as much of its history as is accurately and legitimately possible. Our primary duty is to the specific tribe we are describing. Upon this, certainly all ethnologists are agreed. The vast majority, however, insist that ethnology has another function. They contend that its results should be made subsidiary to much larger problems—to the determination of historical processes and cultural dynamics as such; that they are to furnish us with the raw material for the formulation of general laws. It is the present writer's contention that little warrant exists for thus extending its meaning and that, on the whole, confusion and mischief have followed in its wake.

The only question of importance, then, is to discover some means whereby we can best obtain a complete account of an aboriginal culture. Every ethnologist has realized the marked diversity in both the types of monograph and the kinds of theory and method propounded and must have put this query to himself again and again. How is this to be explained? Personal temperament, special interests, bias will account for part of it; but after due allowance has been made for these factors, a respectable residuum of difference still remains, best to be interpreted, I feel, as the reflection of the investigator's attitude, expressed or implied, toward aboriginal cultures. This must, of course, seem a platitude to most ethnologists, but it is essential that I stress it.

Now three attitudes have been taken toward this purpose of ethnology; first, that it enables us to reconstruct stages in the evolution of culture or, at least, presents us with a point of view outgrown by civilized man today; second, that it demonstrates the enormous diversity in forms of culture developed since the beginning of time; and, third, that it need properly have no purpose, any more than a description of the civilization of Greece or England has a purpose, over and above that of being a specific account of a given culture.

I prefer the word attitude to interpretation because, not infrequently, an ethnologist gives an interpretation that is definitely belied by his manner of describing or discussing aboriginal cultures. In the following pages I have tried, to the best of my ability, to distinguish between the two, for it is of the greatest importance to do so.

Connected with the first attitude is the assumption that aboriginal peoples are inferior in mentality to ourselves. In spite of numerous differences I do not hesitate to include in this group not merely the classical English evolutionists but likewise such a variegated group of scholars as the German Thurnwald, Preuss, and Graebner, the French Durkheim, Mauss, and Lévy-Bruhl, and the English Rivers, Haddon, Malinowski, and Radcliffe-Brown. Not a few American ethnologists, despite their militant attitude toward the older evolutionists, not infrequently seem to share the same view.

The second attitude is that represented by Boas and the vast majority of his school. One of its presuppositions is that nothing is to be predicated of a given culture in advance, but that its specific nature must be demonstrated, step by step. Possibly this formulation of his view is too sharp, but I think it is essentially correct. Fundamentally his outlook is that of the natural scientist. The analogy between cultures and animals is very real to him and he has only recently stated that they differ like so many species or genera. In the course of the examination of his contribution to ethnology, possibly the greatest single contribution of any scholar of the last three generations, I shall try to indicate how this attitude permeates his whole work and how, in spite of his persistent and unavailing protests to the contrary, it has led directly to overt quantitative treatments of culture.

The third attitude has been explicitly stated by only a handful of people, although it is implied in the work of such American ethnologists and theorists as Dixon, Swanton, Lowie, Goldenweiser, Sapir, Spier, and Wallis. It underlies the work of the Danish authorities on the Eskimo and the best and most significant work of the Dutch and Russian investigators. It has always been the basic viewpoint of my own work.

PAUL RADIN

Berkeley, Calif.
August 1933

THE METHOD AND THEORY
OF ETHNOLOGY

By and by anthropology will have the choice between being history or nothing.

F. W. MAITLAND

Chapter I

The Presuppositions of the Ethnological Method in the United States: the Method of Franz Boas

Ethnology should be one of the easiest subjects in the world to define. It is manifestly the study of the culture of aboriginal peoples, more specifically those aborigines with whom the Europeans have come into contact since the fifteenth century. Yet we have only to make this definition to realize that today it has come to mean both more and less than such a definition would seem to imply.

The reasons are not far to seek. Ethnology grew up in a very specific atmosphere. The work that ushered it into existence, E. B. Tylor's *Primitive Culture*, gave it a circumscribed and somewhat subservient position, that of helping to establish specific stages in the evolution of culture. The English theorists who followed Tylor, as well as those English missionaries and officials who subsequently wrote some of the standard monographs, never dreamed of ascribing to their studies any

other significance. When this view was finally
challenged, notably by Boas, it had become so
definitely established that a good part of his
energies and those of his school had to be devoted to
disproving it. In other words, ethnology had again
to assume something of a secondary rôle, that of
examining the validity of the theories of the evolutionary school.

In neither case did this secondary function interfere with the production of excellent descriptions of
aboriginal cultures; but it did lead to the stressing
of a number of problems that were clearly byproducts. For the evolutionist the most important
of these were the comparative method and the
theory of survivals, and for the antievolutionist
the hypothesis of culture areas and the nature of
cultural dynamics—more specifically, diffusion.
The evolutionist definitely insisted that, in spite
of special developments along certain lines, aboriginal cultures represented an early stage or, if you
will, earlier stages in the evolution of culture, and
the antievolutionist wisely avoided the main issues
and insisted that, whatever the facts demonstrated,
they assuredly did not demonstrate any of the
fundamental theses of the evolutionist.

There is no need of opening this controversy
again; it has fortunately been relegated to oblivion.
But its aftermath is still with us and, as I shall try

to point out, has led to the neglect of the very thing with which ethnology is primarily concerned, a truly complete and thorough study of aboriginal civilizations. Before, however, we can properly appreciate what has conduced to the present somewhat deplorable situation, it will be necessary to pass in review some of the main preconceptions characterizing the approach to ethnological data in the United States.

In spite of the manifold and manifest differences between the evolutionist and antievolutionist approach, they do share one thing in common, *viz.*, that they treat the data of ethnology as though they were comparable to those of biology or physics. I am well aware that this will be vehemently denied by Boas and many members of his school, but I think it is quite apparent in their monographs, whether they are conscious of it or not. This then is the first point to be remembered. But there is another point, flowing directly from one of the major positions that had logically to be taken in the controversy with the evolutionary approach, *viz.*, the thesis that we have no right to make any assumptions about the nature of aboriginal cultures. They were to be studied not only without presuppositions but as though we were dealing with a *tabula rasa.* All that we know about culture in our own civilizations and all the evidence we possess about cultural processes in historically documented civilizations were not to be accepted as applicable. If, for instance, it could be proved that cultural diffusion had taken place in Europe, Asia, and Africa, through mass migration and conquest, we were not to claim, *ipso facto*, that such had been the case in aboriginal cultures. The frequent occurrence of certain types of diffusion in the more complex civilizations did not necessarily imply the existence of the same, even as a hypothesis, in the simpler cultures. Similarly, if, in Europe, Asia, and Africa, it could be shown that languages were comparatively few in number and had undergone certain types of transformation, we had no right to assume offhand that a comparable or identical transformation had occurred in aboriginal America, Africa, or Oceania. In both cases this would have to be demonstrated. But how precisely was this to be done in the absence of a documentary record? The answer, as first formulated by Boas and subsequently developed by Wissler, was *by a study of the distribution of culture traits*. This led directly to the creation of a fairly elaborate technique for the determination of culture areas, as well as for the mechanism of diffusion and other cultural processes. But since certain specific types of diffusion and culture transformation could not possibly be demonstrated by the study of the distribution of traits, such as, for example, mass invasions, loss of culture elements, changes effected by the influence of exceptional individuals, these were left out. In other words, in the method devised by Boas, Wissler, etc., the dynamics and the growth of aboriginal cultures were described in terms of an accidentally determined selection of processes.

Now it is in the assumption that everything has to be proved anew, and by the manner in which they determine culture traits, culture areas, and culture centers, that these ethnologists betray their actual point of view.

Let us begin where they begin. What precisely are these aboriginal cultures about which we are to predicate nothing? If we are not to equate them, in a general way, with those cultures about which we possess some knowledge, what assumptions are we to make? The answer apparently is that we are to treat them as *unknowns*, a rather characteristic scientific approach. Of course, they are nothing of the kind. They are *unknown cultures*, not simply *unknowns*. Boas and some members of his school seem to posit this with one breath and deny it with another. As I have indicated above, their attitude implies this: that when we begin the investigation of an aboriginal group, logically speaking, it has no culture and that its culture gradually emerges in the course of the inquiry. Stated thus baldly, this naturally seems somewhat ludicrous and unfair. But stranger things than this occur when a specifically logical and scientific approach is applied to the elucidation of cultural phenomena. The obvious has been demonstrated triumphantly again and again. The concept culture, although methodologically taboo, slips in after the concept *unknown*, from the very beginning, and the investigator proves what he has assumed.

Now we shall all grant that by treating aboriginal cultures as *unknowns*, Boas did an inestimable service to ethnology, because he was then able to show, or, at least, had it within his power to show, that they actually possessed cultures and that those processes inhering in other cultures held likewise for them. This was an exceedingly important fact to demonstrate at a time when the world was bending the knee somewhat obsequiously to crude forms of evolutionism. But after this had been triumphantly done, why was it necessary to persist with essentially the same hypothesis and why, for example, were only certain types of diffusion accepted and only certain developmental schemes tolerated? The answer to this question is intimately bound up with the type of factual presentation he manifestly prefers and which can best be understood by referring to his Kwakiutl and Tsimshian monographs. There we find the bare facts presented without comment, unless it be to indicate the distribution of certain specific traits. Neither the individuals from whom the data were obtained nor the data themselves are evaluated, and this manifestly is not an accident. Surely it is not unwarranted to assume that he wishes the facts to speak for themselves. I feel that we have here come to grips with the real crux of his whole point of view. *Cultural facts do not speak for themselves, but physical facts do.* A pebble is a pebble and a tree a tree. Is he not fundamentally making such a claim for a Kwakiutl text when he gives it without comment or explanation? Is it not a tabulation we have here, of quantitatively defined facts whose properties are to be determined? It is the viewpoint of the natural scientist—more specifically, the physicist. I see no other interpretation.

This interpretation is further confirmed when it is seen how well other aspects of his point of view are thereby explained. We can then understand why he treats cultural facts quantitatively, as discrete entities; why he deals only with single-trait diffusion; why in the comparison of languages he insists that they be regarded as unrelated unless the differences as well as the similarities are explained,[1] and why he prefers to start with the assumption

---

[1] This very demand for a "complete" explanation is a scientific preconception. It is not possible for cultural phenomena.

of *unknowns* and finds no warrant for relinquishing
this principle of interpretation when his *unknowns*
prove to be cultures in our sense, possessed of the
same characteristics as ours and undergoing the
same type of changes.

No one, however, who has studied under Boas
can forget the vehemence with which he has
always insisted that cultural facts were never to
be confused with physical ones. It is apparently his
sincere desire to avoid just that confusion to which
in actual practice he seems to succumb. Manifestly
he views with alarm such expressions of this identification as are to be found in Rivers' *History of
Melanesian Society* or in the elaborate culture-area
theory of Wissler-Kroeber[2] or, finally, in the application of statistical methods as indulged in by the
latter.[3] Something seems to be constraining him to
practice an approach that, theoretically, he con-
demns. The only legitimate inference is that, in
contrast to the culture historian, Boas is scientifically minded—what the Germans call *naturwissen-
schaftlich eingestellt*—i.e., he instinctively treats
every discipline as if it were a natural or mathematical science. Each phase of culture is examined
as though he were asking himself the question:

[2] *Cf.* particularly Clark Wissler, *Man and Culture*, 1923.
[3] *Cf.* also H. E. Driver and A. L. Kroeber, "Quantitative Expression of
Cultural Relationships," *University of California Publications in Archaeology and Ethnology*, vol. 31, pp. 211–256, 1932.

What will result if I approach the matter in this manner? If the approach proves to be suggestive, he considers himself amply repaid and he stops at that particular point where he feels that the analysis indicates a multiple causation for the specific cultural phenomenon he is investigating. The demonstration of the possibilities of multiple origins is the goal he sets for cultural phenomena and it has for him the same function that is served when a value has been assigned to an unknown quantity in an algebraic equation. Now by whatever term one may wish to denominate this type of approach, it is certainly not a cultural historical one.

Equally indicative of the scientific as opposed to the culture-historical method is Boas's relation to the ethnological data. In science we stand beside or, if you will, above the facts. We are not a part of them. But we are a part of the cultural facts we are describing in a very real way. The moment we stand beside or above them, we do them injury; we transvaluate and make them facts of another order. In short, they are reduced to facts of the physical world. The disadvantages attendant upon being an integral part of the phenomena we are describing must seem a fatal defect to the scientific mind. Unquestionably it is. But it is inherent in cultural phenomena and nothing can very well be done about it. This defect is not being corrected by treating them as physical facts. Objectivity, in the sense in which it exists in the natural and physical sciences, is impossible for culture history, except, perhaps, in the domain of material culture. For culture, the ideal of permanency and durability toward which a description of the physical world inevitably strives is unattainable. The more culture historians and ethnologists attempt it, the more suspect their descriptions become. There are too many *imponderabilia*, and these are too intimately connected with its very life blood.

It is because a comparative method always tends in this direction that it always fails. Boas and those trained under him have been the first to recognize this fact, but they do not seem to understand why this method carries so little conviction. They account for its defects and obvious inadequacy by assuming that it destroyed the specific quality of a given culture. But the *malaise* that historically minded individuals feel when reading Elliot-Smith or the works of some of the members of the various quantitative schools of the United States and Germany is due to the attempt of the latter to approximate to the ideals of the natural sciences. That they do not seem aware of it and label their interpretations historical should not mislead us. If those ethnologists who are essentially scientifically minded appear, not infrequently, historically minded, that is, of course, a consequence of the fact that it would be rather difficult, when dealing continuously with cultural phenomena, not to become so. Indeed their inconsistency in this respect, far from clarifying the situation, has made for considerable confusion.

As it is very important to show clearly what I mean when I imply that these ethnologists are apparently historically minded one minute and scientifically minded the next, let me quote at some length a few characteristic statements from Boas, Wissler, and Kroeber. In a well-known paper on the *Method of Ethnology*[4] Boas states "that the whole problem of cultural history appears to be a historical problem. In order to understand history it is necessary to know not only how things are but how they come to be."[5]

Now no historian finds it necessary to inform you of the self-evident fact that culture is a historical process. For Boas to insist upon it seems to imply that there are those who think otherwise. I take it that he is referring to the evolutionists. For reasons not quite clear to me, American ethnologists, in the main, have always assumed that the English evolutionary ethnologists and theorists were not

[4] *American Anthropologist*, vol. 22, pp. 311–321, 1920.
[5] *Ibid.*, p. 314.

historically minded. But this is really not so. Both Tylor and Robertson-Smith,[6] and Frazer after him, are very definitely historically minded. They can be said to have misapplied the ethnological data, but they did it in an essentially historical manner and with an historical purpose in view.

Boas, on the contrary, in spite of his reiterated insistence that culture is a historical problem, does, nevertheless, give us the impression that he is in doubt upon this very question, for in another part of the same paper he adds:

> In the domain of ethnology where, for the most parts of the world, no historical facts are available except those that may be revealed by archaeological study, all evidence of change can be inferred only by indirect methods. Their character is represented in the researches of students of comparative philology. The method is based on the comparison of static phenomena combined with the study of their distribution. . . . It is, of course, true that we can never hope to obtain incontestable data relating to the chronological sequence of events, but certain broad outlines can be ascertained with a high degree of probability, even of certainty.[7]

Here we have the quest for the broad outlines of a chronological sequence and the combination of

---

[6] Robertson-Smith used the comparative method, and whatever he felt could be obtained by the application of the evolutionary hypothesis to cultural facts, for the express purpose of securing data for the history of a specific culture, that of the early Semites.

[7] *Ibid.*, pp. 314–315.

static phenomena with the study of their distribution. This is certainly not the language or the procedure of any accredited historian. It is the method of the comparative philologist, as Boas very correctly observes. But what justification is there for thus equating the historical with the philological methods? None whatsoever. Volumes have been written by historians to show how inadequate and fallacious this latter method is when applied to the history of culture.[8] But Boas is not consistent even here, for, when he expresses himself as satisfied with the broad outlines of the sequence of events, he has given up the philological approach and merged his own with that of the sociologist. Subsequently he speaks of inner developments, due to inner forces within a specific culture, being explicable by reference to acculturation in general:

It is much easier [he states] to prove dissemination than to follow up developments due to inner forces and the data for such a study are obtained with much greater difficulty. They may, however, be observed in every phenomenon of acculturation in which foreign elements are remodeled according to the pattern prevalent in their environment and they may be found in the peculiar local developments of widely spread ideas and activities.[9]

[8] Its validity even for the study of languages has also been attacked, and the consensus of opinion among philologists today seems to be that, at best, their reconstructions are merely probable assumptions.

[9] *Ibid.*, p. 315.

In both instances, the first where he merges his method with that of the comparative philologist and the second where he merges it with that of the sociologist, he does so at that very point where both of them are completely unhistorical. The sociologist, I presume, is not in the least disturbed by the fact that his approach is unhistorical, for he prides himself on the hybrid character of his discipline. The philologist, on the other hand, is only partially aware of the true nature of his method. Instead of realizing that, at bottom, it is a logical mathematical discipline dealing with the time sequences of sound change and the growth of morphology and that its applicability is a definitely circumscribed one, he is tempted to extend its validity unjustifiably. Sapir, for instance, in his analysis of Bloomfield's paper *On the Sound System of Central Algonquian,* concludes his essay with the following statement:[10]

The value in social science of such comparative study of language . . . is that it emphasizes the extraordinary persistence in certain cases of complex patterns of cultural behavior regardless of the extreme variability of the content of the patterns. It is in virtue of pattern conservatism that it is often possible to foretell the exact form of a specific cultural phenomenon.[11]

[10] *Methods in Social Science,* edited by Stuart Rice, p. 306, 1931.

[11] Bloomfield, in the same article from which I have just quoted, p. 306, is much more modest, even for the validity of certain assumptions for

These are far-reaching claims for a well-known scholar, not given to careless statement, to make. It implies that the dynamics of language growth are strictly comparable to those of culture, that a linguistic pattern is comparable to a pattern of cultural behavior—whatever that may be—although, admittedly, each is arrived at in an entirely different manner; that he possesses incontrovertible evidence for the persistence of these patterns, granted that they actually exist, and that he can furnish us with enough examples to justify the statement that the exact form of specific cultural phenomena can often be foretold.

We must conclude, then, that his protests to the contrary notwithstanding, Boas's method is fundamentally unhistorical. How precisely to characterize it is somewhat difficult. That in the main it is a scientific approach is clear. But it is equally evident that it partakes, at times, of other approaches as well. In a previously quoted passage we saw how he equated a cultural fact with a static fact to which a dynamic character was given through inferences drawn from its distribution.[12] This definitely is

philology. He there states: "The postulate of sound-change without exceptions will probably always remain a mere assumption, since the other types of linguistic change (analogic change, borrowing) are bound to affect all our data. As an assumption, however, this postulate yields, as a matter of mere routine, predictions which otherwise would be impossible."

[12] *Cf.* p. 14.

a scientific attitude. When, however, he states that the fundamental problems connected with the general development of civilization can be satisfactorily determined from a study of the dynamic changes and the processes taking place today, he is blatantly a sociologist.[13] He becomes an historian when he says: "Each cultural group has its own unique history, dependent partly upon the peculiar inner development of the social group and partly upon the foreign influences to which it has been subjected."[14] Yet the example he gives is in the approved manner of the sociologist.

A surplus of food supply [he says in his hypothetical case] is liable to bring about an increase of population and increase of leisure which gives opportunity for occupations that are not absolutely necessary for the needs of every day life. In turn the increase of population and of leisure, which may be applied to new inventions, gives rise to a greater food supply and to a further increase in the amount of leisure so that a cumulative effect results.[15]

The foregoing example carries, in addition, a cause and effect connotation reminiscent of the physical sciences and the most rigorous form of

[13] "In short, then, the method which we seek to develop, is based on a study of the dynamic changes in society that may be observed at the present time. We refrain from attempting to solve the fundamental problem of the general development of civilization until we have been able to unravel the processes that are going on under our eyes."—*Ibid.*, p. 318.

[14] *Ibid.*, p. 317.

[15] *Ibid.*, p. 326.

economic determinism. I know that he specifically denies that there is a confusion here with the method of the natural sciences. But I cannot follow him at all in his contrast of the two. "In the natural sciences," he says, "we are accustomed to consider a given number of causes and to study their effects; in historical happenings we are compelled to consider every phenomenon not only as effect but also as cause."[16]

Boas's eclecticism even includes a type of argumentation very popular with the older evolutionists. In considering the origin of totemism, for instance, he says: "The recognition of kinship groups and with it of exogamy is a universal phenomenon. Totemism is not. It is admissible to judge of the antiquity of an ethnic phenomenon by its universality. . . . We may therefore consider exogamy as the condition on which totemism arose."[17]

Others, besides myself, have found it difficult to define Boas's position. Kroeber, for example, feels that his method is that of the laboratory as opposed to the natural scientist. To Kroeber, Boas has torn apart "the web of space and time relations" in order to examine the dynamic elements as

[16] *Ibid.*, p. 316.
[17] "The Origin of Totemism," *American Anthropologist*, vol. 18, p. 324, 1916.

such. This is undoubtedly true, but assuredly the important point involved here is not what Boas has done, but why he has done it.[18] To Radcliffe-Brown, Malinowski, and Father Schmidt, on the other hand, Boas's viewpoint is historical, within their meaning of history. Radcliffe-Brown seems to hesitate and eventually finds it necessary to define it as the study of relations of people and the making of hypothetical reconstructions of such historical processes as migration, diffusion etc.[19]

Kroeber, it seems to me, falls into the same type of confusion, although his position is, on the whole, very frankly and consistently that of the naturalist. He defines the function of history essentially in terms of the historian when he says that "the culture of a group must be more or less known before the history and meaning of an institution can become intelligible. Detached from its cultural mass, a custom reveals as little of its functioning as an organ dissected out of the living body."[20] Certainly no exception can be taken to this. But

[18] *American Anthropologist*, vol. 31, p. 139, 1929.

[19] *The Present Position of Anthropological Studies*, British Association for the Advancement of Science, Section of Anthropology, 1931.

[20] *American Indian Life*, edited by E. C. Parsons, p. 6, 1925. I do not quite understand him when he says that "the method of the evolutionary explanations was deductive. . . . The new ethnology is inductive."—*Ibid.*, p. 5. Surely ethnology, even in his sense, is both inductive and deductive, and the evolutionary method was predominatingly inductive.

the next moment we are told that ethnology is inductive, a term that has no relevancy in culture and is so heavily laden with purely scientific implications as to be exceedingly dangerous. Kroeber uses the word advisedly because for him ethnology is heavily laden with scientific implications. He continues to deal with generalized facts, generalized events, and generalized processes, and he is still capable of stating that "the static view of culture areas can be given a 'dynamic' or processual or sequential significance by the application of culture centers as understood by Wissler."[21] In spite of all his guarded language, he operates with only the familiar single-trait diffusion which is the most certain index of a quantitative treatment.[22] All his specific ethnographical studies bear the definite impress of this predilection.[23]

[21] "Native Culture of the Southwest," *University of California Publications in American Archaeology and Ethnology*, vol. 23, p. 295, 1928.

[22] For innumerable examples, compare his "Native Culture of the Southwest," *ibid.*, pp. 375-398. As an excellent example of a generalized description of generalized processes, let me quote the following: "Evidently then there has been a series of waves northward out of the Gulf region (of the United States), some migrational, some perhaps essentially and actively cultural, which, with a diffusing seepage in the same direction, have given the Northeast what it has other than the simplest."— *Ibid.*, p. 394.

[23] *Cf.* particularly his *Zuñi Kin and Clan*, American Museum of Natural History, vol. 19, pp. 39-207, 1919, and "The Patwin and Their Neighbors," *University of California Publications in American Archaeology and Ethnology*, vol. 29, pp. 253-423, 1932.

In Wissler this confusion of method takes on its fully developed form. First we have culture defined as the "round of life in its entire sweep of individual activities."[24] This is somewhat vague, to be true, but no objection need be taken to it. The moment, however, he becomes specific, all sorts of implications enter. For instance, he states that, in contrast one to the other, the Eskimo and the Hottentot are to be regarded as exhibiting greater originality than the English as contrasted with the French, because the round of life in England does not differ very much from that of France, *whereas that of the Eskimo is completely different from that of the Hottentot.*[25] He is here introducing an evaluational element whose significance becomes clear only when he gives us his characterization of tribal culture. We then discover that, in aboriginal civilizations, we must first determine the nature of a culture trait. A culture trait is "the objective record of a unit of observation, for instance, the fire-making apparatus accompanied by photographs and field notes."[26] A trait, on careful analysis, proves to be "a complex of many processes, all of which bear a functional relation to the end to be achieved."[27] Tribal culture, finally, is

[24] *Man and Culture*, p. 1, 1923.
[25] *Ibid.*, pp. 1–2.
[26] *Ibid.*, p. 50.
[27] *Ibid.*, pp. 50, 52.

characterized by the enumeration of its observable traits, the culture of one tribe being distinguished from that of another by differences in these traits.[28] Some form of sociology and psychology may be involved here, but I can find no trace of what is commonly known as the historical approach. When, continuing, Wissler says that "a culture is not to be comprehended until the list of its traits approaches completeness," and that it was not until a number of cultures had been fully worked out that the problem of culture took shape, we have arrived at the method of the natural sciences.[29] This is the quantitative approach *in excelsis.*

To recapitulate: these three representative American ethnologists are exceedingly eclectic in their use of methods. Sometimes it is an approximation to an historical, at other times to a scientific, method; then it becomes psychological and ends finally as a full-fledged sociological approach. Now I can see no objection whatsoever to eclecticism as such, but when eclecticism means that we never discover when one method is to be employed and when another, it has lost its only justification for existence.

[28] *Ibid.*, p. 50.
[29] *Ibid.*, p. 51. His concept of what constitutes "approximately complete data" is given in a note on p. 51.

Chapter II

The Presuppositions of the Ethnological Method in the United States: the School of Boas

It was the application of the method of the natural sciences to ethnology that led to a different interpretation of its nature and aim from that which it originally possessed. But there were other factors likewise at work. I do not see how it is possible, for instance, to understand the full significance of the quantitative methods in vogue today, unless we bear in mind the influence upon the creators of the American quantitative approach of the great struggle which Boas waged with the evolutionary doctrines of Tylor and Frazer. No modern ethnological school has remained untouched by this controversy in some form or other, whether it be the German *Kulturkreise* school of Foy-Graebner-W. Schmidt, the so-called functionalist school of Radcliffe-Brown and Malinowski, or the diffusionist school of Elliot-Smith-Perry. But none of them envisaged its dangers quite so clearly as

Boas. If, today, that is no longer an issue in American ethnology, this is due entirely to his persistent and telling criticism of its main tenets.

Yet this struggle had a fatal aftermath. In emphasizing the need for some method that would effectively dispose of the evolutionists' favorite hypothesis of cultural stages and discourage the readiness to loose speculation prevalent among them, Boas fell back upon the theory of multiple origins for culture and attempted to apply a rigorous mathematical-scientific method to ethnology which took him farther away from its actual subjectmatter. Indeed, there has been a definite tendency to become mired in accidental and pseudo-problems. Radcliffe-Brown, we have seen, finds it necessary to define Boas's position in terms of hypothetical reconstructions of historical processes.

In order to disprove the contention of the evolutionists, it was necessary to demonstrate that the processes at work in aboriginal cultures were not only those stressed by them, such as development from simple to complex with secondary survivals, but that they were identical with those occurring in every culture. This led to the study of processes as such, as Kroeber correctly observes. But this, as I have already pointed out, had also another effect, viz., of assigning to the study of aboriginal cultures a somewhat secondary rôle. It is quite apparent in the case of Radcliffe-Brown. With Boas and some of his students it is more disguised. Yet we have a right to assume this from the fact that the latter manifestly do not treat aboriginal civilizations as they treat those of Western Europe, for instance. Why make this distinction if culture is culture? Is it not because they feel that aboriginal cultures exhibit certain traits and exemplify certain processes in a more tangible fashion than the so-called advanced civilizations? The interrelations of individuals with individuals, of cultures with individuals, and of cultures with cultures, they definitely imply, are seen there in a more directly recognizable form. This is simply an illusion,[1] fostered by the method employed in the establishment of culture areas and culture centers, and the manner in which diffusion is envisaged. In the case of Radcliffe-Brown and Malinowski, it seems to be due to the persistence of certain preconceptions adhering in the evolutionary hypothesis. In fact, one is, at times, tempted to assume similar preconceptions even among the most ardent of the American antievolutionists and to suspect that the ghost—or is it possibly only the attenuated

[1] Mead in her book *The Coming of Age in Samoa*, p. 8, 1929, is very explicit on this point: "A primitive people," she says, "without a written language, presents a much less elaborate problem (than our own civilization), and a trained student can master the fundamental structure of a primitive society in a few months!"

shadow of the ghost?—of the older evolutionary evaluations still hovers around them, unseen but not unfelt.

It would, however, be a most egregious error to imagine that Boas's importance in the history of ethnology is confined to his theoretical position. We must not take Radcliffe-Brown's characterization of his aims too literally. He is, as we all know, the most assiduous collector of facts. Yet, in spite of his insistence on facts and ever more facts, a certain ill-defined feeling of the nonimportance or nonsignificance, as such, of the specific history of a given culture pervades even the best of his monographs. There are a number of reasons for this which I shall discuss later on. I wish here merely to point out that it is so.

Although Boas would unquestionably give his whole-hearted assent to the original definition of ethnology as the complete study of the aboriginal cultures—each culture for itself—and to the need, in such a specific study, of a full factual knowledge of the tribe, its history, and its relations to other cultures, this ill-defined feeling of the *specific* nonimportance of a *particular* tribe introduces an unhistorical note. A real historian, for instance, would insist that only such part of the historical record be brought into play as bears directly upon the culture as a whole or on the beliefs and customs that are being investigated. The extent to which it would be necessary to stress the mechanisms of intertribal contacts and borrowings would depend upon how materially a given culture had been influenced. He does not find it necessary to begin with the creation of the world. But is not that, in essence, what Boas and Wissler and, to a certain extent, Kroeber are doing when they use every specific "historic" inquiry as a convenient starting point for a study of cultural dynamics in general? But we must not anticipate.

That a thorough knowledge of the history of a culture is necessary for its proper understanding, ethnologists have always recognized, particularly Boas. As we have seen, the problem was how, in the absence of written records, this could be obtained. In fact, could it be obtained? Many historians and critically minded scholars would answer in the negative. Boas, however, answered it in the affirmative. Whatever misgivings may have existed at first, he and all those ethnologists trained by him—and that means the vast majority of ethnologists in America—soon found themselves embarked upon the interesting and frequently uncongenial task of finding a substitute for the time sequence that our own cultures enjoyed. And when they found it, they very conveniently forgot its drawbacks. That substitute, we all know,

was discovered in the inferences and conjectures to be drawn from the manner in which culture traits were found to be distributed and from the analytical investigation of the cultures themselves. To do this, specific criteria had to be developed for interpreting the distributions and clusterings. This led to the well-known formulation for the use of criteria by Sapir,[2] and the equally well-known culture-area concept of Wissler.[3] Boas wisely kept himself free from the extreme forms of both these developments. To him, culture areas represented simply a convenient and initial classification of facts from which specific inferences could not be made, and he has always had a healthy distrust of interpretations based on secondarily established criteria.

In this matter Boas has always been perfectly consistent. Some of the other American ethnologists have not been, particularly Kroeber. His attitude illustrates only too clearly the dangers lurking in too long an adherence to a "mechanism of transient convenience for descriptive purposes."[4] There is always a tendency to forget the purpose of a provisional principle of interpretation. Its con-

[2] "Time Perspective in Aboriginal American Culture," *Geological Survey of Canada, Anthropological Series,* No. 13.

[3] *Man and Culture,* 1923.

[4] "Native Culture of the Southwest," *University of California Publications in American Archaeology and Ethnology,* vol. 23, p. 590, 1928.

veniences are likely to obsess us, and before we are well aware of it we find ourselves enmeshed in a series of pseudo-problems. This, it seems to me, is precisely what has happened to Kroeber. He apparently agrees as to the provisional nature of the culture-area concept and is fully cognizant of the great error involved in making cultural phenomena static. Instead of abandoning the concept, however, when it breaks down completely, convenience triumphs over reality, and he attempts to salvage it. He somewhat uncritically accepts Wissler's slipshod approximation of archaeological to ethnological areas which, at best, merely adds one fallacious description of culture to another. Thus the error is allowed to gain depth. Then he admits the existence of a deadlock but is willing to accept a way out, by taking refuge in the hypothesis of Wissler's culture centers. Yet he must know that the deadlock has resulted just because the culture-area hypothesis broke down. Why not give it up? Instead, as we have seen, the culture centers are used to give dynamic and sequential significance to a static view of culture areas! One pseudo-problem is here piled upon the other. Surely Kroeber must realize that Wissler's culture-center concept is but the refinement of an initial error. What precisely is to be gained by finding points of reference within a variable error?

The only result of all attempts to salvage the culture-area concept has been to strengthen its upholders in the belief that it is incumbent upon their opponents to disprove it.

To all these scholars the only alternative to this concept was chaos. The possibility of establishing some type of sequence for a given culture from internal evidence, from the careful and painstaking study of its specific religion, mythology, social organization, etc., this they rejected as utterly speculative and unscientific. In other words, it was scientific and historical to point out the northern elements in Navajo mythology, but it would be reprehensively speculative to attempt to study Navajo mythology in order to see whether it could throw some light on Navaho history and the growth of Navajo ideas and customs. In thus rejecting this type of interpretation, I think they have made not only a serious mistake but one that has had somewhat momentous consequences for the development of ethnology in the United States. That such a method is beset with the greatest dangers, that the pitfalls are numerous, that it leads to speculation, all this is manifest, but that tangible results of importance can be obtained from it if enough factual material has been collected in the right manner is equally manifest to anyone who attempts it. Whatever be its drawbacks, it is closer to the core of things than the results secured through the manipulation of artificial and static culture areas.

Let me illustrate what I mean from the Winnebago data.[5] Before proceeding, let me state briefly what I conceive to be the fundamental problem of the culture historian.

His primary task is to describe a specific culture as he finds it, without any reference to what has preceded or what is to follow. In other words, he is always to describe contemporary history. If, for instance, he is describing the Italian Renaissance of the fifteenth century, he is not to think of the fourteenth or the sixteenth century. That is a subsidiary and secondary question. For an elucidation of certain aspects of the fifteenth century he will, however, find it necessary to turn back to the fourteenth century, and he may find it exceedingly valuable, in order to understand certain trends of the fifteenth to refer to the sixteenth century. The investigation of processes as such or the attempt to construct cultural typologies not only are outside his province but are likely to interfere with the proper and efficient characterization of the cultural epoch he is portraying. To delimit thus an epoch or period in the life of a

[5] I am, of course, here merely stating the traits without giving any critical elaboration.

nation is avowedly artificial. This much must be conceded to the physiologists of culture. But culture cannot be described in terms of some calculus wherein the complete relations of two ever-moving points are to be determined. All that we can reasonably ask of a philosophically minded historian is that he admit the artificiality of the method and attempt to correct it by reference to what has preceded and what has followed, the latter being of far less importance than the former. In the case of aboriginal cultures we actually have only the present and the possibility of recovering the past.

Bearing the foregoing in mind, let me begin with the account by an old Winnebago of his reincarnations. He speaks there of a method of burial no longer used by his people. How are we to interpret this? The prevalent attitude, among many American ethnologists, would be either to throw out such evidence as utterly untrustworthy and likely to be the product of an archaizing fantasy or to seek for resemblances among other tribes. If, instead, we confine ourselves solely and exclusively to the Winnebago documents, the following facts emerge. We find the same method of burial in a well-known myth where its inclusion cannot very well be explained as due to an archaizing tendency. It is therefore not pure imagination. However, we have no right to assume that there are two independent examples involved here, for the account given by the old Winnebago may very well have been taken from the myth. We may, nevertheless, accept it as indicating that the Winnebago, at one time, employed a method of burial no longer in use. The demonstration of a change of custom in one particular trait would, however, not help us very much. We must, accordingly, seek further, to see whether the myths, rituals, and customs do not give evidence of other changes. We find that they do in a most decisive manner, and the net result is a picture of Winnebago society different from, and in many ways at variance with, that of today.[6] This evidence is obtained directly from the myths, the rituals, specific customs, and the statements of individuals. I cannot here go into the question of the method employed in evaluating the various types of evidence. I am simply using this somewhat schematic representation of the history of the Winnebago culture as an example of a method of approach.

I shall tabulate the results under the following headings: (I) the former structure of society, (II) the transformation of the rituals, (III) the transformation of the mythology, (IV) the transformation of the religion.

[6] Naturally I mean by "today" the culture as it existed three or four generations ago. Cf. my monograph on the Winnebago in the *Thirty-seventh Annual Report of the Bureau of American Ethnology.*

I. *The Former Structure of Society*

1. Marriage with the daughter of your sister.[7]
2. Strong line of demarcation between the families of chiefs and the rest of the population; importance of the daughters of the chief.
3. Different names for certain of the clans.
4. Importance of the waterspirit, elk, and wolf clans, in contradistinction to their unimportance today.
5. Specific places of origin for the different clans as contrasted with the present belief that they all originated in one place.
6. Great importance of agriculture.
7. Specific type of village, different from that of today.
8. Human sacrifice.
9. Cannibalism.
10. Head hunting and use of skull as trophy.
11. Cremation.
12. Buffalo pound.

[7] I cannot resist showing the threefold confirmation this particular detail received. Such a type of marriage is unthinkable today. The reference to it was encountered in a myth and only once. Winnebago interrogated knew nothing about it. Yet there is absolutely no question that the Winnebago, at one time, permitted this form of marriage, as the following facts clearly show: first, the displacement in the system of relationship terms whereby you call the daughter of the daughter of your sister and the daughter of your daughter by the same term, which would result if a man married his sister's daughter; second, the existence of the joking relationship between a man and his mother's brother—the latter would then be his brother-in-law—otherwise this would be inexplicable; and, third, the curious fact that the term for brother-in-law seems to be related to the stem for to-go-on-the-warpath. Now the ideal person with whom you go on the warpath is your mother's brother, who (at one time actually) was your brother-in-law.

13. Types of house.
14. Pottery.
15. Flint arrow points.
16. Use of stone.
17. Use of metal.
18. Use of shell utensils.
19. Construction of linear, conical, and effigy mounds.

II. *History of the Rituals*

1. The Medicine Dance.
   a. Substitution of shell for arrow in "shooting" ritual.
   b. Adoption of the "shooting" bags.
   c. Loss of the shamanistic functions of the members.
   d. Secondary symbolic reinterpretation.
2. The Winter Feasts.
   a. The village bundle.
   b. The personal war bundle.
   c. The secondary association of the Winter Feasts with Earthmaker.
   d. The encroachment of the clan on the ceremonial unit.

III. *History of Mythology*

1. Old and new Hare cycles.
2. The reinterpretation of the Trickster cycle.
3. Displacement of the Turtle as Trickster.
4. The conflict of the older hero cycles with the newer.
5. Displacement of the Waterspirit by the Thunderbird.
6. The older and the newer cosmological notions.

IV. *History of Religion*

1. Changes in the concept of Earthmaker.
2. Earthmaker and Herecgunina (the evil spirit).
3. Changes in the concept of the Waterspirit.
4. Changes in the concept of the Earth.
5. Loss of function of the older deities (the Sun, Fire, etc.).
6. Disappearance of the myths associated with the older deities.
7. Association of evil with the older deities.
8. Characteristics of the older deities that survived.
9. The new deities.
10. Changes in the concept of good and evil as associated with the various deities.

Some of the foregoing traits can be shown to have been lost since the Winnebago came into contact with the Europeans; others can be brought into direct relation with archaeological finds on undoubted Winnebago sites. For a number of features, then, we have a history that takes us back to pre-Columbian times. The culture elements so far mentioned are, however, fairly clear-cut. But there exist in Winnebago civilization certain details of social organization, ritualism, and religion that are ambiguous and where we naturally turn to their immediate neighbors to seek for enlightenment. Frequently we do so because of direct hints contained in myth and ritual, such, for instance, as songs in the Fox or Iowa language, or statements that the Sauk, Fox, Iowa, or Ojibwa Indians introduced such and such a custom or material object. In other instances we turn to these same neighbors, simply because they are neighbors. Let us take the very important question of the nature of the organization of the village. There are two descriptions encountered today, one to the effect that the Upper moiety lived on one side of the village and the Lower moiety on the other, and the second to the effect that the various clans could live wherever they wished. The Winnebago themselves felt the first to be the older type. That in itself would not prove anything. A comparison with the social organization of the Fox, however, shows that the second type of organization was characteristic of them, and, since we know that the Winnebago were in intimate contact with them for a number of centuries, it seems fairly clear that this discrepancy in the description was due to their influence. But even a partial displacement of an older type of village organization by an alien people could not possibly have taken place unless the pressure they exerted and the influence they exercised was exceedingly powerful. We therefore look for other indications of this influence, and we find it everywhere, in varying degrees of intensity. We also discover other tribes, kindred to the Fox, like the Illinois. Both the Illinois and the Fox were hereditary enemies of the Winnebago. This, and the fact that both they and the Fox arrived in Wisconsin much later than the Winnebago, and the complete isolation of the latter from their culturally and linguistically close kin the Oto, Iowa, and Missouri, indicate only too clearly that a serious conflict must have gone on for many generations. What the Winnebago gave their central Algonquian harassers, I do not know, but Fox culture and Fox individuals transformed Winnebago culture along certain significant lines. Yet Winnebago culture seems to have held its own to an amazing degree; and where it did not completely assimilate and reinterpret the foreign elements, old and new stood side by side.

I think that the foregoing illustration of this method, even allowing for the very great dangers inhering in it, should make it clear to everyone that the data obtained from internal evidence can throw tremendous light upon the history of a given culture and that cultural problems assume a far more real and concrete significance when approached in this way than by the method pursued by Boas, Wissler, and Kroeber. Its two prime requirements are that a student have a very detailed and profound knowledge of the culture he desires to portray and that he steep himself in it over a period of years with the same intensity that is demanded of any student of our own civilization.

The failure of these representative American ethnologists to utilize to the full all the internal evidence at their disposal implies more than mere irritation at the speculative element involved in such an approach. It is not really conceivable that they have not recognized the extremely speculative character of their own inferences and reconstructions. Much more is involved here. I feel that they are definitely confused as to the actual viewpoint of the historian. And surely it is legitimate to insist, even at the risk of being termed presumptuous, that whatever good, direct or indirect, may accrue to one discipline from being subjected to the method of another, it is a most unfortunate situation when a predominating number of its accredited students are completely out of sympathy with the spirit of that particular method which has, from the beginning of time, been associated with it. If one is irritated and terrified by all that is indefinite, intangible, and unpredictable in culture, one should keep away from it. The inevitable otherwise happens. The imponderable is made ponderable, facts are made definite, tangible, and precise, and only those aspects of culture are stressed that are definite and concrete, such as, for example, those of material culture. And even here, definiteness is attained at the expense of other and equally important aspects of the data in question. What Boas, in effect, does is to rule out the personal element in aboriginal culture, although that, apparently, is not his intent. He seems well aware of the fact that systematic descriptions of human activities, as given in ethnological monographs, allow us very little insight into the mental attitudes of the individual.

His thoughts and actions [so he states] appear merely as expressions of rigidly defined cultural forms. We learn little about his rational thinking, about his friendships and conflicts with his fellowmen. The personal side of the life of the individual is almost eliminated. . . . The results of her [Dr. Mead's] painstaking investigation confirm the suspicion that much of what we ascribe to human nature is no more than a reaction to the restraints put upon us by our civilization.[8]

But why, let me ask, do we gain so little insight into the personal side of the individual in aboriginal cultures? Does the average historian describe cultures in this fashion? Is it inherent in systematic accounts of man's activities? Clearly not. It has been deliberately omitted. If thoughts and actions appear as expressions of rigidly defined cultural forms, who has made them so? The ethnographer himself, in obedience to some theory either that the

[8] Preface to Mead's, *Coming of Age in Samoa*, pp. xiii-xv, 1929.

rôle of the individual is minimal in aboriginal society, as the older evolutionists and the inconsistent modern neoevolutionists contend; or that it plays a negligible part in every society, as the modern French sociologists and certain American ethnologists like Kroeber and Benedict[9] assume; or because he feels its importance to be definitely subsidiary to the study of human nature as such, as Boas seems to imply here. The method of describing a culture without any reference to the individual except in so far as he is an expression of rigidly defined cultural forms, manifestly produces a distorted picture. To put the individual back again after having first eliminated him gives an equally distorted portrait. He either must be kept in from the very beginning or kept out permanently. The procedure apparently advocated by Boas is neither history nor sociology. It is some form of "conceptuology," if I may coin that term.

Wissler, Kroeber, Sapir, and Benedict, to name but a few, likewise leave the individual out of account, but certainly the last three are well aware of it. Kroeber[10] does so because to him

[9] "Configurations of Culture in North America," *American Anthropologist*, vol. 34, pp. 1–27, 1932.

[10] *Cf.* his "Eighteen Professions" in the *American Anthropologist*, vol. 17, pp. 283 *ff*. 1915, and "The Superorganic," *ibid.*, vol. 19, 1917. In the first of these papers he states: first, that the personal or individual has no

individuals are essentially adventitious excrescences on the supersocietal whole; Sapir because, in spite of his clear perception of the meaning of history and the rôle of the individual, he prefers to operate with an intuited generic man; and Benedict because their recognition would disturb the harmony of a typology of culture. For them to contend that it is not possible to obtain the requisite information is well enough, but why in their monographs and theories do they leave out even the vestiges of the individual's existence? Why could not cultural dynamics have been discussed with reference to individuals—to specific individuals, in fact? There is far more information than they imagine contained in the very records they have collected, and more was at hand for them to gather had they so willed. But what is their attitude toward the specific individual? They consistently reject him

historical value save as illustration; second, that civilization, though carried by men and existing through them, is an entity in itself and of another order of life; third, that the aim of history is to know the relations of social facts to the whole of civilization; fourth, that history deals with conditions *sine qua non;* fifth, that the causality of history is teleological; and, lastly, that only individual minds exist which react on each other cumulatively, the process being merely physiological. In the same issue H. Haeberlin gave a complete refutation of these theses, pointing out, among other things, that for anyone to speak of a history that is not concerned with the agencies producing civilization but with civilization as such, is either a history *à la* Graebner or a philosophy that postulates the entity "civilization" as a Platonic idea, and that it is quite meaningless to say that a certain kind of causality is teleological.

as historically untrue, as a rationalization toward which the human mind unfortunately tends. For that is what it amounts to when, for instance, Kroeber[11] says that

. . . Progress is something that makes itself. . . . Our customary conviction to the contrary is probably the result of an unconscious desire not to realize our individual impotence as regards the culture we live in. Social influence of a sort we do have as individuals. But it is a personal influence on the fortune and careers of other individual members of society, and is concerned largely with aims of personal security, relative dominance, or affection among ourselves. This obviously is a different thing from the exertion of influence on the form or content of civilization as such.

It should not strike us as strange then that these ethnologists reject the individual in favor of psychological catchwords, such as unconscious development, patterns, psychological sets and configurations. That, in the face of all this, they should regard their treatment as rigorous, cautious, and nonspeculative, and any treatment that naïvely includes the individual as an integral and active element in culture as romantic, passes all understanding.

As a corollary to the rejection and neglect of the specific individual, we have the failure to

[11] *Anthropology*, p. 133, 1923.

understand the specific event. What it leads to can best be illustrated by a recent paper of Kroeber,[12] one of the masters of this method of reconstructing the past, entitled "The Patwin and Their Neighbors." We shall concern ourselves exclusively with his summary of the Kuksu cults. According to the avowedly tentative scheme he outlines,

. . . certain ritual practices were diffused from an undetermined center which may have lain in Mexico, but which, if in the United States, is most likely to have been situated among the Pueblos. These rituals probably included initiations of boys, or supernatural impersonations, or both; altars of ground-painting type; fetich bundles; possibly the bullroarer. The impersonations are likely to have been of two types: ghosts of the tribal dead or a race of spirits more or less identified with them; and spirits of a superior or special character, designable as deities and associated with the origin and maintenance of the world. There may also have been the concept that the impersonations, especially of the gods, served to cure illness.[13]

There is no mention here of any specific event or any specific individuals. Doubtless he would retort that he does not know them. But as long as he admits that his whole attempt at reconstruction is tentative and as long as he is compelled to dot his reconstruction with "probables" and

[12] *University of California Publications in American Archaeology and Ethnology*, vol. 29, pp. 253–423, 1932.
[13] *Ibid.*, pp. 417–418.

"possibles" and "likelies," why could he not have said that at a specific time, possibly in the eleventh century A.D., an invasion from the Pueblo areas, of fairly large proportions, brought the above-mentioned practices and ideas to California; that it must have taken place either at a time when most of the indigenous cultures of California were markedly susceptible to new religious influences or have been forced upon the Californians against their will? Or, if there was no invasion, why could he not have said that visiting Californians borrowed such and such practices from the Pueblos or that visiting natives from the Pueblos introduced them and, owing to favorable specific conditions, they became part of native Californian religion? Does he doubt that such things have occurred?[14] I can give him numerous examples from aboriginal America, Africa, and Australia. These hypotheses in which we operate with specific individuals are

[14] Kroeber is not always consistent in his rejection of the individual. It is impossible to be so. It is not therefore surprising to find him say in his *Anthropology*, pp. 192–193, that the "anthropological data are usually unduly deficient in the personal. element. . . . If anthropologists were able to recover knowledge of the particular Pueblo woman who first painted a third color or a glaze on a bowl, or of the priest who first instituted a masked dance in order to make rain, we may be confident that they would discuss these individuals. And such knowledge would throw more light on the history of Southwestern pottery and religion and culture generally than any amount of emphasis on the number of inches of rainfall per year, etc." But why, then, in a hypothetical reconstruction, does he not put the individual in?

no more speculative than the generalized reconstructions Kroeber actually gives; one is no more
inadequate than the other. Both are mere assumptions which, owing to the absence of documentary
evidence, can never be proved.

But it is not overcautiousness or scientific
restraint that makes him refuse to think in terms
of specific events but the fact that, given the
method he has used to arrive at his scheme of
development, there is no room for the specific.
For how has he obtained his initial premise that
certain rituals are basic to the Kuksu cult? By
the simple device of taking the least common denominator of the religions of California. Naturally,
under such circumstances, only the most general
statements are warranted. But he can become
very specific in the use of these general statements
at times, as, for instance, when he tells us, without
qualification, that the foregoing practices and ideas

. . . were diffused westward, and then south and north in
the coast region, as far as north central California, where
they were checked by encountering a culture of fairly
distinct origins and trends, that of the Northwest Coast.
In each area reached, the transmissions became merged
with culture elements already established, and were still
further modified by the development of provincial traits
consonant with the culture of the area. Thus the cult houses,
musical instruments, performers' apparel, largely became
specific, not generic or uniform, in the several regions where

the introductions flourished. These regions were those in which economic prosperity induced relatively concentrated living and inclinations toward organization. The organizing impulses resulted in the formation of societies, perhaps, at times *de novo*. These were essentially luxury growths. . . . In the environs of Sacramento valley, the altar and fetish were lost, new impersonations were created and become dominant, societies became strong, even one new one, at least, being formed; but impersonation of the dead languished and died away where it came in competition with the introduced mourning commemoration held for the specific and recent dead.[15]

I have given this rather lengthy quotation to show how far Kroeber is willing to carry his method of reconstruction. It is evident that we are dealing here merely with the semblance of the specific. All the events he speaks of are generalized events, and they become specific only as a secondary consequence of an assumed scheme of gradations. Having constructed a stairway on the basis of certain presuppositions, Kroeber very properly proceeds to ascend it and then argues, very improperly, that because he has ascended it, he has demonstrated the presuppositions upon which the stairway was originally built.

But we must pause. Our main object was to show that Kroeber does not, any more than Boas or Wissler, employ accepted historical methods in

[15] *Ibid.*, p. 418.

his reconstructions of the past, even where this seems to be his ostensible object.[16] What he is using is simply a modification of the old-fashioned comparative method applied to a somewhat restricted area. How else can one explain the following:

The phenomena (involved in the growth of the Kuksu cult) are highly complex, and demonstrable determinations will necessarily be fewer than probabilities . . . and probabilities fewer than possibilities. There are enough specific and generic similarities between the Kuksu, southern California, and Pueblo cult systems to render pedantic an insistence on the wholly independent origin and parallel development of these. But there are a great number of specific and even generic features which are dissimilar, and these, which constitute the bulk of the systems, cannot be brushed aside as secondary and negligible. They too constitute historic growths, to dismiss which as provincialisms, in favor of those features which lend themselves to a simple unified scheme, would be both summary and contrary to the spirit of historic inquiry.[17]

As I have already pointed out, Boas will have nothing to do with any of these methods, but he

[16] Kroeber seems completely to misunderstand what the historian is doing when he says, "They explain in terms of human thought and action, in other words, of culture. It is true that they dwell more on personalities than anthropologists do. But that is because the materials left them by former historians are full of personalities and anecdotes"!—*Anthropology*, p. 192. And it is surely a most amazing and revealing statement to say that historians have their work made easy for them by the possession of written and dated records.—*Ibid.*, p. 192.

[17] *Ibid.*, p. 419.

is particularly opposed to any approach that attempts to secure even a relative time sequence by the study of the internal evidence contained in myths and rituals. He shrinks back in manifest annoyance, like a true scientist, before the large element of subjectivism involved in such an enterprise.[18] He denies it all validity and turns his attention to the gathering of facts and the application of a purely analytical method to their interpretation. He has never seriously deviated from this type of approach. It found expression in all his own linguistic work and that which he inspired, and in the analyses of art, mythology, and rituals by himself and his students.[19] The inadequacy

[18] So does Lowie. Because the Indians mix legend with fact, he regards tradition as useless. "The general conclusion is obvious"; he says, "Indian tradition is historically worthless because the occurrences, possibly real, which it retains, are of no historical significance; and because it fails to record accurately, the most momentous happenings."—"Oral Tradition and History," *Journal of American Folklore*, vol. 30, pp. 164–166, 1917. The example of the Winnebago given on pp. 245–252 completely disproves this. As a matter of fact, I doubt whether Lowie would subscribe to the statement any longer. It is true that tribes differ tremendously with regard both to the amount of their tradition and to its reliability for the reconstruction of the past. But this is itself a fact of possible historic significance.

[19] *Cf.* "Handbook of American Indian Languages," *Bulletin* 40 *of the Bureau of American Ethnology*, and the following:

F. Boas, "The Decorative Art of the North Pacific Coast Indians," *Bulletin of the American Museum of Natural History*, vol. 9, pp. 125–176, 1897.

F. Boas, *Primitive Art*, 1927.

F. Boas, *The Mind of Primitive Man*, 1924.

A. L. Kroeber, "Symbolism of the Arapaho Indians," *Bulletin of the*

of the results thus obtained was clearly felt by him, and to give them more concrete significance he was led to the study of cultural processes and cultural dynamics, first in relation to specific cultures and then for their own sake. It is this emphasis on the study of cultural dynamics that has become the favorite preoccupation of subsequent ethnological research in America. Here, again, I feel that the conflict with the evolutionary method and doctrines played its part, for a demonstration of the uniqueness of cultural phenomena and of the unpredictable form that cultural processes might assume would destroy the grand schemes of development postulated by Tylor and his followers. But surely, it may be asked, if our subject matter is to be the study of cultural processes, why turn to aboriginal cultures, where the data at best are

American Museum of Natural History, vol. 13, pp. 69–86, 1900.

A. A. Goldenweiser, "Totemism: An Analytical Study," *Journal of American Folklore*, vol. 23, pp. 1–115, 1910.

R. H. Lowie, "The Test Theme in North American Indian Mythology," *Journal of American Folklore*, vol. 21, pp. 97–148, 1908.

P. Radin, "The Ritual and Significance of the Winnebago Medicine Dance," *Journal of American Folklore*, vol. 24, pp. 149–208, 1911.

T. T. Waterman, "The Explanatory Element in North American Mythology," *Journal of American Folklore*, vol. 27, pp. 1–54, 1914.

L. Spier, "The Sun Dance of the Plains Indians; Development and Diffusion," *Anthropological Papers of the American Museum of Natural History*, vol. 16, pp. 451–527, 1921.

R. Benedict, "The Concept of the Guardian Spirit in North America," *Memoirs of the American Anthropological Association*, No. 29, 1923.

poor and where we can never be certain as to what was the "uncontaminated" character of a given culture, *i.e.*, where we have no definite and fixed point from which to start? I cannot imagine a more unfavorable soil for such an inquiry. If the study of processes is to be our primary or absorbing interest, it is much better to confine ourselves to the major civilizations of the world which we know a million times better than the aboriginal cultures and where we have abundant and adequate data. Then we had better stick to Middletown. Those ethnologists like Wissler, Thurnwald, Radcliffe-Brown, Malinowski, Sapir, and Mead, who are making acculturation studies, are, consequently, quite right in limiting their field of inquiry to the adjustment of aboriginal peoples to modern European civilizations, provided they can establish clearly what the aboriginal cultures were at a specific point of time. I doubt whether this can be done with sufficient accuracy to make the experiment worth the while, in view of the much more perfect material they can obtain from our own cultures. But even if they could succeed, it would, in a fashion, constitute the abandonment of ethnological research.

No one felt the dilemma in which the absence of a chronology placed ethnology more keenly than Boas. But there was no halting the somewhat compulsive urge to establish time sequences. Boas himself, while protesting all the time that his classification of cultures or of mythologies into areas was but for purposes of convenience, tacitly assumed that these areas had, on the whole, developed *sui generis*. And that is establishing a time sequence, even if not a specific one. His colleagues and students, however, went merrily on constructing their culture areas and pseudo-time sequences. At first these were on a broad comparative basis; they were, in fact, essentially analytical studies restricted to fairly definite and circumscribed areas. Only relative time sequences, and even those only tentatively, were inferred. These studies were made directly under Boas's inspiration. That was, however, only at the beginning. Then came the crystallizations of the method, in part at his own hands, but mainly by Wissler, Kroeber, Spier, and others, and the numerous studies of trait diffusion. This breaking up of cultures into "constituent" elements gave the latter a fictitious definiteness and separated culture and culture growth from its vital connection with individuals. The smallest unit with which one operated was the group or the subgroup. If individuals were postulated, they were generalized or generic.

Boas protested very vigorously against this development. Indeed it can be said that he has always protested very definitely against all those methods of attack which he himself initiated as soon as he saw where they led. This is not to be interpreted as negativism but simply as an expression of his scientific *Einstellung*, which looks askance at any attempt at synthesis, or any attempt to introduce concreteness into data, as soon as the probable error exceeds that which is permissible in a purely scientific determination.

His criticism of Wissler, Krocbcr, and Spinden, runs as follows:

Recent attempts have been made to raise to a general principle this point of view [*viz.*, that the more widely distributed traits are the older] which, with due caution, may be applied here and there. Spinden in his reconstruction of American prehistoric chronology, Kroeber in his analysis of cultural forms of the Pacific Coast, and, quite recently, Wissler have built up, founded on this principle, a system of historical sequences that appear to me quite untenable. That widely distributed cultural traits develop special forms in each particular area is a truism that does not require any proof. That these local developments may be arranged in a chronological series, that those of the most limited distribution are the youngest, is only partially true. It is not difficult to find phenomena that center in a certain region and dwindle down at the outskirts, but it is not true that these invariably arise on an ancient substratum. The converse is often true, that an idea emanating from a center is diffused over a wide area. Neither may the origin always be looked for in the area of the strongest development. In the same way as we find animals surviving and flourishing in regions far distant from the locality in which they developed, so cultural traits may be transferred and find their highest expression in regions far away from their origin.[20]

Diffusion, which assumed great prominence in all these studies was first treated as though only single traits had always spread, and this is still the prevailing tendency of many ethnologists, particularly of Boas. When this proved to be somewhat inadequate, the concept of culture complexes and culture centers was developed, and the method of interpretation became more and more elaborate. To find one's way in this labyrinth, it was necessary to establish criteria, and it is no more accident that it was a philologist, Sapir, who made the first thoroughgoing attempt to expound the nature and the workings of these criteria.[21] Let us examine some of them.

Sapir prefaces his study with the significant remarks that

. . . one of the characteristic traits of history is its emphasis on the individual and personal. . . . The historical re-

[20] *Primitive Art*, p. 6, 1927.
[21] SAPIR, E., "Time Perspective in Aboriginal American Culture," *Geological Survey of Canada*, Anthropological Series, No. 13. For an excellent and telling criticism compare also W. D. Wallis, *Culture and Progress*, pp. 35–62, 1930.

constructions of the cultural anthropologist can only deal with generalized events and individualities. . . . This limitation . . . need not in the least obscure the application of historical methods to the field of anthropology.[22]

I must insist that if this really were so, if the reconstruction of aboriginal cultures were actually limited in this manner, then it would most definitely preclude the application of historical methods to the field. Even if we were to grant the justification of substituting conceptualized events and conceptualized individuals for real events and real individuals, which no historian would conceivably do because it is at bottom quite meaningless, one might pertinently ask how Sapir had arrived at his notion of the generalized event or generalized individual. He nowhere vouchsafes us this information. But to continue: "These generalized events and individualities introduce a purely quantitative, not qualitative, correction into our initial ideal of historical treatment."[23] If I follow Sapir's argument here, he first admits that history deals with specific individuals and events, that in the reconstruction of the history of aboriginal culture it is impossible to obtain the requisite information with regard to these individuals and events, and that therefore we must operate with generalized

22 *Ibid.*, p. 4.
23 *Ibid.*, p. 4.

events and individualities! Since, however, the latter do not properly exist, we must, so to speak, reendow them with as much reality as we can; and since we cannot give them a qualitative correction, we must give them a quantitative one! In other words, we are asked to devitalize something which we have never known and then to endow this unknown something with a new life and assume that what we have breathed into it is the life it originally possessed. This is certainly a most amazing type of procedure. Of course, Sapir is not the only one who has fallen into this fallacious type of reasoning; it is inherent in every quantitative approach.

After his general remarks Sapir gives a series of aids to be employed in the "formation of a technique in the historical interpretation of data far removed in time."[24] The most important of these are the following:

First, the principle of seriation which postulates that there is a simple-to-complex development and which is best illustrated by the history of artifacts and industrial processes.

Second, the principles bearing on cultural associations. I shall select six of these:

1. Necessary presupposition. This means, for instance, that the throwing stick carries us back

[24] *Ibid.*, p. 4.

much farther into the past than the woven rabbit-skin blanket, because it is so simple an instrument for securing a rabbit.[25]

2. Type of reflection in culture. The more frequent and stereotyped is the reflection of a trait in a culture, the more reason, generally speaking, to assign the cultural element a great age.[26]

3. Relative firmness of association. "The firmer the association, the older the culture element; the looser the association, the more recent the culture element."[27]

4. Maladjustment of culture to environment. As an example Sapir gives the following: "The fact that the grizzly bear as crest is more in evidence among the Tlingit and Tsimshian than among the Haida . . . is almost certainly to be connected with the geographical fact that the grizzly bear is not found in the Queen Charlotte Islands."[28]

5. Frequency of association. "The more frequently an element is connected with others, the older, generally speaking, it will be felt to be."[29]

6. Cultural elaboration and specialization. "The more elaborately developed of two culture com-

[25] Certainly the most devout of the older evolutionists could not ask for more.
[26] *Ibid.*, p. 16.
[27] *Ibid.*, p. 18.
[28] *Ibid.*, pp. 19–20.
[29] *Ibid.*, p. 22.

plexes of a tribe may generally lay claim to the greater age."[30]

The method of interpretation Sapir here outlines has marked affiliations with that of the German comparative mythologists and, of course, with that of comparative philology. It is, in fact, merely a special form of the latter, as Sapir frankly admits. That a clear-headed man like Sapir will go to such lengths simply indicates anew how compulsive is the need we feel for giving aboriginal cultures historical depth. It must be said to Sapir's credit that he apparently realized the futility of such criteria and really qualified everything he said at the end of his essay. "I do not consider," he states, "any single one of the inferential criteria that I have set up as necessarily valid in a specific case. Everything depends upon the specific condition of a given problem. . . . [31] A culture element must not be cut loose from its psychological and distributional setting."[32] In essence this is the same conclusion that Spier draws at the end of his study of the Sun Dance, which is at one and the same time the best example of the quantitative method and its death knell, just as Goldenweiser's

---

[30] *Ibid.*, p. 22.

[31] In other words, upon something else.

[32] *Ibid.*, p. 87. He never returned to it but has applied its general principles to language where they are more at home.

study of totemism is the best example of the purely analytical approach and its *reductio ad absurdum*.[33] But to sum up, Boas's viewpoint is essentially that of the physicist or mathematician, and cultural facts are treated by him as if they were physical facts or mathematical concepts. Here in the predominatingly analytical and quantitative studies that owe their impetus to his teaching, we have the same phenomena again illustrated. Because Sapir is so precise, he presents the viewpoint of all these ethnologists in their honest nakedness. We have generalized events and generalized individualities added to a quantitative treatment. In other words, a concept of the event and a concept of the individual are substituted for the real event and the real individual, and cultural facts are made amenable to quantitative calculations like any measurable object in the external world.

Before we turn to a consideration of the presuppositions of the ethnological method in Europe, it is only fair to state that a number of American ethnologists and ethnological theorists never succumbed to the above-mentioned tendencies, and that some of them were only slightly singed. To the former belong Dixon, Swanton, Linton, and Wallis, and to the latter, Lowie, Spier, Goldenweiser, Gifford, and Radin.

[33] *Cf.* note on p. 137.

Chapter III

The Presuppositions of the Ethnological Method in England and on the Continent

In England we find an ethnological approach characteristically different from that developed in the United States. In spite of the tremendous influence of Tylor and the vogue of evolutionism, no attempt was made by the field ethnologists themselves to reconstruct the past history of the aboriginal cultures investigated, at least not until the time of Rivers.[1] It is true that scholars like Ellis and others speculated somewhat uncritically on the influence of the Mediterranean civilizations on certain African tribes, and that Polynesian investigators had a tendency to wax eloquent about Hindu influences in the South Seas, but anything suggestive of the general chronological schemes of the evolutionists was conspicuous by its absence. From this point of view, the unwillingness of the English missionaries and amateurs to accept the

[1] *Cf.* note 9 on p. 69.

major conclusions of Darwin was very fortunate. The theoretical implications consequently were left entirely in the hands of the professional theorists, like McLennan, Tylor, Andrew Lang, Robertson-Smith, Westermarck, Marett, and Frazer. But even if this separation had not existed, it is extremely doubtful whether those who were entrusted with the collection of the information would ever have developed that interest in general problems and in methodology which is so characteristic of their American colleagues, for they were recruited from entirely different ranks. In the United States professional ethnologists have existed for more than two generations. In England they are of comparatively recent origin. Ethnographic research there was, for a long time, entirely in the hands of missionaries, colonial officials, and traveling gentlemen. That meant, broadly speaking, that ethnology was cultivated by amateurs and was essentially incidental to other work. The type of approach varied consequently from man to man and from group to group. This often led to superficiality, in the case of the gentlemen ethnologists, and to extreme subjectivism, but it also frequently led to monographs of outstanding excellence like the famous ones of Callaway, Codrington, Spencer and Gillen, Howitt, and others.[2] In the case of the

[2] CALLAWAY, H., *The Religious System of the Amazulu*, 1870; *Zulu*

missionaries and officials, all these investigators
possessed one requisite that was disgracefully
lacking among their American colleagues: they
knew the language of the people about whom they
were writing. On the other hand, this very great
advantage was frequently neutralized completely
by the very common assumption, on the part of
even the most broad-minded of these investigators,
that they were dealing with peoples mentally and
morally inferior to themselves. This manifestly
distorted their record and, taken together with the
secondary nature of their interest, made almost all
their descriptions incomplete and inadequate.
But this much must be said for them: that they
were almost always historically minded, that they
never lost sight of the fact that they were dealing
with specific individuals and specific events. When
they attempted to reconstruct the past, speculative
and untenable as these reconstructions generally
were, they were in terms of human beings and not in
terms of generalized individualities and conceptualized events and processes.

The virtues of the English amateur ethnologists
were many. They were practically always people of

Nursery Tales, 1870.

   CODRINGTON, R. H., *The Melanesians*, 1891.

   SPENCER, B., and F. J. GILLEN, *The Arunta*, 1927; *The Northern Tribes
of Central Australia*, 1904.

   HOWITT, W., *The Native Tribes of Southeastern Australia*, 1904.

broad culture even when their personal views were narrow and deeply ingrained. They knew the native languages and they were able to devote years to a given tribe. Since all of them had been trained in some branch of the humanities, they knew what historians meant by history and what were the primary requirements of an historical record; and when they were sufficiently interested and thought the subject worth their while, they could collect data in a manner which must make the professional ethnologists of the last generation blush. Where, for instance, docs any ethnologist give us the information that Bishop Callaway does about his informants, the limitations of their knowledge for the particular work with which they were entrusted, and their personality? Where, in fact, can we, among contemporary ethnologists who pride themselves upon their critical methods and their accuracy, obtain so excellent an account of the religious experience of an aboriginal people as Callaway's account of the religion of the Amazulu? Take, for example, the last work of Boas, clearly the outstanding figure in the ethnography of the last generation, entitled *The Religion of the Kwakiutl Indians*.[3] What does he tell us about the informants from whom he obtained his data? Occasionally their names are given and the group

3 *Columbia University Contributions in Anthropology*, vol. 10, 1930.

to which they belong indicated. Not always that. Nor does Boas add one single word by way of explanation of specific details that are quite meaningless without annotation. Let anyone who is so inclined glance through Callaway's work and note the difference. What holds for Callaway holds for quite a number of other missionaries, although none of them equal him unless it be that remarkable Franciscan monk Bernardino de Sahagun, who in the sixteenth century wrote a monograph on the Aztec in which all the canons of modern historical criticism were scrupulously observed.[4] But administrators, at times, were almost as good. Let me recall but two names—Sir George Grey and A. B. Ellis[5]

Unfortunately what they chose to record was generally utterly inadequate for a comprehensive understanding of a particular tribe, and, as we have already pointed out, extreme subjectivism could, at times, completely nullify their superb qualifications and opportunities. One well-known example of such nullification is R. H. Dennett's *At the Back of the Black Man's Mind.*[6]

[4] *Historia General de las Cosas de Nueva España.* It was originally written in Aztec and translated into Spanish by Sahagun himself. French, German, and English translations exist, the last one not complete as yet.

[5] *Polynesian Mythology,* and *Maori Poetry,* the last one not translated as yet. Three famous volumes, somewhat antiquated today: *The Tshi-Speaking Peoples,* 1887; *The Ewe-Speaking Peoples,* 1890; and *The Yoruba-Speaking Peoples,* 1894.

[6] 1906. *Cf.* particularly Chaps. X and XI.

Such was the situation in English ethnology when the professional ethnologists appeared on the scene. They had all been scientists, of one kind or another, and were somewhat proud of their ignorance of the humanities. The first innovation they introduced they could not very well help under the circumstances, *viz.*, ignorance of the native languages. But there is absolutely no excuse for their failure to realize the importance of knowing these languages and the extent to which this ignorance affected their record. The second element they brought was the so-called scientific method. This was, in large measure, a composite of the general attitude of the natural scientist plus the specific theory of evolution. Since, at the same time, they shared many of the presuppositions of the missionaries, public officials, and traveling gentlemen, their monographs represent, in a sense, not an advance but a retrogression over those of their predecessors. Their one great achievement was the *Reports of the Torres Straits Expedition,* and nothing in these six volumes can even remotely compare with the work of Callaway, Codrington, or even White,[7] in quality, although, to be sure, the picture they draw of native life is more extensive. This does not in the least mean that their work was negligible or that their influence on certain aspects

[7] WHITE, J., *The Ancient History of the Maori*, 1887–1889.

of ethnological research in England has not been for the good. Indeed, if ethnology is taught at a number of English universities today, it is due entirely to the enthusiasm of three representative figures of this school, Haddon, Balfour, and Seligman. They introduced an appreciation for a more systematic treatment of the data than had been customary up to their time, and this has been of inestimable value in its effect on that rather large body of missionaries, public officials, and amateurs, who still occupy themselves with the study of native life and who generally write the best monographs. It is to their influence that we must ascribe such excellent works as Roscoe's *Baganda*, Smith and Dale's *Ila-Speaking Tribes of Northern Rhodesia*, Skeat and Blagden's *Pagan Tribes of the Malay Peninsula*, Talbot's *Peoples of Southern Nigeria*, and Rattray's studies on the Ashanti. The last-named series of monographs, that of Rattray, possess all the merits of Callaway and Codrington, plus a broader outlook and a more systematic presentation. If Rattray can do such work in the spare moments a responsible British official usually finds for the subject, one wonders what he would accomplish if he cared to devote all his time to it. But that has always been the tragedy of British ethnology: that those who were most qualified to do the work were either not sufficiently interested or circumstances made it impossible.

It is to the credit of scholars like Haddon and Seligman that, despite their marked evolutionary leanings, they never attempted to introduce into their work the type of conjectural reconstructions so popular in the United States. The quantitative treatment of ethnological facts found comparatively no encouragement from them, and they kept themselves free from ethnological speculations of the type of Marett and Frazer—too free in fact. Yet England was not, any more than the United States or Germany, to be spared the former. Perhaps that is not to be wondered at, for the first quantitative study of ethnological data was made there, by the founder of modern ethnology, Tylor.[8] Apparently the irritation produced by the lack of a reliable chronology is just too much for any person with a well-developed sense of order or a feeling for logical sequence. W. H. R. Rivers, the ethnologist who attempted to establish such a sequence, was endowed with as inadequate an understanding of the real meaning of history as any of the members of the American quantitative school. He was primarily and fundamentally an

---

[8] "On a Method of Investigating the Development of Institutions," *Journal of the Anthropological Institute* (of Great Britain and Ireland), vol. 18, pp. 245–272, 1889.

experimental psychologist. As he himself has stated, he began as a firm adherent of the current English school. That meant, according to him, an almost complete preoccupation with the evolution of beliefs, customs, and institutions, with little attention paid to the complexity of individual cultures. Suddenly he came to the conclusion that Melanesian society was complex, and that the evolution of its social structure, which he had traced in terms of a comparative study of the systems of relationship, with no regard to the geographical distribution of the individual terms, was inadequate. He therefore turned his attention to the consideration of this second factor and came to the realization that the development of Melanesian society had not taken place in a simple and homogeneous manner, but that it had been exceedingly complex and due to the mingling of two peoples. He proceeded consequently to analyze it into its component elements and subsequently found himself forced to trace the history of each of these component elements, one by one.[9]

Here we have arrived at a fully developed quantitative treatment. We shall leave it for the present and return to its consideration afterwards. Instead,

[9] RIVERS, W. H. R., *The History of Melanesian Society*, vol. II, pp. 1–2, 1914.

let us throw a glance at the development of ethnology in Germany. But before doing so, I would like to say a few words about the unusually important monographs that have been written concerning the main Polynesian groups—Maori, Samoans, Hawaiians, Tongans, Marquesans, and Tahitians.[10] They are in a class by themselves. Owing to the comparative ease with which these languages can be learned and the cooperation of the natives, an amount of material has been amassed, almost always by nonprofessional ethnologists, that outstrips in volume and quality anything that has so far been done on a restricted area except by some of the American ethnologists and the Danish investigators of the Eskimo. Although the excellence of the record is due to very exceptional circumstances, still it constitutes a very pertinent reminder to the professional ethnologist that the ideal collectors of the data are the natives

[10] Much of this is still unpublished. Apart from the early work of the English missionaries and officials (J. White, W. W. Gill, G. Turner, Stair, Mariner, Sir G. Grey, etc.), the bulk of this material has appeared in two series of publications, those of the Bernice Pauahi Bishop Museum, Honolulu (*Memoirs* and *Occasional Papers*), and those of the Polynesian Society (*Journal* and *Memoirs*). Three excellent general descriptions are those of E. Best and E. Tregear on the Maori, and A. Kraemer on the Samoans. Two special studies also deserve to be mentioned, N. B. Emerson's "Unwritten Literature of Hawaii," *Bulletin* 38 *of the Bureau of American Ethnology*, and M. Beckwith, "The Hawaiian Romance of Laieikawai," 33d *Annual Report of the Bureau of Ethnology*.

themselves and that the more the former keeps in the background, the more accurate and authentic will the archives on aboriginal culture ultimately become. As far as the preservation of the record itself is concerned, the ethnologist's rôle should remain predominatingly that of an editor and annotator.[11] But he must do this. Otherwise, as I have pointed out before, the value of the material will be partially if not wholly nullified.

Germany and Austria, like England, developed a class of professional ethnologists very late, but there had always existed a fairly large number of scholars intensely interested in aboriginal civilizations.[12] In the main these had come from the natural sciences, from comparative anatomy and zoology. A few had drifted in from history and the humanities. Until the acquisition of colonies, missionaries and amateurs did not occupy themselves with the subject at all. In short,

[11] What is likely to happen, when he attempts to be more, is best exemplified by the extreme *naïveté*, for example, of the remarks of such excellent editors as Tregear, Best, and Emerson, concerning the mentality and morality of the Polynesians.

[12] The German interest in primitive culture goes back to the Romantic movement of the early nineteenth century and the speculations on the history of civilization which date specifically from the time of Herder. Both tendencies were reenforced by the colossal figure of Alexander von Humboldt and the great historians of the early and middle nineteenth century. The two representative works embodying these tendencies are T. Waitz, *Anthropologie der Naturvölker*, and J. Lippert, *Kulturgeschichte der Menschheit.*

ethnology was an academic subject there entirely. It is not surprising then that theories, couched in the customary philosophical terminology, were definitely in the ascendant. These theories centered around two men, one of them an outstanding figure in the history of geography of the nineteenth century, Friederich Ratzel, the other a vastly overrated and muddle-headed thinker named Adolf Bastian, a man of tremendous capacity for work and an almost equally tremendous capacity for not digesting the data. The first stood primarily for the theory that similarities in culture were to be interpreted as due to diffusion, and the second for the theory of psychical unity, *viz.*, that the same ideas, beliefs, and customs have been repeated again and again, at different times and among different peoples. All German ethnology since their time has revolved around the discussion of these two theories. The deadlock was broken only by Foy-Graebner's culture-strata (*Kulturkreise*) hypothesis, which is really a special form of Ratzel's diffusion theory. It is true that Ratzel himself might have been somewhat horrified at the idea of establishing a culture stratum on the basis of quantitatively determined criteria, but he would, in the main, have approved of Graebner's principal contentions.

When German ethnologists first began to do fieldwork, they were deeply imbued with these theories; indeed, their theoretical presuppositions were merged with the presentation of their facts in such a manner that it is often difficult, in the extreme, to tell where the one begins and the other ends. For some inexplicable reason, German ethnologists have always proceeded on the theory that every specific investigation of a tribe has to be tortured so that it can be used as an illustration of some universal tendency of the human mind. But with all due deference to the amazing skill of many Germans at metaphysical formulation, it does not always follow that, because a thinker is confused, he is wrestling with problems. In their desire to attack the major and basic problems of culture and culture growth, they frequently forgot to gather enough data to attack even the minor and insignificant ones. As a result of this unfortunate metaphysical terminology—for it is often nothing more—one encounters in even the best work of the academic ethnologists a somewhat irritating pretentiousness, of which, I am certain, they are unaware. This pretentiousness, this naïve assumption that fundamental problems can be envisaged and satisfactorily discussed merely because one happens to be interested in them, leaves a critically minded reader with the unpleasant feeling that the facts are always highly colored or subjectively distorted, that the record has been tampered with from the very beginning. This does not destroy their usefulness except for those phases of culture where it is absolutely vital to know precisely what an informant has actually said, as in descriptions of religion, for instance.

To this undue preoccupation with inadequately formulated general problems, we must add the somewhat unsuccessful attempt, on the part of the academic ethnologists, to enter into a sympathetic *rapport* with the cultures they are describing, an attempt which generally ended in either sentimentalism or extreme subjectivism. Both have interfered with the primary business of getting the facts completely and correctly. It has also meant an expenditure of unnecessary time and energy on the part of scholars who were excellent observers— time which, from the point of view of ethnology, might far more profitably have been devoted to collecting facts. This is particularly true of such an excellent field worker as Preuss. In other words, it has led to fragmentary accounts of cultures and to premature generalizations.[13] Another cause con-

[13] They have, however, written, easily the best handbook on ethnography which we possess today, *Illustrierte Völkerkunde*, edited by G. Buschan, 2d ed., 1922, and, under the general directorship of G. Thilenius, given a detailed and meticulous, if somewhat uninspiring, description of the material culture of one area, Micronesia.

tributing to the inadequacy of their ethnographic characterizations is their woeful inability to describe social organization, Thurnwald perhaps excepted. None of the outstanding academic ethnologists of the last generation has given us even partially complete sketches of a tribe. Preuss[14] has described the religion and mythology of the tribes he investigated, Thurnwald[15] the social organization, and Ankermann, Krause, etc.,[16] have been content with minor essays. The really adequate studies of aboriginal cultures have been made by missionaries and outsiders who had comparatively little interest in the relative merits of the diffusionism of Ratzel, the elementary ideas of Bastian, or the mythological obsessions of Ehrenreich.[17] Possibly T. Koch-

[14] PREUSS, K. T., *Die Religion der Cora*, 1912; *Die Religion und Mythologie der Uitoto*, 1921.

[15] THURNWALD, R., *Forschungen auf dem Salomoinseln und dem Bismarckarchipel*, 1912; *Die Gemeinde der Banaro*, 1912.

[16] ANKERMANN, B., "Kulturkreise und Kulturschichten in Afrika," *Zeitschrift für Ethnologie*, vol. 37, 1905; "Totenkult und Seelenglaube bei Afrikanischen Völkern, *ibid.*, vol. 50, 1918.

KRAUSE, F., *Die Kultur der kalifornischen Indianern*, 1921; "Zur Besiedelungsgeschichte der nordamerikanischen Praerie," *Korrespondenzblatt der deutschen Gesellschaft für Anthropologie*, etc., vol. 44, 1913.

[17] SPIETH, J., *Die Ewe Stämme*, 1906; *Die Religion der Eweer*, 1911.

WESTERMANN, D., *Die Kpelle*, 1921; *The Shilluk*, 1911.

STREHLOW, C., "Die Aranda und Loritza-Stämme in Zentral Australien," *Veröffentlichungen aus dem städischen Völker Museum*, Frankfurt am Main, vol. 1, parts I–III, 1907–1910.

GUTTMANN, B., *Das Recht der Tschagga*. This is the best study of

Gruenberg is an exception, but his work was, on the whole, superficial.

As far as the personal preconceptions of these scholars are concerned, none of them regards the mental endowment of aboriginal peoples as equal to that of so-called civilized man, and all of them operate with some kind of evolutionary scheme. Yet with all these defects, their fundamental approach is that of the culture historian, Ankermann excepted, and this must always be said to their credit.[18]

No account of German ethnology would be complete without some remarks about three of its most interesting figures, Karl von den Steinen, Paul Ehrenreich, and Felix von Luschan. The first of these was probably the most gifted ethnologist his country has ever produced. He wrote a work on the aboriginal tribes of southern Brazil, which will probably always remain one of the classics of ethnography, and a monograph on the art of the Marquesans. Yet his studies remained fragments, and his influence was negligible because he refused

---

aboriginal law we possess.

PESCHUEL-LOESCHE, E., *Volkskunde von Loango*, 1907.

[18] PREUSS, K. T., *Die geistige Kultur der Naturvölker*, 1923.

THURNWALD, R., *Psychologie des primitiven Denkens*, 1918; *Primitive Kultur* in the *Reallexikon der Vorgeschichte*, edited by Max Ebert, 1928. In this last article Thurnwald's uncritical neoevolutionism comes out very markedly.

to waste his time on unprofitable discussions. The second, Ehrenreich, began as a physical anthropologist, became an excellent field ethnologist, and ended as a comparative mythologist. His fundamental critique of physical anthropology has been forgotten, his field work was never emulated, but his highly speculative discussions of mythology have exerted a wide and somewhat unwholesome influence on his contemporaries. The third was a physical anthropologist. He was, however, also an excellent ethnologist, and his work on the material culture of Africa deserves to be remembered for a long time. Yet, in all probability, although essentially not a theorist, he will be longest remembered for having, together with G. Thilenius, introduced into ethnology the thoroughly baneful concept of convergent evolution.

Most of the ethnologists we have so far been discussing were, as we have just pointed out, strongly influenced by both Bastian and the evolutionary method. The movement ushered in by Foy and Graebner,[19] on the other hand, was definitely anti-Bastian and claimed to be both

[19] It is well to remember that up to the present all German ethnological field workers, with the exception of Ankermann, the exceedingly erratic L. Frobenius, and a few missionaries definitely trained by Father Schmidt, have consistently rejected the viewpoint developed by Foy, Graebner, and Father Schmidt.

antievolutionary and historical.[20] Actually it is no more historical than Rivers's method or that of Wissler, to which it has some superficial resemblances. As it is fundamentally an illustration of a quantitative approach, we shall return to it later on. Here we wish simply to make a few brief remarks about the claims made for it by its ablest living proponent Father Schmidt. With Graebner the desire for chronology became an obsession and the obsession a dogma. In his last work Father Schmidt leaves us in no doubt upon the matter. According to him, Graebner's work can be divided into three parts. "The first of these deals with the criticism of sources and provides the means of establishing the facts with exactitude and fidelity. The second treats of interpretation and leads to discovering the true meaning of each fact. The third . . . gives an account of combination." Now combination is one of those marvelous principles that a benign Providence sends to theorists in distress and proves that "the two objects to be compared belong to the same cultural unit."[21] It is by means of the "process of combina-

[20] Cf. in addition to Graebner's book, mentioned before, the last work of Father W. Schmidt, The Origin and Growth of Religion, 1931, particularly pp. 219–250, where he gives a complete bibliography in which he includes everyone who has ever mentioned the word history, as adherents of his point of view.

[21] SCHMIDT, W., ibid., p. 230. According to Graebner, "Hitherto, direct interpretation has been alone in vogue. I feel perfectly certain that,

tion" that "indirect interpretation" can take place and "indirect" interpretation is the corner stone of Graebner's system, for it enables those who are properly gifted to compare objects belonging to the different cultural units which are inconveniently separated in space.

Graebner's work falls into four divisions: the first, where he gives us the criteria through whose help the various culture contacts can be arranged into definite strata; the second, where he indicates the manner in which these culture strata are connected with one another through juxtaposition and intermingling; the third, where we learn the rules for the establishment of a chronology for the different strata; and the fourth, where we find the determination of the process which enables us to arrive at the causal succession of the particular cultures and the reasons for their development.[22]

There is something compelling in the effrontery with which Graebner lays down the laws that govern culture growth, and this is probably the reason for his very great influence in Germany and Austria. It cannot be too definitely stressed, however, in view of the claims made by Father

---

if tested by this requisite, a large part of the ethnological work which has been done, particularly in the field of the history of religion, loses much of its value, if it does not become entirely negligible."—Quoted from Schmidt, p. 231.

[22] SCHMIDT, W., *ibid.*, p. 231.

Schmidt, that the *Kulturkreise* theory of Graebner has not been accepted by any ethnologist outside Germany, with a few negligible exceptions.[23] Graebner's formulation has led to more pseudo-problems than all the other theories put together. Ethnologists have been far too kind to him, particularly those whose leanings are definitely toward some form of quantitative treatment of cultural data. Even Boas,[24] for instance, who sees through Graebner's fallacies clearly, is not severe enough. Instead of examining the foundations of his method, showing their complete inadequacy and the fallacious nature of his reasoning, and then paying no attention to it, scholars have permitted themselves to be beguiled into examining the extent to which his predicated culture strata hold true.[25] It is but another illustration of the fatal propensity of ethnologists for establishing points of reference within an error.

[23] *Ibid.*, pp. 223–229. Whatever weight might otherwise have been attached to Father Schmidt's critical judgment must disappear in the light of the following extremely naïve remarks: "[Graebner's] *Methode der Ethnologie* is based on E. Bernheim's *Lehrbuch der historischen Methode* which is much to its advantage as regards construction and handling of the subject"!—Schmidt, *ibid.*, p. 228. Certainly comment is unnecessary here.

[24] Article "Anthropology," in *Encyclopedia of the Social Sciences*, 1930.

[25] *Cf.* for example, Heine-Geldern's attempt in his article, "Urheimat und frühste Wanderungen der Austronesier," Anthropos, pp. 543–619, 1932.

The Dutch ethnologists to whom we must now turn, although their work is well enough known outside their own country, have never been adequately appreciated. In part this is due to the fact that the peoples with whom they dealt have been so markedly influenced, on the whole, by Hindu and Mohammedan civilizations that they were not properly regarded as aboriginal in the strict sense of the term; in part it is simply due to the fact that they wrote in Dutch. Be this as it may, the slightest acquaintance with their work must make it patent that their monographs are, on the whole, the equal of the best English and American. The overwhelming majority of the Dutch ethnologists were recruited from the humanistic disciplines; all of them knew the language of the peoples they studied, and most of them were able to spend many years of intimate intercourse with them, in the capacity of either government officials or missionaries. Their attitude toward the natives was typical of that of Western Europeans, although not quite so pronounced. In addition, they have generally kept themselves aloof from active participation in any of the major controversies—evolutionism, diffusionism, and psychic unity. Always remaining strictly historical, they have never been beguiled into formulating cultural problems in terms of the physical and natural sciences. Their one great defect is that they have not seen fit to publish their data in text and that they have not published enough detailed monographs.[26]

The Danish and Russian ethnologists have all the merits of the Dutch, and since, in addition, they have absolutely no racial prejudices—this is particularly true of the Russians—and have also realized the necessity of obtaining and publishing their material in text, they come as close to fulfilling all the conditions for a perfect ethnological record that one can reasonably expect. The Danish task was, of course, rendered comparatively easy because all their efforts were limited to one tribe, the Eskimo. Scholars and missionaries have been

[26] Their number is very large. The most important are the following:

Wilken, G. A., *De Verspreiden Geschriften*, 4 vols., 1912.

Kern, H., *Verspreide Geschriften*, 1915.

Kruijt, A. C., *Het Animisme in den Indischen Archipel*, 1906.

Nieuwenhuis, A. W., "Die Veranlagung der malaiischen Völker des ostindischen Archipels," in *Internationales Archiv für Ethnographie*, vol. 21, Supplement, vols. 22, 23, 25, 1913–1921.

Hurgronje, G. Snouck, *Het Gajoland en zijne bewoners*, 1903, and *The Achenese*, 1906.

In addition we must mention the following journals and dictionary:

Tijdschrift voor Indische Taal, Land, en Volkenkunde, 1853 ff.

Tijdschrift voor Nederlandsch Indie, 1838 ff.

Bijdragen tot de Taal, Land, en Volkenkunde van Nederlandsch Indie, 1853 ff.

Nederlandsch Indie oud en Nieuw, 1916 ff.

Encyclopaedie van Nederlandsch Oost-Indie, 4 vols., 1917–1921.

Katalog des Ethnographischen Reichsmuseums, 16 vols., 1919–1923.

studying them for two hundred years so that it can be said that the archives they have amassed about them are perfect of their kind. We know more about the Eskimo than about any other aboriginal people. The data have been presented in text and free from the disturbing influence of speculations and theories and, since so many investigators have participated, we have here all the controls that a critically minded individual has a right to demand.[27] The Russian work is not quite so complete, but its range is much larger, covering as it does all of Siberia. In addition to a number of very able works by missionaries, of whom Veniaminov is perhaps the best known, many of those who participated in the conquest of Siberia have left valuable accounts of the natives—valuable because they were so free from the normal prejudices of Europeans. Beginning with the last quarter of the eighteenth century, we find a whole series of excellent ethnographers, of whom the most important are Pallas, Castren, Radloff, and, toward the end

[27] The Danish interest in the Eskimo is, of course, very old. We need not go any further back, however, than the two great missionaries of the eighteenth century, Hans Egede and David Crantz. Their remarkable descriptions of Greenland are still authoritative. Most of the data since then has been published in two great series, the *Meddelelser om Grønland* and the *Reports of the Fifth Thule Expedition*. The most important names associated with this work are G. Holm, H. Rink, W. Thalbitzer, H. P. Steensby, K. Rasmussen, and K. Birket-Smith.

of the nineteenth century, Bogoras, Jochelson, Sternberg, etc. The last three have very definite theories, but they have kept them strictly separated from the actual data.

The French, in spite of their enormous colonial empire, and the excellent work of the early missionaries, have never been specifically interested in aboriginal cultures, with the exception of those of Indo-China and northern Africa, if one can call these aboriginal. What they have done there is of the very highest quality but does not fall within the domain of ethnology proper. Their work on the native tribes of West Africa and Madagascar is not in the same class with that of the other nations. Since the days of Comte they have been fairly exclusively interested in theories of social development and their somewhat belated concern with ethnology seems to be due to the bearing theorists felt it would have on much larger problems. In the history of ethnological theories the school founded by Durkheim and so ably continued by Mauss, Hubert, Lévy-Bruhl, etc., has been of paramount importance, but it cannot be said to have stimulated ethnological research until within the last few years. Neither can it be said that these scholars, with the exception of Mauss, have been keenly interested in the many problems connected with the acquisition of a proper, authentic, and complete record.[28] Somewhat in a class by itself is the work of the late Erland Nordenskiöld.[29] It is concerned primarily with typology and restricted to material culture. The dangers of such an approach are manifest, but Nordenskiöld himself realized this and was extremely cautious in the inferences he drew. He kept himself remarkably free from the errors into which so many ethnologists, who have made material culture their specialty, have fallen—for instance, Wissler and Graebner. He always remained an historian with a clear perception of what was the rôle of an historian. Yet there are so many lacunae in all attempts at plotting distributions, and these are likely to be so vital for the picture of any culture, that it is somewhat difficult to see

[28] The recent creation of an Institut d'Ethnologie is likely to have far-reaching effects upon the development of real ethnology in France, provided it does not play too markedly into the hands of the theorists. A publication like that of Leenhardt, *Notes et documents sur le Néo-Calédonien*, 1930, is an excellent augury. So too is the work of the late M. Delafosse and his pupils.

[29] His most important monographs are the following:

Eine geographische und ethnographische Analyse der materiellen Kultur zweier Indianerstaemme in El Gran Chaco, 1918.

The Ethnography of South America Seen from Mojos in Bolivia, 1920.

The Changes in the Material Culture of Two Indian Tribes under the Influence of New Surroundings, 1924.

what useful purpose the plotting of distributions can serve, apart from giving temporary classifications. In the hands of less cautious and more uncritical ethnographers, Nordenskiöld's method is bound to lead to all the fallacies that we stressed in our criticism of Wissler and Kroeber.

Chapter IV

The Factors in the Determination of the Ethnological Record

We have thus far limited ourselves to indicating the preconceptions underlying the treatment of aboriginal civilizations by the majority of ethnologists. It must now be our task to point out what conditions, apart from these preconceptions and temperamental preferences, fostered such a treatment. For it is only fair to say that not a few ethnologists were ill at ease with the results into which they had been led. There are a number of factors involved here: first, the inevitable and unavoidable pioneer character of the early researches; second, the professions from which many of the ethnologists of the last generation were recruited; third, the peculiar relation in which an ethnologist stands to his data; fourth, the manner of collecting the data; fifth, the present character of aboriginal cultures; and, last, the present distribution of culture traits. To the foregoing must be added the specific attitude of the world at large toward aboriginal peoples and aboriginal cultures, for this has often diverted attention from the real work at hand to the educational task of correcting misconceptions as well as ludicrous and unjustifiable assertions frequently made by exceedingly intelligent individuals.

It goes without saying that, like most new subjects, the older monographs and descriptions leave much to be desired.[1] Since native cultures were everywhere dying out, the cry was necessarily for material, no matter how collected. Even when a certain amount of critical control began to be exercised, the unfortunate exigencies of the situation often prevented anything like an adequate critique of the sources or any systematically organized exploitation of the resources. It was a case of everyone for himself, and this meant, at bottom, antiquarianism at its worst, or possibly at its best. At any rate, it was antiquarianism with all its implications. Where the data were obtained by a missionary or a partially or fully trained investigator from other fields, the situation was somewhat different. At times a full sketch was aimed at, while at other times only special aspects were studied. In the main, however, because of

[1] I am beginning, roughly speaking, with the founding of the American Bureau of Ethnology in 1879 and, for the early volumes of this series, to which my remarks alone apply, I always except that very remarkable ethnologist J. O. Dorsey.

its tangibility and concreteness, and because information upon it was easily obtainable, material culture was almost always stressed, so what was originally an accidental emphasis became a permanent trait of all descriptions. In Europe, far removed geographically from aboriginal civilizations, accident likewise determined the stress that was laid upon material culture. There, however, it was the natural desire to describe the objects in the museums.

Most of these researches, in short, bore definitely the impress of their pioneer character.[2] Potentially the greatest danger here lay in the fact that the pioneer descriptions were never, strictly speaking, comparable. One description might be detailed along one direction and the next along another and, since circumstances frequently prevented further study, the picture of a given culture thus remained inadequate and one-sided. Later, when the essential pioneer character of many of these portrayals was recognized, it was often too late to correct them. The interest in special problems and special areas had by that time developed, and the complete description of a culture became subordinated to other ends. All this, of course, is well-known.

[2] Most of what I am here saying applies specifically to the history of ethnology in the United States. Exceptions, of course, occur. I need only mention Lewis H. Morgan and Horatio Hale.

What is generally forgotten, however, is the direction this pioneer work has given to later studies. One of its main characteristics, we have seen, was an overemphasis on material culture and on special aspects of aboriginal life. In addition it bequeathed a whole series of pseudo-problems to the next generation. Let me dwell upon one only, the assumption that there were, north of the Rio Grande, fifty-nine distinct linguistic stocks. This has, as we all know, become one of the corner stones of later American ethnology.

Now how precisely did the early American ethnologists arrive at this determination, which was for so long a time almost axiomatic? Its history is well-known. The founder of the American Bureau of Ethnology, J. W. Powell, was the first to promulgate it on the basis of material which had been collected under his supervision. Powell was neither a natural-born philologist nor in any way prepared either to plan such a survey or understand the results after they had been obtained. Individuals just as unprepared were entrusted with carrying it out, Gatschet being the only exception. A list of English keywords was prepared and sent to all the various agents, government officials, and missionaries, who had any contact with the Indians. They filled in, next to the English word, what they thought was the Indian equivalent.

Since they often knew practically nothing about the native languages, this was often some form of the word in question, or occasionally, a phrase in which the word occurred. The amateur linguists in the Bureau then interpreted the lists and arrived at a definite classification into fifty-nine stocks. As a provisional makeshift it was remarkably good. But Powell was a soldier, used to giving orders. The word provisional did not exist in his vocabulary, and so the linguistic stocks stood as final. It was immediately adopted without the slightest murmur, and, although the manner in which it was set up was well-known to everyone and although everybody realized that it had been based exclusively on a lexic comparison of uncritically obtained data, no one ever seriously questioned it until Dixon and Kroeber's[3] predication of Hokan and Penutian. The latter's conclusions were almost immediately attacked as ridiculous and unjustified, and Boas and Goddard laid down the amazing dictum that it was incumbent on linguists to disprove the potpourri Powell had foisted upon us before any attempt could be made to establish genetic relationships of the type Dixon and Kroeber proposed. Surely the only proper attitude was to have realized that Powell's classification at best

[3] DIXON, R. B., and A. L. KROEBER, "New Linguistic Families in California," *American Anthropologist*, pp. 647–655, 1913.

showed that we had no right to make any inferences
from the data—either that the languages were
related or that they were unrelated. Why should
we be asked to disprove an unproved assumption?
The only explanation, of course, is the old one, that
it was one of those numerous theses that had been
emotionally and uncritically accepted as corrob-
oration of a definite theory, *viz.*, multiple origin,
a theory which lies at the basis of all Boas's work
on aboriginal cultures.

But here I am interested only in the question of
methodology. Powell's classification proved nothing. When Dixon and Kroeber and subsequently
Sapir questioned it, Boas's reaction was to attempt
to find other explanations that would explain the
similarities in vocabulary and structures which
these scholars had pointed out. He insisted that
vocabularies and structural peculiarities could be
borrowed, that it was as necessary to account for
the differences between two languages as for the
similarities; all of which is obvious enough. That,
however, they were not true problems is evidenced
by the fact that he would not draw, or allow
others to draw, the simple inferences flowing
naturally from the predication of the borrowing of
vocabularies or morphological elements, etc. The
series of problems, minor and major, which was
thus brought to the fore, while important and even

vital, really had nothing to do with the case in question, for their manifest purpose was to bolster up Powell's classification. Clearly the only logical and scientific procedure to have followed would have been to examine the basis upon which Powell had originally made his classification. This is precisely the one thing Boas did not do. And this is what I mean by saying that some of the problems developing in connection with the pioneer work were pseudo-problems.

But it is not only a heritage of pseudo-problems that this pioneer work left: it also initiated trends, mechanically followed since, which a more generous-minded critic would possibly designate as traditions. One of these trends, as indicated before, was the emphasis upon material culture. It must be remembered that the extreme richness of the data on material culture was simply an accidental function of the ease with which such material could be obtained. Since there is a very natural tendency to overestimate the difficulties experienced in collecting the data, this fact was later forgotten, and a secondary interpretation for the richness of this type of information developed, as so frequently is the case with such interpretations and evaluations, under cover of a point of view. This point of view, that it was within the realm of material culture that aboriginal man's most significant achievements lay, was intelligible enough. It fitted in admirably with the prevalent attitude of the evolutionist and antievolutionist that aboriginal man was essentially concrete minded, a belief still shared by many ethnologists and theorists. Since the method of approach of these pioneers was essentially that of the natural sciences, it fitted in for other reasons as well. But more important than anything else was the fact that it attracted an ever-increasing number of students who were primarily and exclusively interested in material culture. In Germany we find the same overemphasis. There, however, it was due to entirely different causes. Having no colonies and no tradition of rich and cultured amateurs as was the case in England, students of ethnology naturally fell back upon the excellent material in their museums.

It is necessary for me to stress these various factors in detail because it is essential for the reader to envisage clearly what different strands have gone into the development of the ethnologist's prolonged and insistent preoccupation with material culture. There are certain disciplines where this is unavoidable, as in prehistory, for instance. It is not unavoidable in ethnology and was even less unavoidable three generations ago. Assuredly others, besides myself, must have been struck by the fact that, whereas it hardly seems necessary for a student of Greek or Roman culture to know much, if anything, about the details of their methods of fishing or preparation of food, it is regarded as quite essential for an ethnologist to know them. Why this insistence upon *Privatalter-tümer?* If ethnologists regard them as more important in the simpler than in the more complex civilizations, well and good. Let them say so. Some would acquiesce. The majority would demur. The more critical would undoubtedly say that, at bottom, this is to be ascribed to the simple fact that a more complete record of the material culture of a tribe can be obtained than of any other aspect of their life. But this is, I feel, a pure illusion. And even if it were true, it would in no way prove that material culture is more important among them than among us. The richness of the data is an unfortunate accident and it behooves us to be continually upon our guard against overevaluating this phase of their life. The lack of appreciation and understanding of the rôle of the individual in aboriginal civilization and the naïve application of an antiquated form of the theory of economic determinism are traceable directly to its influence, not to mention the various quantitative interpretations so popular today.

As an example of the damage it has done, let me contrast the enthusiasm evoked by the ingenious devices connected with the harpoon of the Eskimo as opposed to the casual way in which ethnologists refer to their poetry. And surely all the most intricate inventions made in connection with harpoons will not tell us one-tenth as much about the Eskimo as the following poem:[4]

> I call to mind
> And think of the early coming of spring
> As I knew it
> In my younger days.
> Was I ever such a hunter!
> Was it myself indeed?
> For I see
> And recall in memory a man in a kayak;
> Slowly he toils along in toward the shores of the lake,
> With many spear-slain caribou in tow.
> Happiest am I
> In my memories of hunting in kayak.
> On land, I was never of great renown
> Among the herds of caribou.
> And an old man, seeking strength in his youth,
> Loves most to think of the deeds
> Whereby he gained renown.

Or the love song of Ikigaitt, whose aunt has refused to let him marry his sweetheart:[5]

[4] RASMUSSEN, K., *Report of the Fifth Thule Expedition*, vol. 7, No. 2, p. 70, 1921–1924

[5] THALBITZER, W., *Légendes et chants Esquimaux du Groenland*, 1929.

Quand elles me sont apparus, les filles du bateau
Quand du sommet de l'Ikigaitt, elles sont été visibles
Oh! comme elles pleuraient mes chères soeurs,
Je les ai vues pleurer.

Et ma tante, la méchante soeur de mon père, je l'ai vue
    s'envanouir,
C'est elle qui ne me voulait pas, elle ne me voulait pas.
C'est sa faute si je deviens le beau-fils des glaces de l'in-
    térieur,
Si je cherche la solitude,
C'est elle, qui m'a refusé la douce petite amie qui m'avait
    dit oui:

Quand elle se met contre ma bien aimée, que puis-je faire?
Je me fâchais quand elle mangeait la bonne chère
Et que moi je devais vivre de lichen
Et à la fin me contenter de moules.

On peut être fâché quand elle s'habille de chaudes fourrures
On peut être fâché quand elle dort sous l'édredon chaud.
Et moi je devais me contenter de la peau de mon kayak
    comme couverture,
Et maintenant j'ai seulement la peau de mon kayak comme
    couissin.

The pioneer period in American ethnology, which
contained such intellectually robust figures as
J. W. Powell, W. G. McGee, D. Brinton, C. Thomas,
and O. T. Mason, was succeeded by that over which
Boas presided. To appreciate more fully the contribution for good and evil with which he and his

school are associated, it is important to remember that very few of these scholars came to ethnology directly. Practically all of them were recruited from the older disciplines and they were attracted to it because, for various reasons, they were dissatisfied with their particular subjects. Essentially, then, they were rebels, or, at least, dissenters. Ethnology seemed to offer them unlimited scope for new vistas, where they could unfold their energies untrammeled by outworn methods of interpretation and eternally reinterpreted facts. Many of them came from the natural sciences. To these dissenters and natural scientists, either the one or both, an unkind fate entrusted the destinies of the new ethnology in its formative and glamorous period. There is, unquestionably, nothing quite so fascinating and satisfying as the prospect of being freed from the old entangling alliances and to feel that the old order no longer prevails and that the world is to be discovered all over again.

The scientists and dissenters went to work in earnest. All that we knew of cultural growth and change in the civilizations of Europe and Asia had no applicability for the aboriginal cultures of America or Africa or Oceania or, to be more precise, was not brought into the purview at all. If Europe and Africa and Asia showed a very small number of linguistic stocks, what bearing, they

contended, did this have on aboriginal America?
There, distinct stocks might grow in luxuriance.
If linguistic development suggested certain persistent tendencies in the Old World, why should
they do so in the New? In this lack of interest in
all that the history of the Old World cultures had
taught us so laboriously, we have the note introduced by both the dissenters and the scientists.
It was an excellent prophylactic, suggestive,
stimulating, necessary, if you will, but it was an
illusion. The dissenters could no more throw off
their past or deny their knowledge of culture
growth—at least, those who possessed it—than
those ethnologists who had been recruited from
the natural sciences could discard their method
of approach. This knowledge crept upon them
unawares and robbed them of the fruits of their
new adventure in the hour of triumph. The study
of diffusion and the analytical dissection of aboriginal cultures taught them, only inadequately,
principles of interpretation that had been adequately demonstrated, over and over again, in
Europe and Asia. The innovators found themselves
laboriously proving the obvious. Naturally they
would not admit it, and so they found it necessary
to postulate generalized events and generic individuals, to assume that a vocabulary could be
borrowed apart from morphological elements and

morphological elements apart from vocabulary; to predicate that resemblances were due predominatingly to what they called convergences; to claim that variability and change were universal everywhere, but that, nevertheless, the clan organization or the grammatical structure of a language had remained constant and intact from the beginning of time. In short, they found it necessary to insist that aboriginal cultures and languages were somehow of a different order from our own and yet of the same.

But even if these ethnologists had been the most orthodox of Western European culture historians, they would have been confronted with a very peculiar and specific situation. It goes without saying that no historian studies a people in whom he is not fundamentally interested and in whose civilization and fortunes he cannot to some extent participate. When a civilization is quite alien to his own and participation in it strictly impossible like the Chinese, for example, he approaches it with respect, and by dint of intensive application he can become fairly at home with it and avoid some of those glaring mistakes that are likely to creep into any description of a culture in which one is unable to take part directly. What holds true for a European student of Chinese civilization holds true to a far more devastating extent when an ethnologist essays to study aboriginal cultures. They have no written language and consequently none of the earmarks of culture that a literate scholar assumes as self-evident. The people themselves are, today, generally impoverished and disorganized, materially, spiritually, and morally. It is making an unusual demand on the academically trained student that he respect their achievement and equate it, after a manner, with his own. And, of course, he never really does. True participation is simply out of the question and romantic participation obscures the situation completely. For any ethnologist to imagine that anything can be gained by "going native" is a delusion and a snare. Nor is the situation materially altered when the word realistic is substituted for romantic as, for example, Mead seems to have done.[6]

Some may be content with a purely external relation and call their lack of contact objectivity. The majority rightly reject this as a subterfuge and instinctively identify themselves with their data. This is not a psychoanalytical identification, not a

[6] *Cf. Coming of Age in Samoa,* and *Growing Up in New Guinea.* Boas in the foreword of the former book states that "we feel grateful to Miss Mead for having undertaken to identify herself so completely with Samoan youth that she gives us a lucid and clear picture of the joys and difficulties encountered by the young individual in a culture so entirely different from our own." Coming from Boas, this statement seems almost inconceivable.

katharsis for those weary in heart and mind, but an instinctive substitute for some approximation to that direct participation without which an analysis of culture is a frame without body or living breath. Of the advantages that accrue from such an identification I need not speak. That it partakes of the romantic is clear. But there are other dangers, perhaps less obvious. First of all, it does not bridge the gulf between the investigator and the data, a fact that is frequently forgotten, and, second, it is apt to set free within him irrational tendencies and egotistical trends that are the common heritage of man but to which an academically trained individual falls an easier victim than most others, and to which he, at times, gives a more naïve expression.

Ordinarily it is a work of supererogation to dwell on such frailities, but in any honest examination of ethnology this must be done, for these frailities have both colored and interfered with the record. Hypersensitiveness is not a virtue that can expect to be respected in such matters. It cannot be too strongly stressed not only that the field ethnologist collects the facts but that his description is most likely to remain the final picture of a given culture, from which no appeal can be made. What more natural than that this semidivine function which has been thrust upon him should make him feel that the facts are peculiarly his, obtained by the sweat of his brow. For anyone to question them is not merely an impertinence but a direct aspersion upon his character and veracity. This attitude, particularly prevalent in the United States, that the specific field of inquiry represents an ethnologist's private preserve wherein no one else may hunt has done inestimable harm and frequently has meant that a tribe has been described by only one person. The implications are self-evident. And when it is further remembered that this individual attempts to study every phase of the subject—language, art, religion, mythology, material culture—and that he almost always attempts to do so without a speaking knowledge of the language of the tribe under investigation, then this lack of control must strike an outsider as unbelievable, indeed almost as amazing as the fact that ethnologists have tolerated it for so long a time. Manifestly to overcome the difficulties confronting an ethnological investigation, it would require the cooperation of a group of supermen. That any one individual should aspire to do it single-handed is awe inspiring. Surely it is folly, but folly of heroic proportions, and that must be the excuse for his temerity.

It has sometimes been contended that the dangers attendant upon a tribe's being described by one person have been exaggerated, that, somehow, in a manner not quite clear, a description proves itself. Clearly such a contention can emanate only from those who are on their last line of defense. Otherwise one might be compelled to assume that their folly was not of heroic proportions.

In short, in ethnology, an identification which was a pardonable substitute for participation led, in the last analysis, to that most undesirable of results, a blocking of critical control and the obscuring of the rôle exercised by the investigator in the grouping of facts which had themselves been previously subjected to some form of selection.

If, now, we turn from the characterization of the investigators to the records themselves, we are immediately struck by the wide diversity of objectives they exemplify and the differences in the method of collecting data they indicate. The only question with which we are directly concerned here is the degree to which the methods of collecting were adequate for the securing of accurate information and the extent to which this information was kept distinct from the investigator's comments or reinterpretations. Both questions are of fundamental significance.

It is, or should be, a primary requirement that the data be obtained in the original, and this method has been followed sporadically since the time of Sahagun. But it has been systematically insisted upon here in America only since the influence of Boas began to make itself felt. It is, of course, a condition *sine qua non*. Owing to circumstances over which the investigator often has no control, this primary requirement is, however, frequently not fulfilled. This is unfortunate. But, unfortunate or not, it must be clearly recognized that every type of information suffers to some extent, if it is obtained in translation or what professes to be translation, and that some of it is rendered almost useless for certain types of intensive work. Even when investigators are fortunate enough to enlist the active services of natives in securing their facts, if they are obtained in translation, much of what would normally be gained by such a procedure is lost. Information on material culture, for obvious reasons, suffers least. That on religion and literature, on the other hand, loses almost all of its significant character in translation. And if a widespread impression exists today that little attention has been paid, in aboriginal civilizations, to religious speculation or to distinctions customary in our own religious thought or that primitive literature is only folklore in our sense of the term, that, I cannot help feeling, is due to the unauthentic manner in which the data have been gathered. For it is just as unauthentic to obtain an

American Indian prose epic or poem in English as it would be to obtain the Morte d'Arthur of Mallory in German or Villon in Russian.

It is because of this essentially unauthentic nature of the data that they apparently lend themselves so well to quantitative tabulation à la Wissler and Graebner. Admittedly it is difficult and arduous to obtain the desired material in text, but there is no other way if our primary object is to obtain a complete picture of a culture. Any other method is totally inadequate and misleading and plays directly into the hands of the antiquarians. Those ethnologists who obtain all their information in their own language, without any knowledge of native idioms, may honestly feel that they are making the proper allowances for their deficiency, but it is, strictly speaking, impossible. First of all, they cannot properly be aware of the full extent of their deficiency and, second, the results obtained in this manner are far too "convenient" to be discarded in favor of data which partake of all the indefiniteness and lack of rigorousness that emerge when the contact of the investigator with a culture is intimate.

How inadequate and misleading such a method is likely to be, and how easy it is for its results to be interpreted as corroborative of specific attitudes toward aboriginal culture in general, is beautifully illustrated in aboriginal literature and religion. Offhand, I believe most ethnologists would grant that much is lost, but they would still contend that enough remains to justify the obtaining of information on these two subjects in translation or, what it generally amounts to, paraphrasing. Something remains, undoubtedly. But what is it? In the prose literature it is a knowledge of the plot, the episodes, the themes, and the motifs of a given tale—excellent material for distributional studies, but for nothing else. But, let me ask, was it ever intended to be anything else? I sincerely doubt it. The investigator begins with the presupposition that he is dealing with folklore, and, since folklore is not literature, properly speaking, his method, he feels, is fairly adequate. The moment, however, we get a representative and accurate record in text, as among the Eskimo, the Navajo, the Kwakiutl, the Maori, we find that aboriginal peoples, like ourselves, have both their literature and their folklore and that, stylistically, the one is treated quite differently from the other. In the one case we are dealing with an artistic production where the content is possibly only a subsidiary consideration and in the other with traditionally handed-down themes and plots that have been subjected to very little reinterpretation. When obtained in translation, all this is lost, and literature and folklore are merged in one inextricable whole. It is not to be wondered at, then, if the widespread belief prevails that aboriginal literature is simply mythology, and that it lacks most, if not all, of those traits that would make it comparable with our own literatures. The insistence upon texts is not, therefore, simply a piece of pedantry, as some critics would have us believe, but a preliminary precaution for the attainment of accuracy. That it is even necessary to call attention to this fact is the saddest commentary that can possibly be passed on ethnologists.

It is true, however, that texts as such are merely an introductory requirement for accuracy. Accuracy does not inhere in a fact merely because it has been obtained in text. That would indeed be philological pedantry. Certainly we are entitled to some information about the individuals from whom the texts emanate. This is very rarely given and texts either become entirely subordinated to philological purposes or their value becomes completely neutralized. The vast majority of texts gathered in the United States have been collected by professional philologists and they may very rightly feel that it is not incumbent upon them to be ethnologists. That does not correct their inadequacy for ethnological use and does bring with it the obvious corollary that philologists should not then attempt to be ethnologists. In short, just in those cases where we have texts, a disturbing element is introduced by the fact that they have been collected by philologists whose objective is entirely different from that of ethnologists, and who frequently collect their material for very specific purposes. Indeed the selection begins at the very fountainhead, for a good linguistic informant may be very insufficiently acquainted with the details of his culture. Distortion is piled on distortion.

To correct the almost universal deficiency that he is unable to speak the native languages, the ethnologist has, at times, attempted to learn enough of the native idiom to control a translation. This is, of course, a great advantage, but it is obviously not enough. There is no substitute for a speaking knowledge of a language. Since even the ability to control a translation is none too frequent, the data are obtained through interpreters or from bilingual informants. Frequently these interpreters obtain their information directly from the best versed older individuals in the group and pass it on to the investigator, so that a partial corrective is made, even if in this unsatisfactory and roundabout manner.

But there are other factors besides the investigator's ignorance of the native languages and his precise relation to the sources of his information, which must be specifically studied if we wish to obtain a clear picture of his methods of field work. In the history of the major civilizations of Europe, Asia, and Africa, the preservation of the sources is due to chance, an obvious and serious defect, which is only partially rectified by the wealth of material. In ethnology, on the other hand, the preservation is consciously directed. That is why some knowledge of the personality and preconceptions of the investigator are vital and that is why the type of objective and the influence of institutions and bureaus of research dealing with ethnology are a definitely limiting condition. A cursory glance at the five great series of ethnological publications in the United States—the Bureau of American Ethnology, the American Museum of Natural History, the Field Museum of Natural History, the University of California Publications in American Ethnology, and the Reports of the Jesup Expedition edited by Boas—is sufficient to demonstrate this.

Let us take, for example, the famous studies on the societies of the Plains and the Sun Dance, published by the American Museum of Natural History.[7] Of the tribes concerned in the former only two, the Blackfoot and the Crow, and in the latter only four, the Blackfoot, the Crow, the

[7] *Anthropological Papers of the American Museum of Natural History*, vol. 11, 1916.

Arapaho, and the Cheyenne, had ever been studied as units. In other words, the objective here was a distributional investigation and nothing else. That the Crow, Blackfoot, Arapaho, and Cheyenne had been studied in considerable detail was an accident. The director of the two enterprises, Dr. Wissler, was either oblivious of or indifferent to the possible distortions of fact and perspective that this might introduce into the very study he was making. He frankly states that the study of the Plains societies

. . . was originally projected on the assumption that as a whole these organizations . . . were a phenomenon of cultural *diffusion and that a close analytical study of them in detail would reveal the approximate place and relative time of their origins.*[8] As these assumptions were not published or made a part of the instructions to field workers,[9] it cannot be claimed that the data were selected according to this criterion. On the other hand, each investigator was left to follow the natural unfolding of his own problems. . . . We believe, therefore, that at least in one respect the plan has resulted satisfactorily, *viz.*, to furnish independent concrete reports of fact. . . . Our point of view is strictly that of the present day' anthropologist and we have not the least

[8] The italics are my own.

[9] Although I do not care to make too much of this point, it should be borne in mind that practically all the field workers involved were either members of the staff of the American Museum or connected with it in some semiofficial capacity. In other words, the specific object Wissler had in view was very well known to them.

doubt but that sociologists could also discuss the same data in a different manner.[10]

Does Wissler mean that others are to use the data that have been selected and prejudged in connection with a specially circumscribed problem? Wissler could feel certain that the preparation of the ethnologists participating in the investigation was adequate for obtaining the bare facts in all their detail. That is all he apparently wished. Yet, in both cases, customs and rituals of a perplexing complexity were involved in which the rôle of the individual and numerous intangible factors must have had a determining influence. Most of the collaborators in the investigation seem to have had little appreciation of this aspect of their problem.[11] But let me call attention to one more point. Wissler states that his assumptions were not part of the instructions given to field workers. Now a naïve outsider might conceivably ask, under the circumstances, whether field workers are ever given instructions as to what they are to get?[12]

[10] *Anthropological Papers of the American Museum of Natural History,* vol. 11, p. vii.

[11] With the exception of Lowie and Spier, who, if they do not specifically say so, at least indicate their serious doubts as to the efficaciousness of this method.

[12] This is not true, in the main, of the English and Continental ethnologists, both because much of their work was and still is done independently and because institutions do not even remotely attempt to give their scientists "instructions."

But to proceed to the next fundamental question, the relation of the investigator to his informant. Our ideal may very well be to secure all the possible facts, but every investigator soon realizes that the facts he is likely to secure depend, to a marked degree, not merely upon his competence, his knowledge, and his interests but to a factor frequently overlooked, his personality. No matter how objective one may strive to be, where there is such a close bond as the one existing between the ethnologist and his important informants, personal considerations are likely to enter which are apt to color his judgment, if they do not, occasionally, entirely warp it. It is well, then, for the ethnologist to recognize this fact and attempt to guard against it. Otherwise he is apt to regard one good and personally attractive informant as of paramount importance and, since so few tribes are ever described by more than one person, the investigator's judgment must stand.[13] The more informants, the better—that is clear. But the more informants one has, the more contacts one has to make and, paradoxical as this may seem, the more

[13] The vast majority of English and German ethnologists do not seem to be in the least aware of the influence of the personality of the investigators both upon the selection of informants and upon the information they are likely to give, and their descriptions are frequently suspect just for this very reason. They have attempted to substitute, for this lack of contact, the most tenuous of objective procedures, questionnaires.

danger there exists of minor errors, whose cumulative effect can be tremendous. In the United States, at least, this has been tacitly recognized and investigators have preferred to make ethnologists out of their informants. That is, they have trained their most promising native collaborators as best they could and confined their own efforts to arranging and editing—frequently, unfortunately, not editing—the data obtained by them. This is, for example, true of the large collections of texts gathered by Boas on the Kwakiutl and Tsimshian, by Michelson on the Fox, and by myself on the Winnebago, to name only a few.

In those cases, nevertheless, where to all intents and purposes the natives have themselves become the investigators, new difficulties arise, for then it is essential to know not only the relation of the white ethnologist to his informant but, likewise, the relation of the latter to his sources of information.

Now it may seem to some that I am unnecessarily querulous and hypercritical. Such, however, is not my desire. If I insist upon these points so definitely, it is because I feel that our whole duty is toward keeping our record as clear from discernible personal distortions as that is humanly possible. We cannot keep them all out, because most of them are not easily recognizable. Nor am I insisting upon anything that would not be regarded as a minimum critical caution in any historical investigation making the slightest claim to accuracy.

However, it is not enough for the investigator to determine for himself the qualifications of his informants or the limitations of their knowledge; it is his duty to specify them. The failure to do so, together with the very frequent failure to distinguish carefully between the record as obtained and the discussion of it, constitutes one of the most glaring and inexcusable defects of the majority of all monographs on aboriginal peoples. No introductions on the method of field work or on the critical controls to be observed, such as Malinowski and Mead indulge in,[14] can make amends for this

[14] MEAD, M., "More Comprehensive Field Methods," *American Anthropologist*,

MALINOWSKI, B., *The Argonauts of the Western Pacific*, 1922. Malinowski, in spite of the fact that he so clearly envisages the methods that must be adopted, completely overestimates the rôle of the ethnologist in presenting and fixing the record. That is, of course, to be expected in his case, because he begins with definite preconceptions both as to the nature of the mentality of aboriginal peoples and as to the purpose of anthropology. When he says that his *corpus inscriptionum Kiriwiniensium* can be utilized by others besides himself, he does not indicate that this *corpus* has been selected by him and that he, apparently, was interested in the magical formulae connected with the *Kula*. If, as he states (p. 25), the goal of the ethnologist is to grasp the native's relation to life and his vision of his world, it is a piece of unwarranted conceit on the part of the investigator to relegate to the end, the "collection of ethnographic statements, characteristic narratives, typical utterances, items of folklore and

offense against the elementary requirement that others have an opportunity of scrutinizing the record *as it was obtained.* Let the investigator discuss and comment upon it to his heart's content. Indeed, the more the better. But these discussions must be entirely separate from the original data.[15] In such matters there can be no compromise. As has been pointed out repeatedly, the factors conspiring to distort the picture of an aboriginal culture are rather formidable. Let the ethnologist, at least, not consciously add to the difficulties. And he is doing so most emphatically when he combines facts and interpretations into one inextricable whole.[16] If he has already done this in

---

magical formulae" which are to serve as a *corpus inscriptionum* (p. 24). How can any outsider fill in the *imponderabilia* of actual life himself, no matter how thorough, detailed, and minute his observations may be? Furthermore, it is a complete misapprehension of what an historian considers the test of accuracy and the true nature of a primary source to think that a chronological list of *Kula* events witnessed by the observer would remove any obscurity that might remain as to the sources of his data (p. 15).

[15] Of course, the proper method would be to have as frank and outspoken a critique of the qualifications of investigators as is traditional in history. It is easy enough to see why that has not developed in ethnology. Naturally every ethnologist makes judgments about other ethnologists as rigorous and as harsh as any that exist among historians, but these today are confined to the glamorous publicity of private conversation.

[16] Boas has, of course, stressed this again and again. My criticism, in his case, is that he partially neutralizes the value of his data by not adding critical notes. On pp. 8–10 I have attempted to draw certain implications

the field, *i.e.*, in the actual gathering of the data
as some ethnologists are inclined to do, we should
know this and assess his account accordingly.
The records are, after all, in the same category
as the archives of history. They may be dull,
repetitious, uninspiring, dead. So, frequently, are
the archives. Yet we have no right to touch them,
even to the extent of rearranging them in the
interests of clarity. They should undoubtedly
be explained, rearranged, commented upon, and
the breath of life be instilled into them. But this
must be done apart from the records themselves.
Now in spite of the self-evident nature of this
demand and in spite of the great influence Boas has
wielded in the United States, there are very few
ethnologists besides himself who have conformed to
this simple requirement, and only one, as far as
I know, who has secured all of his information in
text.

The philologists have done much better. In a
case like that of Michelson, where, for the last
twenty years his Fox informants have been filling

---

for his unwillingness to do so.
    The unexcelled record that Michelson has obtained from the Fox
Indians, constituting possibly the most detailed account that has ever
been secured from an aboriginal tribe and which was made possible by the
existence of a syllabary among them, suffers in a similar fashion, *i.e.*, as
far as the ethnologist is concerned. Michelson is a philologist and his
ethnological comments are of a fragmentary and incidental nature.

volume after volume in their syllabary, all the
conditions for an accurate account free from the
disturbing influence of the investigator are present.
But, after all, Michelson is a philologist and only
incidentally interested in ethnology. The same
holds true for the other philologists who have
secured remarkable records.[17]

European ethnologists, the English, German, and
French, have been the greatest sinners in this
respect. Such famous studies as Rivers's *Todas*,
Codrington's *Melanesians*, Junod's *Thonga*, Smith
and Dale's *Ila-Speaking Peoples of Northern
Rhodesia*, Roscoe's *Baganda*, Peschuel-Loesche's
Loango, Malinowski's *Trobriand Islanders*, and
even Rattray's otherwise excellent monographs
fall short in this one particular. It is not merely a
matter of formal arrangement. No one has the
right to obliterate the exact form in which his
information was received. Strangely enough, those
ethnologists who have of late protested most
vehemently against the older type of monograph
and who have discoursed most vociferously and

[17] It may with some show of fairness be contended that the facts can be
kept distinct from the comments in a running description of a culture.
That is the method of one of the best ethnologists the United States ever
produced, J. O. Dorsey, and that is also the method of such excellent
ethnologists as Lowie, in his work on the Crow, and Spier, in his monograph on the Klamath. But unless it is backed by a knowledge of the
language, as in the case of Dorsey and Lowie, it is, on the whole, an
inadvisable practice.

militantly against their inadequacy—Radcliffe-Brown, Malinowski, Mead—have in their own work entangled their data in such a maze of discussions, impressions, reinterpretations, and implications that it is even more difficult to get to the original record than it is in the case of the worst offenders among their predecessors.[18]

Having now passed in review briefly the various aspects of the relation of the investigator to his sources of information, we have next to examine the nature of the present condition of these sources themselves, a subject of more than usual importance in ethnology because it is the goal of every ethnologist to study an aboriginal culture as it presumably functioned before it had been seriously influenced or disturbed by contact with the major European and Asiatic civilizations. He must therefore make some attempt to determine what the characteristics of this presumably older culture were—a task of no small magnitude. This task will, of course, differ considerably in various parts of the world. My remarks, on the whole, apply to the aborigines of North America.

[18] That greater difficulties arise in the investigation of a tribe whose culture is still functioning than in the study of semimoribund civilizations is clear. But that does not absolve the ethnologist from fulfilling his primary function of presenting the facts in the words of the informant and of keeping record and comment distinct.

We must first be clear about one point, *viz.*, at what particular period in the history of a given tribe to begin. Shall we, for instance, begin with the discovery of America, roughly speaking with the first half of the sixteenth century, or shall we begin with the first contact of a given tribe with Europeans? The new influences must have been felt from the very beginning and have extended far beyond those tribes with whom Europeans came into direct contact. Not only was there an introduction of new objects but disturbances of all kinds took place over a wide stretch of territory. Now the question that must be answered is, first, whether we are to regard this as something quite different from anything that had ever occurred before or not? The effect of the European invasion has been to destroy fairly completely many of the tribes with whom it came into contact or, at least, to distort their cultures markedly and to impel them along lines of development which we customarily assume were entirely new to them. The introduction of the horse has always been used as the stock example of the influence of such a new factor. But did not similar things happen before? Did not the Iroquoian tribes, like the Mohawk and their immediate kindred, completely destroy the Hurons—just as completely in fact as the European culture destroyed many an Indian tribe? And did

not the Algonquian invasions change and distort
the cultures of the various Siouan tribes with whom
they came into contact in Wisconsin, Michigan,
and Minnesota? What, in other words, I am trying
to make clear, is that it is quite unwarranted to
argue that, because we can demonstrate the
presence of European artefacts or influences, we
are necessarily dealing with cultures that are in
process of deterioration or that can no longer be
regarded as aboriginal in any sense of the term.
These cultures have no more lost their aboriginal
character because of European influence than, for
instance, the Mississauga Indians of southeastern
Ontario lost their aboriginal character because
they were so markedly influenced by the Iroquois.

It is well, then, not to allow our very natural
desire to think of a given tribe apart from European
contact beguile us into a search for the "primitive"
tribe, untouched and undefiled.[19]

In North America, most parts of South America,
and practically all of Polynesia, no aboriginal
culture has been fully functioning for the last

[19] The present tendency to study aboriginal cultures in their relation
to those of Europe is absolutely sound, but the dilemma, unfortunately,
still exists: with what tribal picture are we contrasting the existing "hybrid" culture and how has this picture been obtained? It is, likewise,
essentially incorrect to study these cultures as exemplifications of the
principles underlying acculturation, instead of studying them as cultures
illustrative of certain phases of acculturation, it being really immaterial
whether they are hybrid, semimoribund, or degenerate.

three generations. It is, of course, exceedingly dangerous to make such a statement, for it implies that we are adopting certain specific criteria as indicative of cultural health and cultural disease. As a rule, we take the condition of the economic life as such a criterion. We cannot apply this too rigorously, however, for the Eskimo have preserved their economic life intact and yet can be said to have "deteriorated" in other respects, and the Pueblos of the Southwest have completely lost their old economic order and yet have preserved other aspects of their life intact; at least, they are actively functioning. Let us then say that what we generally mean by insisting that a specific aspect of culture has broken down is that this has been given up and that nothing apparently has taken its place. Where to draw the line between this and cultural change is somewhat delicate. Perhaps, here in the United States, the feeling exists that such a partial breakdown is merely the prelude to a complete absorption of the aboriginal group into our own culture, that there is no possibility of such a group making an adjustment comparable to that of so many African tribes, and that it is this that we have in mind. Whatever be the situation, however, it is fairly clear that one or a number of aspects of a culture may cease to function without impairing the healthy function of the others. Still, the breakdown of the old economic order and the old social organization, considering the highly integrated nature of the majority of aboriginal civilizations, must have had the most far-reaching effects. These must be taken into account, although it is not always easy to determine what they are. I think the best we can do is not to speak carelessly of a complete disorganization of the social order but, better, of a supplanting of one type of social organization by another to which the natives have not as yet become adjusted, but which enables them to live in security. In other words, all that we need remember is that we are studying a tribe in a state of rapid transition and that the present transitional state differs only in degree from other transitional states through which many of the tribes must have passed, not infrequently, long before the coming of the Europeans. It is, of course, exceedingly unfortunate that we should be compelled, in the vast majority of cases, to study aboriginal tribes only during such a period in their history, but that in no way affects the question of their functioning. In attempting a characterization or a reconstruction of the history of a particular tribe, however, this atrophy of one or more of its aspects must be duly recognized.[20]

[20] I am, of course, speaking of the reconstruction of their specific history in so far as this can be done through internal evidence and not reconstruction of the order of Wissler, Kroeber, Graebner, Rivers, and Perry.

To assess the records properly, we must consequently bear in mind not only the direct European influence but also those changes which have developed within each tribe indirectly, as a result of the new situations that have arisen. This is hardly the proper place to comment upon so intricate and vast a subject in detail, and I shall therefore confine myself to a few examples.

The Winnebago Indians, when first encountered by the French or, better, when they were first heard of by the French, lived in a fairly large number of villages in eastern Wisconsin, practically scattered across the state from Green Bay to the Illinois line and southwest to Lacrosse. By the middle of the eighteenth century they had been forced into a comparatively small area with at most three distinct villages. After 1865 fully one-half of the tribe were forcibly transferred to Nebraska and confined within a restricted district of about three hundred sixty square miles. As a consequence of this shrinkage and restriction, the inhabitants of what had originally been distinct villages, with very definite traditions, were thrown together pell-mell, and all local differences were merged into a new hybrid unity. Similarly, there has been a very marked hypertrophy of ceremonialism, first, because the requirements for entrance into the various ceremonies became much easier, and, second, because ceremonialism was, until recently, the one phase of their life still actively functioning. Doubtless numerous other examples will occur to the mind of every field worker who has given the matter any thought.

It naturally follows from the foregoing that the informants upon whom we have to rely are frequently relating matters that they themselves only know from hearsay, and this must, of course, decrease to some degree the accuracy of their information. But it also brings with it other dangers. The informants, *i.e.*, the ultimate source of our information, hand on to the investigator their generalizations and syntheses. Theory and practice are thus frequently confused in an inextricable fashion at the very fountainhead. The monographs on the American Indians abound with just such examples, which, in many instances, go back to the informants themselves. Here again we are dealing with a normal cultural phenomenon which must have occurred again and again in the history of every group. It is not a sign of degeneracy or hybridization or decline. To so designate it is to betray a lamentable ignorance of common historical processes. Not to recognize it, however, and not to allow for it is likely to lead to a serious distortion of the record.

The somewhat contemptuous attitude taken by a number of ethnologists toward those cultures which have been in direct or indirect contact with the major European and Asiatic civilizations for the last two hundred years or so has led to a marked neglect of the study of certain areas and to a belated and romantic search for the "untouched" tribes. But there are no untouched tribes for the ethnologist or the historian. And what precisely would be gained if we found them? Apparently there must still lurk in the minds of these ethnologists some feeling that the untouched tribes will reveal mysteries that the "touched" ones have lost. Does a culture become significant in direct proportion to the privations one suffers in investigating it, or is it indeed that our friend the attenuated ghost of the older evolutionists refuses to be completely laid and that the quest for the primitive and unadulterated tribe still continues?

Now if the present condition of aboriginal cultures is such as I have depicted, what prospects, it may be asked, has a distributional study of being moderately correct and what portions of such a record are likely to be more correct than others? Because of the importance attached to these distributional studies in the United States and Germany, even at the risk of repetition, let me again recapitulate what it is the proponents of this method attempt to do.

Their purpose is not that of the mere enumeration of traits and its utilization for specifically circumscribed areas, as Nordenskiöld has done for South America, but an enumeration of traits for the avowed object of establishing certain types of diffusion and of arriving at an "historical" reconstruction. The basic requirement for any such approach, even granting its legitimacy, is an accurate and adequate record. But how can the record be even remotely accurate in view of the disturbing factors that have been pointed out above? And even if it could be demonstrated that the distribution obtainable today is fairly accurate, what right have we to assume that it would have held two hundred years ago? How, for instance, do we know what traits have disappeared? How do we know what traits have had a transient existence, and what a more or less permanent one, in a given region? In other words, I, for one, do not feel that it is even strictly feasible to make an enumeration in the manner of Nordenskiöld. Certainly distributions have significance, but their significance depends upon their accuracy and their completeness, and their accuracy and completeness depend upon innumerable and often specific conditions about which we are inadequately informed. Finally, even if we were to grant a certain validity to Wissler's and Kroeber's trait tabulations, with what type of traits are they actually dealing? The answer must be: with tangible and concrete objects or with customs and beliefs that can easily be given a unit character or upon which they have forced a unit character. Points of view are necessarily excluded and so are all the intangible elements that go to make up so large a part of what we consider essential for any correct characterization of a culture. Now, to give a custom or a belief a unit character, untold mischief is done to it. It is not merely that we are transforming a cultural into a physical fact but that we are frequently giving only a small portion of the particular custom or belief, and that we delude ourselves into believing either that we are stating the complete custom or that we are giving its essence.[21] The only excuse to be advanced for such a procedure is that both Wissler and Kroeber are very frank in their insistence that

[21] For an excellent criticism of this type of methodology, compare Allport and Hartman's analysis of Chapin's *Cultural Change* and Kroeber's "The Principle of Order in Civilization as Exemplified by Changes of Fashion," *American Anthropologist*, vol. 22, pp. 235–263, 1919. The authors quite rightly insist that the only question involved is "whether the attempt to measure and interpret cultural growth as one would handle the explicit objects of natural science will, in practice, justify the methodological assumptions upon which it is based."—*Methods in Social Science*, edited by S. A. Rice, p. 336.

cultures are to be treated on the analogy of animal and plant species; *i.e.*, they are to be given a habitat with a specified range; their characteristics are to be properly described and their subspecies and varieties are to be neatly ticketed.

Summing up then the discussion we have had in the last few chapters, we can say this: That both the presuppositions underlying the treatment of aboriginal cultures, as well as the method by which the data were secured and the actually available information obtained by ethnologists in the United States and Germany and, to a lesser extent, in England all conspired to identify cultural facts with those of the natural sciences, whether the ethnologists were aware of it or not, and that this has led directly to the popularity that the quantitative approach enjoys today.

Chapter V

The Quantitative Method in Ethnology

All quantitative treatments of culture can be traced back to three essentially distinct types of approach: the equating of the data of culture with those of the natural sciences; the analysis of a culture into its constituent elements; and the attempt to establish time sequences. In the history of ethnology this last came first, for it developed in connection with the application of the evolutionary theory to the growth of culture.

The great English ethnological theorists began with the assumption of stages roughly comparable to the paleontological record as envisaged in the third quarter of the nineteenth century. That meant the necessity of establishing a series of criteria for each stage and implied furthermore a developmental evaluation of these criteria. In the scheme of animal evolution this was comparatively easy. There the gradual differentiation of the various organs, and of the nervous system in particular, could be legitimately regarded as indications of progressive increments of growth. For the history of culture this was not so simple. We need not, however, inquire too closely into the precise justification for the selection of specific criteria in the scheme of cultural evolution and simply point out that, in the main, they predicated two: the growth and differentiation of religion from animism to ethical monotheism and that of social organization, from the totemistic clan and mother-right to the individualized monarchies and republics, and father-right. From these two basic assumptions, it was then a moderately simple task to discover the transitions between the two limits of the series. To do so, however, it was necessary to postulate a definite theory of survivals, and this, in its turn, led to auxiliary hypotheses. Tylor, with his admirable sanity, realized quite early the opportunity this opened up to subjectivism of all kinds. He attempted therefore to devise some means for obtaining a more precise gauge for determining the succession of cultural stages. The method he perfected he embodied in a classical paper entitled *On a Method of Investigating the Development of Institutions.* Therewith the youthful and somewhat blustering discipline was delivered up without further ceremony to the tender mercies of the statisticians.

In this famous essay Tylor, on the basis of the
tabulation of the data bearing on the development
of a number of customs, such as exogamy, descent,
and change of residence, pointed out that the
coincidence of certain of these traits was greater
than that to be expected according to laws of
ordinary chance. Thus, for instance, in the sixty-
five tribes where the husband resided permanently
with the wife's family, there were fourteen cases of
ceremonial avoidance between him and her relations. The law of probability required only eight.
In sum, said Tylor, "There is a well-marked pre-
ponderance, indicating that ceremonial avoidance
by the husband of the wife's family is in some way
connected with his living with them."[1] The fundamental difficulty in all such inferences is that of
determining how often the presence of a given
trait is to be counted as an independent example,
and that, in turn, depends upon a number of
factors, of which the principal one is possibly the
rôle assigned to diffusion. Tylor disregarded it
completely. While he was well aware of the limitations of the statistical method and warned his
readers against assigning reasons for the connection
of apparently correlated facts which were only
analogous to the real reason or corresponded to it
partially or indirectly, yet he does seem to have

[1] *Op. cit.*, p. 247.

believed in the possibility of a statistical treatment yielding fruitful results for the reconstruction of historical sequences. He dealt, of course, with broad lines of development.

However, we are not here concerned so much with the correctness of his inferences as with the applications of his method.[2] To the associations of such traits as matrilocal residence and the avoidance of the wife's family, Tylor gave the name *adhesions*, and the discovery of *adhesions* has become the corner stone of all distribution studies since his time.[3] How this concept was used by Wissler, Kroeber, Rivers, Elliot-Smith, Perry, Graebner, and Schmidt, we shall point out shortly. Suffice it to say that with all these scholars it became a purely quantitative determinant.

But let us now turn to the second of our types of approach, the analytic method of Boas and his students. Boas had clearly two objects in view: first, to examine in detail and intensively the precise nature of a given aspect of culture and, second, to utilize the results thus obtained in order to refute the unilinear schemes of development that until

[2] "To discover *adhesions* one must proceed to work out the distributions of complexes among the successive tribal cultures and then correlate these distributions. In this way one may discover what trait-complexes are associated."—C. Wissler, *Man and Culture*, p. 67.

[3] *Cf.* also the admirable presentation and critique of the method in W. D. Wallis, *op. cit.*, pp. 36–42.

very recently were the order of the day. He had in mind specifically the theory according to which geometrical designs had developed from realistic patterns by a process of gradual deterioration; the theory according to which all mythological themes and motifs had their origin in an attempt at explaining natural phenomena; the evolutionary theory according to which totemism was a stage through which all primitive peoples had passed; and, lastly, the theory according to which secret societies, the world over, had developed out of the the men's house and age classes.[4] Such an exclusive preoccupation with analysis as this was bound to produce certain distortions no matter how well aware the individual ethnologist was of all the dangers inherent in such an approach. These dangers were of three kinds: first, after breaking up an art style, institution, or ritual into its constituent elements, the analyst forgot to reunite them; second, the results of such an analysis, because they seemed externally definite and specific, had a marked tendency to invest the individual elements with a false fixity and an essentially spurious individuality; and, lastly, the elements themselves were evaluated and used as criteria to determine both what was essential and what

[4] For a list of the main essays of Boas and his students bearing on these points, compare note 19 (p. 50).

unessential, in a given ritual or institution, and to construct historical sequences. All these distortions tended in the same direction, that of converting cultural facts into unit characters amenable to a quantitative treatment. That this did not happen to a far greater extent than was actually the case was due to the fact that the majority of the ethnologists responsible for these analytical essays subsequently repudiated their conclusions.

Instead of a general discussion of the merits and demerits of the analytical approach, I shall confine myself to a presentation of two of its examples, Goldenweiser's *Totemism* and my own *Ritual and Significance of the Winnebago Medicine Dance.*[5]

Goldenweiser set himself the task of inquiring into the legitimacy of regarding totemism as an integral phenomenon, both historically and psychologically, as the English theorists and field ethnologists contended. Five main features were taken as symptomatic: (1) an exogamous clan, (2) a clan name derived from the totem, (3) a religious attitude toward the totem, (4) taboos, or restrictions against killing, eating (sometimes touching and seeing) the totem, (5) a belief in descent from the totem. These features he then proceeded to analyze in order to demonstrate their essential independence of one another. It never occurred

[5] *Cf.* note 19 (p. 50).

to him that, logically and scientifically, it was his primary duty to show first why he gave each one of these features a unit character. He himself pointed out that it was not at all self-evident why one should throw together such a heterogeneous assemblage of elements—an institution, a religious attitude, a genealogical belief, a custom like taboo, and a specific type of naming. But he does not seem to have realized, at the time, that they were only heterogeneous because he had arbitrarily given each feature a separate unity. So little indeed was he aware of his initial hypothesis that he equated the phrase *organically interrelated* with the concept *integral phenomenon* that the English ethnologists had used in speaking of the various features found in totemism. It may therefore be said that his treatment was a quantitative one from the very beginning.

Under the circumstances it was, of course, not very difficult to show, by carefully selecting his tribes, by leaving out all reference to diffusion, and by the use of a logical-psychological definition of what constituted factual identity or similarity, that practically no one of the five features given above was absolutely essential for totemism. But even to do this he had to be somewhat unfair in the choice of his examples. He began, for instance, with a comparison between the totemism of

Central Australia and that of British Columbia, in other words, with an example of what might be called classical totemism—that of Central Australia —and an admittedly confused and aberrant form —that of British Columbia. For each he tabulated ten features: exogamy, totemic names, taboo, descent from the totem, magical ceremonies, reincarnation, guardian spirits, art, rank, and the number of totems, and then he was surprised at the striking contrast.

> Only in two points—exogamy and totemic names—does there seem to be any agreement, but even here the conditions are not really analogous. A certain religious attitude, in the broadest sense, is found in both areas; but in Australia it is, outside of mythology, also dimly perceptible in the attitude . . . towards the living animals, plants, etc., while in British Columbia the religious element must be sought in the ceremonies and myths.[6]

By applying the foregoing method he was able to satisfy himself that all the so-called "symptoms" of totemism were extremely variable both in themselves and in the manner in which they adhered to one another, and that an indeterminate number of elements of culture could become secondarily associated with them. He was thus led to ask himself the very reasonable question: "If totemism includes, roughly speaking, everything,

[6] GOLDENWEISER, A. A., "Totemism," pp. 51–52.

is totemism itself anything in particular?"[7] That it most emphatically was something, it was, of course, impossible to deny. This something he found in the theory advanced by Tylor and Boas, that its peculiarity lay not in the sum of the totemic elements nor any individual element, but in the relation between the elements, and that the intimacy between the associated features could never have become so absolute had they not become linked with definite social units, of which they then became the prerogatives and the symbols. Each of the "symptoms" themselves, Goldenweiser insisted, was complex historically and psychologically, as well as variable. In each totemic combination, however, there were forces at work which tended to correlate the several heterogeneous elements. Not only this, but we likewise find that, in spite of their distinct history, the various totemic complexes of Australia, America, and Africa show a considerable degree of similarity—a similarity to be explained as the product of a convergent evolution.[8]

Yet even this very general and conceptualistic analysis is found to be too indefinite, and so Goldenweiser proceeds to do away with the term *religious*, for there are cases of totemism, he insists, where the religious element is nil. He consequently substi-

[7] *Ibid.*, p. 53.
[8] *Ibid.*, p. 95.

tutes for the phrase *objects and symbols of religious value*, the phrase *objects and symbols of emotional value*. The term *social units* he finds likewise too vague, in view of the fact that the objects and symbols in question were originally of emotional value primarily for individuals and had become transformed into social units only through their totemic association. The definition of totemism must therefore read as follows: *Totemism is the process of specific specialization of objects and symbols of emotional value.*[9]

In other words, Goldenweiser committed three of the cardinal sins inherent in the purely analytic treatment of cultural data: first, he converted cultural facts into quantitative units; second, after first artificially breaking up the totemic complex into its constituent elements, he equally artificially reunited them; and, third, he pushed his analysis to its furthest possible point and reduced it to a *reductio ad absurdum*. It is small wonder then that, being a man with a strong historical sense, he shortly afterwards repudiated the whole method.

In my study of the Winnebago Medicine Dance[10] the errors committed were of a similar type and, as in the case of Goldenweiser, were an outcome of the analytical approach. There I began with a compari-

[9] *Ibid.*, p. 97.
[10] *Journal of American Folklore*, vol. 24, pp. 168 *ff.*, 1911.

son of certain of the similarities between the Winnebago ceremony and that of their immediate
neighbors, and the problem I set myself was that of
determining what justification existed for postulating an historical identity between the ceremonies in
question on the basis of these similarities. I
accordingly proceeded to break up the Winnebago
ceremony into a number of constituent ritualistic
complexes which were sharply differentiated from
one another. These then were compared with the
ritualistic complexes disclosed by the study of the
identical ceremony among the Ojibwa, Menominee,
Dakota, and Omaha tribes. This resulted in the
same type of distortion previously brought out in
the critique of Goldenweiser. Certain elements were
given too great a unity and definiteness and others
too great an indefiniteness. And herein, in fact,
lies one of the fundamental defects of any purely
analytical attack. It is left to each investigator to
determine what he is to call identity and what not.
Manifestly this problem is basic to all the social
sciences, as well as to history.

We cannot enter into any discussion of it here.
All I wish to point out, for the present, is that those
ethnologists who indulged in this method do not
seem to have been sufficiently aware of the difficulty; were not, indeed, in the least cognizant of
the fact that what was involved here was nothing

less than one aspect of the very troublesome and persistent problem of form versus content. They cannot very well be blamed for not attempting to solve it, for it is the reef on which many a philosophy has foundered. But they should most emphatically be reprimanded for treating the matter as lightly as they did and attempting to reconstruct the history of a specific institution or ritual without due regard to the nature of the difficulties that lay concealed within it. Stated rather broadly, what they actually did was to invest certain of these complexes with a definite form and insist that content did not matter and then, reversing their procedure, invest others with a specific content and insist that form did not matter. This is a very old game indeed—that of playing the head against the tail. We shall see later on that, in a disguised form, it reappears in most of the quantitative methods and even in an approach which is ostensibly a revolt against them, such as that of Benedict, for instance. The criterion of form was destined to play a great rôle in one of the major examples of the quantitative method, that of Foy-Graebner. This much must, at least, be said to the credit of the latter: that they did realize that a problem was contained therein.

But to return to my analysis of the Winnebago Medicine Dance. As in the case of Goldenweiser, not even the most refined analysis could do away with certain similarities. These I very conveniently classified into specific and general. The specific, with some show of reason, I credited to the influence of the neighboring tribes and the general to that gift of the gods, convergence.

Now this ascription to *specific* resemblances, particularly when they occurred between contiguous tribes, of significance for the study of diffusion and ultimately for the reconstruction of historical sequences was the bridge which connected Boas's analytical with Wissler's distributional method. To this we shall now turn.

I have already discussed the main presuppositions inhering in Wissler's and Kroeber's method of reconstructing culture sequences. Here I wish simply to give a number of concrete examples of their procedure. Let me, however, mention again the main postulates with which Wissler operates. They are, first, that the wider the distribution of a trait, the older is its age; second, that there is a zonelike distribution in the form of concentric circles extending from the culture center to the periphery; and, third, the analogy of culture with the biological sciences.[11] Bearing these in mind,

[11] "Though the phenomena we deal with are complex and variable, they can be dealt with empirically, reduced to statements of sufficient exactness, consistently classified and their geographical distribution plotted."—

let us proceed to the presentation of the analysis of the very best example of the distributional approach, Leslie Spier's *The Sun Dance of the Plains Indians*.[12] Here the problem emerges clearly and definitely: to trace the relations between the various Sun Dance ceremonies by an analysis of the distribution of the traits found among them. He begins with the very reasonable assumption that the ceremony is a "synthetic product." This assumption is arrived at by having recourse to the very familiar device of giving a unit character to specific rites and then comparing them. If the comparison indicates that a sufficiently large number of traits are to be found outside the specific Sun Dance area, then the hypothesis of the ceremony being a "synthetic product" is justified. When, however, it is justifiable to ask, Does a ceremony become entitled to the designation of Sun Dance? The answer, I think, would definitely indicate that, over and above the number of traits in common, another factor enters, *viz.*, the observer's evaluation of them, so that some are regarded

---

C. Wissler, *ibid.*, p. 58. In another passage of the same book (p. 61) he makes the following claim for his method: "These inspiring triumphs of sound method in archaeological research serve to bring home to us the homely truth . . . that stone objects . . . are like skeletal remains of dead cultures, which, whenever rearticulated, will reveal the outlines of the living form."

[12] As indicated before, Spier, long ago, repudiated the method.

as more intrinsic than others. In short we find here again two of the characteristics of the analytic method in full bloom. A third characteristic is introduced when Spier passes over the more general objective phases of the dance, such as those referring to the procedure, structures, and regalia, and confines himself strictly to a study of the details.[13] Thus, for instance, we have eighty-two traits tabulated under twelve rubrics varying in type from *altar* to *vomiting induced*. Not the slightest word is said about the reasons for giving each of them a unit character, although in view of the fact that they are subsequently used to determine statistically the nature of the relationship of the various tribes, this does call for some comment. Spier specifically stresses this point. "One must clearly recognize in interpreting it [the tabulations] that complexes, such as the buffalo hunt, are given no more weight than such minor traits as the finger plume."[14] From a study of the various ceremonial procedures he then comes to the conclusion that "the scores agree in a highly suggestive manner, being more frequent for tribes in proximity

[13] Spier, *ibid.*, p. 463. "[The objective phases of the dance] do not prove altogether satisfactory in indicating historic relations. In the first case there is considerable uniformity even in detail in all the dances. Then again isolated elements, rather than complexes of which they form a part, are shared by a number of tribes."

[14] *Ibid.*, p. 477.

to the central group and decreasing as we approach the border of the Plains. "[15] He finds that the minor traits show a type of diffusion similar to that of the major ones, widespread and somewhat random, and that some member of the central group shares in the particular trait of any group selected. The minor traits themselves are regarded as elaborations of the fairly uniform fundamental procedures. From this he infers that they had either been diffused from different parts of the Plains or from the central group. Like all the students of Boas, Spier was somewhat perturbed by the apparent denial of tribal individuality which an analysis of this kind implied, and he is very careful to state that the evidence for such individuality is considerable. But he could envisage it, naturally enough, only in connection with modifications of the specific character of the procedure. Since he determined beforehand what was the regular procedure and the specific character of the ceremony, precisely as I had done in the analysis of the Medicine Dance, this was not very difficult.

From the analysis of the procedure, Spier then turned to the question of the organization of the Sun Dance. He found two types, one based on individual ownership and one based on a fraternity of owners. True to the principle that what is more

[15] *Ibid.*, p. 479.

widely distributed must be historically older, he argued that the first was older because "of their respective distributions and because the individual organization appears again as the basic element in the fraternity."[16] As a result, the central tribes are again proved to be the true nucleus of the ceremony.

And now for the final *dénouement*. Although he discovers that the central group—Arapaho, Cheyenne, and Oglala—have the most highly elaborated type of procedure and organization, these rites have taken on no new form. The significant fact is not that they share the common stock of traits but "that there is a measure of coherence in their own performances."[16] Here we have one of Sapir's criteria cropping out. To justify this assumption of "logical coherence," Spier has to reduce the whole ceremony to one *essential* activity—that of "erecting a pole within an encircling structure before which the votaries dance."[16] The one disturbing feature—torture—is ruled out as an essential element. This is not easy, and Spier succeeds in eliminating it only by presenting such weak arguments as the following: that, "except among the Dakota, none of the principal dancers are tortured; that only a minority of their associates

16 *Ibid.*, p. 491.

perform it and must specially vow to do so";[17] that "Curtis found it far less in evidence among the Cheyenne, etc., than with other tribes."[17] By eliminating the torture feature something was gained besides the mere reducing of the ceremony to its least common denominator, for the Oglala could then be dismissed from the group of tribes who originated the dance, because of the emphasis they placed on torture. In a somewhat similar fashion the Hidatsa and Arikara, who fall in the same group as the Arapaho-Cheyenne, could be ruled out as the true nucleus because they built a special structure for the Sun Dance. "Their important ceremonies are almost invariably held in the permanent Medicine lodges [and this] may be taken as presumptive evidence of its origin among a nomadic tribe."[18]

Having thus established a historical sequence for the various major rites and their secondary embellishments, Spier turned to the question of how these developments were to be explained. Here, of course, he could operate only with the most general of processes, and he ends by confessing that, "only a more precise knowledge of the function of the innovating individual, of his cultural equipment, the character of his milieu and the extent of his

[17] *Ibid.*, p. 493.
[18] *Ibid.*, p. 498.

contribution,"[19] can be of any avail. He does not, however, seem to have realized that the validity of his whole factual analysis depends equally upon such knowledge.

We have so far discussed the application of the analytical and distributional method to a specific type of social organization, a specific ceremony within a tribe, and a specific ceremony within an artificially delimited culture area. I shall now turn to Lowie's attempt to apply both approaches to the elucidation of a very complex problem connected with the Plains age societies.[20]

In the magnificent series of studies by Lowie, Wissler, and others, an unparalleled mass of data had been accumulated for the precise purpose of determining the nature of the mutual relations of the various systems of Plains' society. They had been grouped into two types: those that were graded and those that were ungraded. Like Spier, Lowie begins with the "simpler" phenomenon, the ungraded societies, and specifically with those whose constituent elements approximated to the graded societies. Having determined their interrelations among themselves and their relation to the graded series, he then proceeds to a consideration

[19] *Ibid.*, p. 532.
[20] *Anthropological Papers of the American Museum of Natural History*, vol. 11, pp. 881 *ff.*, 1916.

of the graded systems in order to determine, as he states, "their historical unity or diversity, chronological sequence, and chronological relations to the ungraded systems."[21]

To a far greater extent than in the case of Spier, Lowie at every point gives the reasons for his classifications. If he uses the grading as differentia, it is because he feels that the absence of grading is correlated with an absence of system. This logical deduction he then finds corroborated by the conditions for entrance into the societies, the graded ones requiring an age qualification and an entrance fee and the ungraded ones, with two exceptions, requiring none. The two exceptions are then accounted for. Now, whether Lowie's explanation for the two exceptions holds or not, I should like to stress the point that in all analytical studies an attempt is always made to have distinctions as sharp and clear-cut as possible. These investigators and theorists never seem to have realized in the least that cultures, on the whole, are rarely clear-cut and distinct, that it is only by a process of elimination and abstraction that they become so, and that with each such abstraction comparison with other cultures becomes less justifiable. What holds for culture as a whole

[21] *Ibid.*, p. 881.

applies much more rigorously to special units within a culture.

The reason for this obsession for sharp outlines is, of course, to be sought in the twofold purpose all these students constantly had before them: the determination of diffusion and the construction of a chronology. Let us take as an illustration the mutual interrelations of the Tukala and Mawatani societies of the Iowa, Ponca, and Omaha, where we have apparently reliable evidence that the Omaha obtained the two societies from the Ponca, and the Ponca from the Dakota.[22] Yet in spite of these well-known facts, Lowie concludes that the Iowa organizations, about which we have no historical information, are closer to the Dakota than the Omaha because they share the traits of rivalry and of the mutual theft of wives with the Ponca, whereas the Omaha do not possess them. Since the Ponca are known to have borrowed their organizations from the Dakota, and the Dakota possess these traits, the problem is regarded as boiling down to the simple question as to whether the Dakota or the Iowa were the borrowers. Both the Oglala Dakota and the Iowa are found to have two leaders, four women singers, two waiters, a similar haircut, and the bravery obligation. In addition, Tukala apparently means nothing in

[22] *Ibid.*, p. 885.

Iowa and has a specific meaning in Dakota, and, finally, the Iowa organization is far less elaborate than the Dakota, the traits it shares with the latter as well as those it lacks being common to the Dakota Tokala, and the Kit-Fox society of tribes farther north. We must consequently assume, concludes Lowie, that the Iowa adopted the society from the Dakota. By means of identical logical argumentation, Lowie then finds that all the military organizations of the southern Siouans merely had a marginal significance, that they occurred in a rudimentary or vestigial form, and that they were of relatively slight importance in tribal life.[23]

Step by step, Lowie then takes us through all the societies and determines the nature of their relationship within the various tribes, on the basis of specific criteria. Wherever possible, he also attempts to determine the relative age of the various societies within the same tribe. It is quite noticeable that in the latter case the distribution of the names of the societies is used as a criterion.[24] Certainly this is not self-evident.

After thus eliminating tribe upon tribe as the possible originators of the graded societies, he

[23] *Ibid.*, p. 890.
[24] "The great age of the Kit-Foxes, Crow-Owners, and No-Flight is attested by their occurring with the same native designations, not only among the Eastern Dakota, but the Assiniboine as well."—P. 907.

narrows down the problem to whether the Blackfoot originated it and transmitted it to the Village
tribes who then passed it on to the Arapaho, or
vice versa. His argumentation is so typical of the
very best traditions of the analytical distributional
school that I shall quote it *in extenso:*

The hypothesis of a Blackfoot origin is, of course, *a priori*
as probable as any other. There are, however, empirical
reasons to the contrary. In the first place, the system of the
village tribes is far better integrated and homogeneous,[25]
making the Blackfoot system, in spite of its quantitative
development, appear as a deteriorated replica. To be sure,
this argument alone cannot be considered decisive, for it
might be plausibly contended that a looser association
would precede as a necessary stage the perfect coordination
of the Mandan and the Hidatsa organizations. However,
there are additional reasons in favor of the view here taken.
The ceremonial surrender of the wife, a custom shared by
all the graded systems, occurs only in the Kit-Fox Society
of the Piegan and the equivalent Horn Society of the Blood.
It stands, moreover, as an anomaly in the ceremonial life
of the Blackfoot proper while among the Village people it
is simply a constituent of ceremonialism that is automatically introduced into the particular form of ceremonial
transfer connected with the Age societies. The probability,
then, is overwhelming that the Blackfoot are the borrowers
of the usage. But it is hard to conceive that the notion of
the ceremonial surrender of a wife should have been bor-

---

[25] It is perfectly amazing how this criterion crops up all the time, and yet
examples of highly integrated organizations that are young and unin-
tegrated ones that are old must occur to everyone at a moment's notice.

rowed without the concrete culture elements in the transfer of which the principle found expression. The probability is, then, again in favor of Mandan-Hidatsa priority.[26]

Now what conclusions can be drawn from such an intensive application of the analytical distributional method to this enormous mass of specially selected detail? Two, says Lowie, one with regard to the conditions prevailing in the Plains that led to the special development of graded societies, and the other with regard to the actual course of their development. In both instances he is compelled to give generalized descriptions. The tendency to form societies, he finds, is throughout North America correlated with a certain complexity of social and religious organization. The first specialization was then the development of a particular type of "military" organization in the Northern Plains. Apparently these military organizations did not antedate the religious ones, nor were they graded. Age grading thus turns out to be a very special feature of any limited distribution arising out of the serial ranking of previously ungraded organizations.

But if the inferences as to the conditions are of the most general kind, those as to the actual tribes to be credited with the origination and spread of

[26] Pp. 948–949.

the graded societies are specific enough. In the order of time we have the following scheme:

I. Ungraded military societies.

II. Village tribes introduce grading into the foregoing and transmit this feature to the Hidatsa.

III. Hidatsa transmit the same to the parent stock from which both the Arapaho and the Gros Ventre have sprung.

IV. Hidatsa, at a later time, transmit the graded societies to the Blackfoot, who must have been in close contact then with the Village tribes.[27]

The type of "historical" conclusions drawn by Lowie are very modest indeed compared with those which Kroeber drew by the application of what is the distributional-statistical approach in its full vigor, plus the injection of the biological analogies that always hover around Kroeber's viewpoint.[28] There is no need of discussing his viewpoint in further detail here, except to point out that generalized inferences become even more generalized, and that, in spite of the recognition, for instance, that the rich cultures north of the Rio Grande owe very much to southern Mexico, still the old

[27] Lowie has since taken a much more cautious attitude toward the justification of drawing conclusions of this kind on the basis of an analytical distributional method.

[28] "Native Cultures of the Southwest," *University of California Publications in American Archaeology and Ethnology*, vol. 23, pp. 375–398, 1928, and "California Culture Provinces," *ibid.*, vol. 17, pp. 151–169, 1920.

procedure persists, of a development from the simple to the complex. He pictures the culture growth of the Pueblos of the Southwest as follows: union of lineages into clans and of clans into towns; loss of most of the political autonomy of the lineages; loss of most of the territorial property; elaboration of ritual organization with differentiation of official functions; the partial segregation of religious and profane houses, and the multiplication of initiating cult societies. Then we have the extension of the fetish concept until even the individual members of the cult societies possess their own fetishes. The lineages, in the meantime, have reconstituted themselves on a maternal instead of a paternal basis of reckoning. Kroeber even hazards an interpretation as to when this happened: "In connection with the permanent attachment of women to houses or their coming to their own houses. . . . There is nothing in recent Pueblo society to contravene such a resolution of its history."[29] He then compares his reconstruction with the culture of the present-day Shoshonean tribes of California and even risks a correlation with the various periods in Pueblo archaeology. The Basket Maker periods II and III and Pueblo I are the eras of small groups essentially restricting themselves to limited tracts. Pueblo I and II repre-

[29] *Native Cultures* . . . , p. 384.

sent the period of the first drawing together of lineages into groups, and Pueblo III the consolidation into large pueblos presumably containing several multiple-lineage clans.[30] In spite of the fact that he himself feels that these reconstructions and correlations are somewhat hypothetical, he thinks that at most they are merely premature, and that they illustrate the possibility of the cooperation between the archaeological and ethnological approaches!

In the field of intangibles [he says] there is no reason why the archaeologist should refrain from using the distributional inductions of ethnology; nor why the ethnologist should hesitate to buttress his findings as to the history of culture forms and organization by converting, as well as may be, the tangibles actually established by the excavator, into their corresponding intangibles.[31]

Surely no comment is necessary here, except to indicate that the analytical distributional method, in the hands of a naturalist of culture, must inexorably lead precisely to this debacle, and that none of the older evolutionists or the most uncritical of the German and English diffusionists have ever indulged in more unjustified speculations.

The studies so far considered have dealt with attempts at historical reconstruction on the basis

[30] *Ibid.*, p. 385.
[31] *Ibid.*, p. 386.

of trait analysis and distributions which tacitly assumed the hypothesis of multiple origin for the main elements of specific cultures, Kroeber possibly excepted. It requires little ingenuity, however, and only a slightly different manipulation of the data, to arrive at the opposite conclusion, *viz.*, that these distributions can be most adequately explained on the hypothesis of a diffusion from one center. This is what Perry, Elliot-Smith, Rivers, and Foy-Graebner-Schmidt attempted. I shall begin with Rivers.

From an analysis of the complexities of Melanesian society he drew two inferences: first, that social organization was the most stable of all elements in culture; and, second, that the higher, *i.e.*, the more complex elements of culture, were almost everywhere due to the presence of a group of immigrants who had brought them. His emphasis accordingly was upon the study of the contact of peoples, and this gave to his investigations a prevailingly dynamic character. To prevent falling into the error of Boas, who postulated continuous change and fluidity, he predicated an essential unchangeability for social organization. He next proceeded, in the most approved manner of the quantitative method, to break up Melanesian culture into its component elements and to group them chronologically into distinct strata. But instead of dividing them into numerous culture areas as Wissler had done for North America, he divided them into two cultural strata, using, of course, criteria quite different from those of Wissler. How he established these two strata is well-known. It was characteristic of his method that he began with a comparison of the terms of relationship. He found two distinct types: one diffused rather widely through Melanesia and Polynesia and the other limited to Melanesia. Within the latter area he found great diversity. He then attempted to show that these two types of relationship systems were correlated with certain specific traits of social organization. He postulated as the earlier type of society dual organization with matrilineal descent, communism, and gerontocracy, out of which, later on, a number of complex new forms had developed that could be best explained if we assumed that individual marriage had arisen in these societies. The group of relationship terms encountered in Melanesia was found to be used for just those relationships which, he insisted, would have been most definitely affected by the course of the societal evolution which he believed he had discovered. To account for this development he had recourse to the influence of an immigrant people. These immigrants play a great rôle in Rivers's theory. Now it so happens that the more complex cultural traits were unquestionably diffused throughout this area by definite waves of immigrants. But Rivers's treatment of these immigrants is utterly unhistorical. For him they remain essentially a concept, the mechanism by which a dynamic character can be given to cultural data that otherwise would have to remain static. He found further evidence for the rôle played by these immigrants, in secret societies, the use of kava and betel, the mode of disposal of the dead, etc. This naturally led to subjective evaluations, and the old story was repeated, of including some and of discarding other elements depending upon how well they fitted into a preconceived scheme. How hard occasionally he was put to it is best exemplified by his treatment of the variety in the modes of the disposal of the dead as found, for example, in Australia. He dogmatically denies that this variability is due to local elaboration.

There are few customs [he says] in which man is more conservative than in his treatment of the dead. Among ourselves a new kind of funeral rite, such as cremation, only makes its way very slowly and as the result of strenuous propaganda. It is the intimate relation of the rites of death with the most sacred beliefs and sentiments of mankind, which account at once for the extraordinary persistence of features of these rites and for the success with which immigrant peoples succeed in carrying their rites into a new home. Wherever we find diversity of funeral rites, we may safely conclude that there has been diversity of culture.[32]

Australia was indeed something of a stumbling block. To account for its culture, he had, for those traits showing great variability, artificially to center his interest on a single feature, the diversity of burial customs, and, for those that were undifferentiated, like material culture, to invoke his very useful and convenient principle of the disappearance of the useful arts.

In short, Rivers was led to commit the same type of error that we emphasized before in connection with the discussion of the various members of the Boas school and, to a certain extent, of Boas himself. That his criteria dealt with the mechanism and nature of contact, instead of the determination of culture areas and culture sequences, and that he attempted to account psychologically and psychoanalytically for the great fascination exercised by the "immigrants" upon the simpler peoples is utterly immaterial.

The principle of accounting for diversity by operating with two units, one stable, complex, positive, and dynamic, and the other indeterminate, simple, negative, and static, received its most articulate and *simpliste* expression in the

[32] "The Problem of Australian Culture," *Psychology and Ethnology,* p. 163, 1926.

diffusion theory of Perry and Elliot-Smith.[33] According to this theory, as is well-known, all the most significant features of primitive culture— dual organization, the clan, agriculture, irrigation, pottery, metal working, stone working, architecture, sun worship, the higher forms of religious and ceremonial life—originated in Egypt and were then spread by groups of immigrants over the face of the earth.

Perry's method of demonstration can perhaps be best characterized by the famous line of Goldsmith:

And drags with each remove a lengthening chain.

You begin, say, with twenty elements, and, if nineteen are found in the next culture to be considered, this culture is to be equated with the first, and, if five are found in the marginal area, that is as it should be, for much is often lost on a long journey.

I have claimed [Perry insists] that the archaic civilization was put together, and that it spread, by a continuous process; that, in fact, the growth of communities and of cultural elements proceeded by definite steps, each of which was a consequence of those that preceded it. I have, further, claimed that most of the elements of the archaic civilization were built up in Egypt. In the domain of ideas . . . the Egyptians went from one idea to another as the organized body of thought in their possession led them.

[33] *Human History*, 1929.

. . . Given that this is true, and that Egyptian thought was built up ultimately from concrete facts of every-day experience, and that it has, in its inception, no element whatever of speculation, it is obvious that communities which derive their culture from Egypt would adopt a different attitude towards the ideas originating in Egypt, from that of the Egyptians themselves. The peoples influenced by the archaic civilization rejected large parts of the culture, and, in fact, chose those elements that harmonized with their own experience. They selected, for instance, the ceremonies connected with agriculture, leechcraft, burials, house-building, because they understood, from the people of the archaic civilization, that without these ceremonies things would go wrong. The sun was to them a matter of indifference simply because, it may be argued, nothing had ever occurred in their experience to cause them to elaborate ideas with regard to it. The sun had risen and set daily for untold years, and was accepted as a matter of course, as was the rest of nature. Only when men arrived with an organized system of ideas built up around the sun was any attention at all paid to it. And, what is more, it would seem that after the disappearance of the Children of the Sun, the sky world remained in men's thoughts because of the life that it was supposed to contain. Otherwise, it would evidently have disappeared from thought all through the region, as it has in the case of the Pueblo Indians, where the life, in the form of the "breath-body" goes to the underground land of the dead.[34]

What can be said of this type of speculation and argumentation except to repeat the exclamation of an ancient predecessor: *Sancta simplicitas!*

[34] *The Children of the Sun*, pp. 479–480.

We have reserved for the last the well-known *Kulturkreise* theory of Foy-Graebner, and we shall discuss it in terms of its last authoritative presentation, that of Father W. Schmidt. As I have pointed out elsewhere,[36] the *Kulturkreise* theory is in many ways evolutionary, in spite of its avowed antagonism to the older method. With this phase of the theory we have here no concern, except to point out that it inherited part of its quantitative bias from the older hypothesis. The task these theorists set themselves was identical with that of Wissler, Perry, and Rivers: the establishment of spacial and temporal relations between cultures. Unlike the American school, however, they dealt with world distributions and connections, and, unlike Perry, Elliot-Smith, and Rivers, they were not in the least interested in operating with two units, one of which was a historically documented and complex civilization. True to their German background, they preferred to begin by the establishment of principles. Thus we have the criterion of form, quantity, continuity, degree of relationship, etc.

By the help of these criteria and others of the same tendency, we are able to determine the spatial connexion of cultural areas, and to do so by an objective process, free

[36] *Social Anthropology*, pp. 20–21. For a specific demonstration of the marked evolutionism contained in Father Schmidt's point of view, see the excellent paper of Lowie, "Queries," *American Anthropologist*, vol. 35, pp. 288–296, 1933.

from subjective judgements of value and developmental series constructed *a priori;* and with scientific certainty, without any excessive heaping up of merely possible hypotheses, whether or not the areas in question are separated by areas of different culture.[36]

To establish a temporal connection Father Schmidt, summarizing Graebner, commences with the simple consideration that "where two cultural areas of different character touch one another, then either they will overlap at the borders, and so produce crossings, or else they will merely touch at the edges and so produce the phenomenon of contacts."[37]

We need not dwell here on the rôle played by purely subjective elements in the determination of what constitutes identity or adequate quantitative resemblance or on that played by the assumption of stability and mass migrations, for that has already been stressed *ad nauseam.* Instead, let us see what it is Father Schmidt insists an investigator

[36] SCHMIDT, W., *The Origin and Growth of Religion*, p. 232, 1931.

[37] He continues, "It is obvious that forms arising either out of a crossing or a contact must be more recent than the parent forms. This is the first objective ethnological criterion of time, and may lead to still further chronological results; for those forms due to mixture or contact in which the two components are still clearly to be recognized as such are thereby shown to be less ancient than those in which the component elements have blended into unity, since this process must needs demand a longer time."

It would seem that Father Schmidt is here combining a type of paleontological argumentation with that of Mendelianism.

must leave on one side, in order "to determine the inner development of an object, an institution, or an area."[38] According to him, to arrive at an undisturbed picture of inner development, we must reject all those elements that are due to an external cause, for instance, all those that are due to what he calls crossings. But not only that.

No element belonging to one culture can have any inner connection with the analogous element in another culture, so far as its development is concerned. For the many-sided peculiarity of a culture is the result of its separate and independent existence throughout a considerable extent of time, apart from all other cultures. Consequently, the development of its several elements has been wholly independent likewise, and not in any way affected by the analogous elements of another culture, or in any way affecting them in their development.[38]

With regard to the origin of the individual forms, the theory lays down the two following rules:

1. Cultural elements are to be explained only from ideas and associations appertaining to the culture to which it belongs.

2. With the specific culture only the older forms of a given element are specifically significant for explanations as to origin, for they reflect most accurately the various influences, physical and

[38] *Ibid.*, p. 236.

mental, to which the original appearance of that particular element is to be ascribed.[39] What such fictitious precision leads to is characteristically enough indicated by the three stages this school predicates. In the first, the primitive, we have the so-called Food Gatherers, where the men obtained food by hunting and the women by collecting plants. In the second stage, the exploitation of nature begins, women passing to primitive horticultural pursuits. Society is then organized on an exogamous matrilineal basis. Where the undivided family and patrilineal organization exists, the men develop from a hunting to a cattle-raising stage, while in the culture where an exogamous patrilineal society is found, totemism arises, which, adds Father Schmidt somewhat naïvely, "is a kind of animal worship."[40] The three stages, primitive, primary, and secondary, are further differentiated, each into three cultures, and we are treated to the interesting information that the

[39] *Ibid.*, p. 237. Father Schmidt, however, criticizes Graebner on three points. They are the following: "First, different individual elements of culture have different capabilities of dissemination. Second, especially close and accurate observation is needed where crossing and contact take place; for here tendencies of an arbitrary and nonorganic kind are formed, for instance, in mythology. Third, there is need for particularly accurate grasping of the combined factors of comparison, and care to recognize aright what element is really the nucleus of the phenomenon studied."— P. 237.
[40] *Ibid.*, p. 238.

"primitive" Eskimo once possessed exogamy, and that all the three primitive stages have very conveniently been combined into one in South America. What can one possibly say to such schematization except to reiterate our previous characterization that with Graebner and his followers the search for chronology became an obsession and the obsession a dogma?

Chapter VI

The Reaction against the Quantitative Method

Although the vogue of the quantitative method is with us today, its star is visibly beginning to set. In part this is the fate that inevitably overtakes unsound interpretations; in part it is but the natural reaction to any approach that robs cultural facts of their vitality, of their humanness, of that specific quality which makes them cultural and not biological or physical. We are all willing to forego the pleasures of surreptitious definiteness for one whiff of reality. Boas, I think, has always realized this, but apparently he dreads to visualize what would happen if ethnology were ever divorced from a rigorous logical and scientific method. He would have heartily subscribed to Lowie's statement, made many years ago to be sure, that ethnology should aspire to the exactness of the natural sciences, at least as far as logical method was concerned. Otherwise it would become a branch of *belles lettres*.[1] But let us accept the soft imputation. History has frequently been accused of the same frailty, and yet its association with the dreaded *belles lettres* has not seriously interfered with the correctness of the pictures Thucydides drew of Greece, Gibbon of Rome, and Burckhardt of the Italian Renaissance.

The reaction against the quantitative treatment of culture has taken two significant forms; first, an avowed attempt to describe culture as an integral whole with due regard to the proper interrelation of all its parts, and, second, an attempt to define it as a specific configuration. Significantly enough, the term configuration has been borrowed from Gestalt psychology.

The first revolt is associated with the names of Radcliffe-Brown and Malinowski in England, and with Mead in America. The German anthropologist Thurnwald is always included in this group by both Radcliffe-Brown and Malinowski, for reasons not quite clear to me. As far as I can see, the only bond uniting these ethnologists and theorists is their avowed critique of the quantitative method and its applications. The approach of each one of them is essentially distinct. Radcliffe-Brown is inconsistently a sociologist seeking for "laws," a

[1] "Social Organization," *American Journal of Sociology*, vol. 20, p. 95, 1926.

historian, and a neoevolutionist, and it is not always simple to tell which one of these facets of his point of view he is employing; Malinowski is fairly consistently a sociologist who occasionally relapses into the older evolutionism. He is always unhistorical. Mead is essentially a journalist in the best sense of the term, and Thurnwald is a sociologist and a neoevolutionist with a psychological vocabulary not always very clear. All of these investigators insist that, in contradistinction to their predecessors, they are as much interested in the implicit elements of culture as in the explicit ones. In making this claim they are manifestly wrong. Every modern qualified ethnologist has always been interested in the implicit features of culture. The difficulty has always been that few of them were able to stay with any group long enough to disentangle these implicit elements, granted, indeed, that it is possible for an outsider to do so. Since neither Radcliffe-Brown, Malinowski, nor Mead has ever stayed with natives for any longer period than those ethnologists whom they so seriously criticize, if indeed they have always stayed there so long, it might be well to examine the nature of that precious technique they developed which has enabled them to penetrate so much more deeply into the intricacies of aboriginal culture than their contemporaries. Let us see what it is.

Radcliffe-Brown blandly informs us that

. . . the meaning of an element of culture cannot be discovered by asking the people themselves what it means. . . . The meaning can only be defined when the culture is seen as a whole of interrelated parts, and this can only be accomplished by one who is able to take an objective view of it, the ethnographer or descriptive ethnologist in fact.[2]

The new anthropology, called by him comparative sociology, insists upon the following. I give them in his own words:

1. It rejects all attempts at conjecturing the origin of an institution where there is no information based on reliable historical records.[3]

2. It rejects all attempts to provide psychological explanations of particular social and cultural phenomena in favor of an ultimate psychological explanation of general sociological laws.

3. It describes social and cultural phenomena in sociological terms.

4. It regards culture as an integrated system and examines the functions of social institutions, customs, and beliefs of all kinds as parts of such a system.

[2] "Present Position of Anthropological Studies," British Association for the Advancement of Science, p. 17, 1931.

[3] That, in spite of his resolve, he occasionally lapses into historical inferences, Lowie has conclusively shown in the above-cited article, "Queries."

5. It gives us valuable information about the unformalized aspects of culture.
6. It applies to human life in society the generalizing method of the natural sciences.
7. It is functional, generalizing, and sociological.[4]
He finds fault with previous field workers for confining their task to the simple observation and recording of the facts in as precise a manner as possible, instead of attempting at the same time to discover their meaning. Meaning, for him, can be attained only when we know the interrelations of an element of culture with other elements, and when we know the place it occupies in the whole life of the people, and this signifies, of course, not only their visible activities but also their thoughts and feelings.[5] As an example he informs us that the "essential" meaning of the Sedna myth of the Eskimo "lies in its relation to the division of the year into two parts, summer and winter, and the effects this division has on the social life."[6]

It would take us too far afield to comment in detail upon all the questions raised by these somewhat dogmatic utterances. That we are far removed from the quantitative method is apparent, although the precise nature of the method that has taken its

[4] *Present Position* . . . , pp. 16–17.
[5] *Ibid.*, pp. 16–17.
[6] *Ibid.*, p. 17.

place is not always apparent. But what bearing have the principles laid down here on the fundamental problem of how to obtain the requisite information on the implicit elements of culture? Radcliffe-Brown informs us that, as a result of more extended and methodical observation, Malinowski and Mead have obtained valuable data about the unformalized aspects of the cultures they investigated. Yet when we turn to their monographs we find that Malinowski, for instance, has nowhere given us an even approximately complete account of the people he visited, and that the works in which Mead has embodied her results are simply impressionistic sketches. We are given no body of texts and no presentation of the facts in such a way that they can be critically controlled. In other words, we have subjective judgments and evaluations substituted for the old-fashioned type of observation and recording in as precise a manner as possible, for which these scientists seem to have so much contempt.

Although there are a number of important points in which Malinowski and Radcliffe-Brown are at one, fundamentally they are interested in entirely different problems. Both, in a sense, are crying for the moon. Where Radcliffe-Brown, however, seeks data for the formulation of laws, Malinowski desires it in order to elucidate the nature of cultural functioning.[7] He frequently speaks of the cultural processes being subject to laws, but he means something quite different from Radcliffe-Brown.

The cultural process is subject to laws, and the laws are to be found in the function of the real elements of culture. The atomizing or isolating treatment of cultural traits is sterile because the significance of culture consists in the relation between its elements and the existence of accidental or fortuitous culture complexes is not admitted.[8]

But granted that we have this *perpetuum mobile*, how are we going to describe it? The moment that we arrest this movement of the wheel of life, we introduce a distortion. Malinowski calmly disregards, as of course he must, this fatal difficulty.

As an example of this meaning, he takes the simplest kind of an artefact, the digging stick, and attempts to show that, though it may be identical in physical nature with the walking stick and the punting pole, it is quite distinct from them, for it fulfills a different function. "It is the diversity of function, not the identity of form, that is relevant to the student of culture," he claims.[8] But on his own theory everything is relevant to the student of culture. Now what functions do these irrelevances fulfill? And does he mean to

[7] Article "Culture," *Encyclopaedia of the Social Sciences*, p. 625, 1932.
[8] *Ibid.*, p. 625.

contend that the temporary lack of use of a digging stick is not of significance, that it is then not functioning at all? Does he further mean to imply that there may be no relevant significance to the identity of form of the three types of stick he mentions? How does he know this? As a matter of fact, he does not know it. And in uncritically separating them, he may be falling into that very error of atomizing and isolating cultural traits that he stigmatizes as so sterile.

But it is not this uncritical philosophizing that renders so much of his theorizing disconcerting; it is the realization that he completely fails to recognize the inconsistencies into which he is continually falling. Certainly we should not expect so intense an apparent opponent of trait complexes to operate with "real component units." What does it avail him, then, to speak of the systems of human activities called institutions, of their centering around a fundamental need, of their showing a pronounced amalgamation of functions, and having a synthetic character?[9] The fat is in the fire, and he is embarked on the most dangerous of journeys. The moment one begins with unit characters, one is definitely committed either to an historical approach, a statistical approach, or an atomistic approach, *i.e.*,

[9] *Ibid.*, p. 626.

independent invention. He prefers the last, as the
following quotation indicates:[10]

> These secondary regularities of form which cannot be
> accounted for by the primary function of the object . . .
> are to be explained by the cultural context. . . . A digging
> stick may be weighted, sharply pointed or blunt according
> to the character of the soil, the plants grown and the type
> of cultivation. The explanation of the South Sea outrigger
> may be found in the fact that this arrangement gives the
> greatest stability, seaworthiness and manageability, con-
> sidering the limitations in material and in technical handi-
> craft of the Oceanic cultures.

Here we have arrived at a point of view essentially identical with Boas's earlier formulations of
his method. Why a new term like functionalism
should be applied to it is not at all evident, nor can
I see that it is in any sense an advance upon the
latter or that Malinowski is aware of the presuppositions inhering in it. To go through the motions
of an elaborate and ornate argumentation, to pile
up truism upon truism, and to indulge in belle-
tristic distinctions that have no content, hardly
constitute an effective introduction to an avowedly
new and revolutionary approach.

Here in the United States the most articulate of
recent criticisms of the quantitative method has
come from one of Boas's younger pupils, Margaret

[10] *Ibid.*, pp. 626–627.

Mead.[11] I am at one with her in her criticism of the inadequacies of the ethnological record; in fact, a good portion of this essay is an attempt to point them out. I likewise heartily agree that the inexplicit, the unformulated, and the uninstitutionalized aspects of culture are of importance to an understanding of the whole of culture.[12] Whether they are as important as the traditional institutions depends entirely upon the culture. It most emphatically does not follow as an axiom. She is certainly to be congratulated upon eschewing conjectural historical reconstructions. To eschew conjectural reconstructions, however, does not justify us in being unhistorical, and Mead is entirely unhistorical. By this I mean what every historian means: the description of a culture in such a way that we feel we are dealing with real and specific men and women, with real and specific situations, and with a real and specific tradition. In addition, even if we realize that the history of a culture is unprocurable, no description ever carries conviction unless its recorder is convinced that it has had a history. Now, in spite of the superficial impression to the contrary, Mead is not dealing with specific individuals or situations but with generalized ones.

[11] "More Comprehensive Field Methods," *American Anthropologist*, vol. 35, pp. 1–15, 1933.
[12] *Ibid.*, p. 15.

It is she who gives them their uniqueness, and that is something fundamentally different.

But it is not really her program as such at which I cavil; it is the amazing assumption that any outsider can obtain the type of information she specifies except after an intensive study of a lifetime. Indeed, I seriously doubt whether an outsider can ever obtain it. And yet both she and her husband Reo Fortune claim to have accomplished all this in investigations that never lasted longer than a year and generally were of shorter duration. That she carefully organized her method of approach does not give her the qualifications which only a long and protracted residence and a complete command of the language can possibly bestow. Of what avail is it that she says,

> Behind every general statement about the behavior of children in Manus and Samoa lies a long line of observations, which are not made at random and recorded casually, but are made systematically about a selected group of children, on points which preliminary investigation has shown to be most significant. . . . In Manus I studied the effect of the personality of fathers upon the personality of the sons whom they have reared.[13]

Any adequate study of this kind, even under the most favorable conditions, can be done only after many years of intensive application. What one

[13] *Ibid.*, pp. 11-12.

gets within a year, or for that matter within five years, even if endowed with unusual penetration into the personality of others, is bound to be superficial and largely subjective. And that is precisely what her published work demonstrates. Nor does this constitute the slightest reflection upon her ability or her integrity. How could it very well be otherwise? Like Radcliffe-Brown and Malinowski, she too is crying for the moon. But most of us learn early in life that it cannot be procured and that stamping with our feet is not very effective.

Mead's approach is essentially a broad sociological one, with a definite leaning toward the acquisition of case histories. We all know how unsatisfactory they are among ourselves. For Samoans and the inhabitants of Manus they would manifestly be ten times as inadequate.

The revolt of Benedict against the quantitative method is fundamentally different. She may protest against historical reconstructions which seem to her naïve and *simpliste* as vehemently as she wishes, but her whole temperament is that of a culture historian to whom the history of a specific group has significance and validity. Her difficulties lie in the fact that she is trying not to be one. Her error consists in attempting a succinctness of characterization that fails because it is too refined. It is the essence of a civilization

that she attempts to distill, and, to prevent its
volatilization, she dogmatically includes and excludes in an unjustifiable and arbitrary manner.
A real danger lurks in such a procedure, *viz.*,
that of flying in the face of unpalatable facts that
tend to disturb the desired harmony. She not
only flies in the face of these facts; she calmly
leaves them out. Quite apart from this, it is
doubtful whether distilled syntheses of this kind
are ever applicable to culture. Fascinating as they
may be, they are of extremely problematical value.
It is conceivable that they may hold for individuals,
but they certainly do not hold for a specific
culture, and Benedict has applied them not merely
to a specific culture but to a whole area.[14]

As has been already indicated, Thurnwald is
always included in the same school as Radcliffe-
Brown, Malinowski, and Mead. Apparently this is
done because, like theirs, his is a general sociological
approach. But he does not seek for laws like
Radcliffe-Brown, define culture in terms of function like Malinowski, or attempt to stress the
implicit side of culture at the expense of the
explicit like Mead. Fundamentally he seems a
straightforward evolutionist who still takes refuge
in schematisms and thinks of aboriginal peoples in

[14] "Configuration of Culture in North America," *American Anthropologist*, vol. 34, pp. 1–27, 1932.

terms of stages of culture. That he uses modern psychological terminology, is willing theoretically to grant the individual a far greater rôle than did the older evolutionists, and culture a greater fluidity, does not alter the situation. All the objections that have been urged against this point of view by Boas and his school apply with redoubled force to this attempt to reinvigorate an erroneous and a futile method.[15] What distinguishes Thurnwald from the other ethnologists with whom his name is so often associated is his skill as an ethnographer, his willingness to record observations minutely and in text, to furnish us with some means of control for his statements, and, lastly, to exclude his theoretical preconceptions from his actual field work. It is just conceivable that Thurnwald is merely retaining the formulae of the evolutionary approach and that actually he has renounced all its older implications, just as, after a fashion, Marett has done in his theoretical essays.

One characteristic of this whole revolt against the quantitative approach is the abandonment by its representative ethnologists of what they designate as the "old-fashioned" monograph. Yet, with all their defects, these monographs were specific

[15] *Psychologie des primitiven Denkens,* 1918, and article, "Kultur" in Ebert, *Reallexicon der Vorgeschichte,* 1924–1929.

and contained an enormous mass of pertinent information. In their place, Radcliffe-Brown, Malinowski, Mead and Fortune have substituted a fund of information incomparably smaller, a preoccupation with problems that are difficult to properly attack and evaluate even in our own culture where the conditions are infinitely more propitious, a pretentious impressionism, and a counsel of perfection.

Chapter VII

Reconstruction from Internal Evidence and the Rôle of the Individual

It must not be supposed that the first protest against the quantitative method came from Radcliffe-Brown or Malinowski or Mead. Long before them, exception had been taken by the ethnologists best qualified to protest, those who had used it and found it inadequate and erroneous. A culture historian like Lowie clearly looked at it askance from the very beginning, and his reconstructions of Plains societies were but a half-hearted concession to a dominant mode. As we have pointed out before, men like Goldenweiser and Spier, after valiantly testing its applicability, gave it up completely. Kroeber himself gives it up in part. Yet I do not feel that he is essentially an historian; unless it be that for some inexplicable reason he has insisted upon neutralizing his inherent interest. Judged by his writings certainly it would be better to say that he has made inroads upon the historical approach rather than accepted its implications.

His may be the face of history, but it certainly is the voice of the natural sciences.

It would, however, be a completely false envisaging of the situation if the culture historian were asked to disprove the contentions of the adherents of the quantitative method. Ethnology deals with culture, and that should effectively dispose of any attempt to graft upon it a method appropriate to and developed for the natural sciences. Whatever hesitation has hitherto existed in this regard is due to the fact that, with very few exceptions, ethnologists have refrained from drawing the proper inferences from this predication. They have taken away with one hand what they have given with the other. But culture is culture, and the analysis and description of Kwakiutl culture must be made according to the same principles as that of our own civilizations. The task, let me insist, is always the same: a description of a specific period, and as much of the past and as much of the contacts with other cultures as is necessary for the elucidation of the particular period. No more. This can be done only by an intensive and continuous study of a particular tribe, a thorough knowledge of the language, and an adequate body of texts; and this can be accomplished only if we realize, once and for all, that we are dealing with specific, not generalized, men and women, and with specific, not generalized, events. But the recognition of specific men and women should bring with it the realization that there are all types of individuals and that it is not, for instance, a Crow Indian who has made such and such a statement, uttered such and such a prayer, but a particular Crow Indian. It is this particularity that is the essence of all history and it is precisely this that ethnology has hitherto balked at doing. It is a mistake to believe that it cannot be done any more. Let me give but one example. A Winnebago named John Rave introduced the Peyote cult to his tribe. He dictated to me an account, in Winnebago, of his conversion to the new religion and his attempts at spreading it among his own people. This document assumed its proper perspective only when it was viewed in a specific sense. Then it was manifest that I was dealing with a well-articulated and consistent body of doctrine, with definite internal indications of its growth; that this body of doctrine was at conscious variance with the older Winnebago sacramental system; that it represented the conscious and personal fusion of older and newer beliefs; and that the determination of what was to be included and what omitted was as much, if not more, due to the personality of Rave as to the generalized workings of the traditional background.

How much can be attained by the intensive study of a single document, provided one is adequately acquainted with a particular tribe, I shall now attempt to show at some length by three examples taken from the Winnebago: the document I have just mentioned, a myth called *The Chief's Daughter and the Orphan*, and a semilegendary account of events for which we have corroborative published evidence. In our first example we are dealing with contemporary trends and developments, in the second and third with the past.

I. INTERPRETATION OF THE PEYOTE DOCUMENT

The value of beginning with a document cannot be too strongly stressed.[1] In elucidating culture we must begin with a fixed point, but this point must be one that has been given form by a member of the group described, and not by an alien observer. This is, of course, a truism to the historian. Unfortunately even excellent ethnologists sin against it all the time.

---

[1] My method is, in short, one which is essentially identical with that developed by Mauss in his lectures and his last publication in *L'Année sociologique* and brilliantly exemplified by Eduard Norden in his *Die Geburt des Kindes*, a study of the famous *Fourth Eclogue* of Vergil. This is not meant to imply, however, that I approve of the manner in which Mauss injects his sociological preconceptions into the elucidation of a document, or of the excessive use made by Norden of "Interpretationen und Combinationen." But these criticisms do not affect their method of approach.

Let me then begin with Rave's account of his conversion to the Peyote cult. This is a hybrid form of Mexican catholicism that has been secondarily modified by the inclusion within it of elements taken from the cultures of certain American Indian tribes. From a stylistic and artistic point of view this document can be broken up in the following way:

1. *Introduction*

Brief account of meeting in 1910.

2. *Conversion*

First eating of peyote; object within him.
Second eating of peyote; visions and hallucinations.
First prayer: Intellectual realization of peyote as cause.
Third eating of peyote.
Second prayer: Connection of God and Son of God with the Peyote.
First realization of his conversion and the powers it gave him.
Vision of his family and the evils of drinking.
Third prayer: Inward realization; complete surrender.
Testimonial of the uniqueness of his experience.
His desire to convert the Winnebago.

3. *Testimonies*

Curing of Rave's disease.
Curing of disease of Rave's wife.
Curing of Black Waterspirit's consumption.
Curing of He-who-gathers-men's sins [evil habits].

Statement of its all-curative effect; disease and sins.

The secondary [?] creed, belief in God.

Quotation of He-who-gathers-men's testimony as to his cure.

Conversion of the rich and important members of the Medicine Dance, John Harrison and Squeaky-Wings.

4. *Exhortations*

Reiterated expression of gratitude to the Peyote for its psychical cure and expression of contrition for past sins. Recital of simple secondary creed.

First exhortation to all to come and be cured, to try it in person.

Second exhortation to all.

Third exhortation: How it has changed his character.

Fourth exhortation: Reiteration and insistence upon Peyote's curative power. Simple creed at the end.

Expression of personal gratitude.

Fifth exhortation: Watch the peyote eaters. Try to understand them.

Ceremony to come to an end.

Final prayer: Secondary creed.

In the very brief introductory account which prefaces the document proper, six objects are mentioned which indicate at once the intricate nature of the religious syncretism involved. They are the peyote, the "chief stick," the Bible, the bird-feather fan, the fire, and the water. The peyote and the Bible are new. Yet the term applied to the peyote equates it immediately with the old medicinal herbs, and the inclusion of the Bible with these other objects gives to the latter a new significance. The "chief stick," in both designation and meaning, is taken bodily from two of the older rituals, although its precise shape is new. The bird-feather fan is old in concept but new in shape and in its secondary implications. The rôle of the fire or fireplace is old, but it has lost its ritualistic designation. The shape of the fireplace itself represents a new element. Finally, the rôle of the water is simply the attenuated survival of the ritualistic meal. At the end of the introduction there is an injunction against *going out* and an exhortation to *remain quiet*. These are not simply meaningless words but represent on the contrary a taking over of certain tenets of an older religious theory.

We pass now to Rave's eating of the peyote. He describes this as follows:[2]

During 1893–1894 I was in Oklahoma with peyote eaters. In the middle of the night we were to eat peyote. We ate it and I also did. It was the middle of the night when I got frightened, for a live thing seemed to have entered me. "Why did I do it?" I thought to myself. I should not have done it, for right at the beginning I have harmed myself.

[2] For a full description of the Peyote cult, see my article "The Peyote Cult of the Winnebago Indians: A Study in Borrowing," *Journal of Religious Psychology*, vol. 7, 1913, and Chap. XVI of my monograph on the Winnebago Indians, *Bureau of American Ethnology Report* 37, 1923.

Indeed, I should not have done it. I am sure it will injure me. The best thing will be for me to vomit it up. Well, now, I will try it. After a few attempts I gave up. I thought to myself, "Well, now you have done it. You have been going around trying everything and now you have done something that has harmed you. What is it? It seems to be alive and moving around in my stomach. If only some of my own people were here! That would have been better. Now no one will know what has happened to me. I have killed myself."

Just then the object was about to come out. It seemed almost out and I put out my hand to feel it, but then it went back again. "O, my, I should never have done it from the beginning. Never again will I do it. I am surely going to die."

As we continued it became day and we laughed. Before that I had been unable to laugh.

The following night we were to eat peyote again. I thought to myself, "Last night it almost harmed me." "Well, let us do it again," they said. "All right, I'll do it." So there we ate seven peyote apiece.

Suddenly I saw a big snake. I was very much frightened. Then another one came crawling over me. "My God! where are these coming from?" There at my back there seemed to be something. So I looked around and I saw a snake about to swallow me entirely. It had legs and arms and a long tail. The end of this tail was like a spear. "O, my God! I am surely going to die now," I thought. Then I looked again in another direction and I saw a man with horns and long claws and with a spear in his hand. He jumped for me and I threw myself on the ground. He missed me. Then I looked back and this time he started back, but it seemed to me that he was directing his spear at me. Again I threw myself on the ground and he missed me. There seemed to be no possible escape for me. Then suddenly it occurred to me, "Perhaps it is this peyote that is doing this thing to me?" *Help me, O medicine, help me! It is you are doing this and you are holy! It is not these frightful visions that are causing this. I should have known that you were doing it. Help me!* Then my suffering stopped. *As long as the earth shall last, that long will I make use of you, O medicine!*

This had lasted a night and a day. For a whole night I had not slept at all.

Then we breakfasted. Then I said, when we were through, "Let us eat peyote again to-night." That evening I ate eight peyote.

There are three things to be borne in mind here: first, the object within him; second, the hallucination about the snakes; and, third, the vision of the "devil." The discussion of what he precisely means by speaking of an object having entered him would take us too far afield and be problematical at best. The hallucination about the snakes, however, brings up more concrete questions. To have a vision of a snake meant disaster in the old visionary experiences, and apparently this was its association in Rave's mind. The second snake connotes something different. The designation applied to it is associated with one of the most sacred of the old Winnebago spirits, the waterspirit. The long tail and the spear at the end of the tail were characteristic of this spirit. The third vision, that of the devil, is a hodge-podge of old and new. The term applied to the devil by the Winnebago has an uncertain etymology. The accepted folk etymology is interesting but manifestly untenable. There the word is analyzed as meaning "he of whose existence one is doubtful." In all probability, however, it means "the real horned one" and represents a medley of the Christian figure of the devil and an old Winnebago spirit called Red-horn.

There is an interesting point here, Rave's fears and his precise relation to the figures in his hallucinations. To explain his fears as part of a cultural pattern, or in such general psychological terms as an instinctive reaction to something unknown, would be utterly inadequate. They can be explained only in terms of a knowledge of the specific individual John Rave, of his character in general, and of the specific state of mind with which he approached this particular ordeal. It might be imagined from the rationalistic manner in which he speaks here that he was wholly concerned with finding some explanation for his hallucinations and that they left him as soon as he had arrived at the conclusion that the peyote had induced them. Yet it is exceedingly unlikely that he was not aware of the effects produced by the peyote. What we have here is a retrogressive rationalization which had become stereotyped in the course of seventeen years. He was an utterly disoriented individual when he first partook of the peyote. From his earliest childhood the attempt to establish a *rapport* with the spirits had filled him with terror. He had never succeeded in securing a successful vision at puberty. It is this same terror that seized him at the peyote meeting. When the spirits who appeared to him are the dreaded snake and the equally terrifying waterspirit, both of which spell death, and these in turn are followed by the devil himself, his fear knows no bounds. Presumably it is then that he remembers what he had previously been told by the peyote worshippers and understands both the significance of the figures of his visions and the power of the peyote. In other words, for the first time in his life he has seen the Winnebago spirits face to face. He has been blessed. So he breaks out into a prayer of gratitude, using the old Winnebago ritualistic terminology, and equating the peyote with both the powers of the old curative medicines and the blessings supposed to flow from membership in the Medicine Dance.

The struggle, too, has its significance. It is both old and new. In the puberty vision-quest the spirits were at times pictured as pursuing one. To be captured by them meant success. The new note, here, is the evil intent of the spirits. But even this is not entirely new, for the evil spirits are always regarded as desirous of destroying an individual. In fact, in the older puberty visions the first three spirits who appeared to the faster were regarded as false ones. Only the fourth visitant represents the true one. In Rave's hallucinations, it might be said, the Peyote is this fourth spirit. Such a conception is entirely alien to the old background. Finally, let me point out that the idea of a place of refuge mentioned by Rave and, indeed, the exact term he uses are taken directly from the major ceremony of the Winnebago, the Medicine Dance.

These constituents of Rave's conversion to the Peyote were thereafter to be dramatized. Conversion was to consist of the presence within an individual of some object that refused to come out, of visions and of hallucinations outside one, and of an articulate recognition that the peyote was the cause of these phenomena—was God. So the official theory became a codification of the specific things that happened to John Rave, and only by possessing some knowledge of John Rave's life could this have been properly understood.

An examination of the terminology of the prayer is even more illuminating. The phrase *Help me!* appears both in the puberty vision prayer and in all myths where the hero is in difficulty. *You are doing it* belongs to the vocabulary of the doctor.

I should have known it is taken from the old prayers. However, there it is the spirit who is supposed to recognize the human gift, not the reverse. *They let up on me* is taken from the old myths and is regularly used when the evil spirits who are pursuing the hero give up their pursuit. The specific term used for *holy* here is part of the doctor's vocabulary. *As long as the earth shall last* is an old ritualistic phrase, and *I shall use you* is part of the regular prayer formula.

Yet in spite of the fact that there is not a single new term involved here, this is a completely new prayer in form, content, and spirit. Compare it, for instance, with the following example of a typical old prayer to the Earthmaker, the Winnebago supreme deity: "Harken, Earthmaker, our father, I am about to offer you a handful of tobacco. My ancestor concentrated his mind upon you. The fireplaces with which you blessed him; the small amount of life you granted to him; all the blessings you bestowed upon my ancestor, that I ask of you directly. Also that I may have no troubles in life."[3]

In Rave's prayer there is no mention of tobacco, no calling upon any of the older spirits, none of the old metaphors, nothing of the old ritualistic modesty. The fundamental point, of course, is the

[3] *Ibid.,* p. 447.

omission of tobacco, *i.e.*, the repudiation of the whole older theory of offerings and of the mechanism whereby an individual could be brought into relation with the spirits. That this was not accidental is proved by Rave's hatred of tobacco in every form. For him there was to be no intermediary between the worshipper and his God, and there was to be no other requirement except a confession of sin, a contrite heart, and complete surrender. But let us continue with Rave's account:

In the middle of the night I saw God. To God living up above, our Father, I prayed. *Have mercy upon me! Give me knowledge that I may not say and do evil things.*[4] *To you, O God, I am trying to pray. Do thou, O Son of God, help me, too. This religion, let me know. Help me, O medicine, grandfather, help me! Let me know this religion!* Thus I spoke and sat very quiet. And then I beheld the morning star and it was good to look upon. The light was good to look upon. I had been frightened during the night but now I was happy. Now as the light appeared, it seemed to me that nothing would be invisible to me. I seemed to see everything clearly. Then I thought of my home and as I looked around, there I saw the house in which I lived far away among the Winnebago, quite close to me. There at the window I saw my children playing. Then I saw a man going to my house carrying a jug of whiskey. Then he gave them something to drink and the one that had brought the whiskey got drunk and

[4] The text actually says "In view of the evil things I have done," but my Indian interpreter preferred to use the words as given above.

bothered my people. Finally he ran away. "So, that is what they are doing," I thought to myself. Then I beheld my wife come and stand outside of the door, wearing a red blanket. She was thinking of going to the flagpole and was wondering which road she should take. "If I take this road, I am likely to meet some people, but if I take the other road, I am not likely to meet anyone."

Indeed, it is good. They are all well—my brother, my sister, my father, my mother. I felt very good indeed. *O medicine, grandfather, most assuredly you are holy! All that is connected with you, that I would like to know and that I would like to understand. Help me! I give myself up to you entirely!*

For three days and three nights I had been eating medicine, and for three days and three nights I had not slept. Throughout all the years that I had lived on earth, I now realized that I had never known anything holy. Now, for the first time, I knew it. Would that some of the Winnebagoes might also know it!

The second prayer, beginning with *Have mercy upon me!*, is, I think, later in date than the first. The phraseology is still patently old, but the spirit seems more markedly Christian. In other words, the religious syncretism has gone one step farther. Let me, as in the first prayer, analyze and comment upon the constituent elements. The phrase *Our father who is above* is a combination of the old epithet for Earthmaker and the Christian formula. It is certainly Christian in intent, for there is no exact parallel to such a simple declaration in the old ceremonies. The words *Father, have mercy on me* are likewise mixed Winnebago and Christian, but they are certainly Christian in intent. *I have no right to say it in view of what I have done* is probably a modification of the old ritualistic modesty, but it really is new for all that, being partly just personal, partly Christian. The term applied to God is the old Winnebago appellation for Earthmaker. The verb translated by *to pray* really means *to call upon* and is a new terminology with new implications. *Son of God* is of course entirely Christian. The term *this religion*, literally *this work*, is the old ritualistic phraseology. So, likewise, is the epithet *Grandfather*, as applied to peyote. It was regularly used in connection with the herb societies. There is a very interesting word used to describe the quietness that came upon Rave after he had finished his prayer. It is very rare and means specifically the rest and peace that comes suddenly after turmoil. It expresses quite admirably the welcome exhaustion that follows in the wake of the hallucinations induced by the peyote.

This second prayer is characterized by the following facts. It has a fixed form; there is a supplication to God, a supplication to the Son of God, and a supplication to the peyote. It is immediately followed by what constitutes the completion of the conversion. This completion of the conversion consists of four parts: the ineffable happiness that befalls Rave, the longing for his family and the vision he sees of them, the prayer of gratitude and complete surrender, and the definite declaration that he had at last attained to a knowledge of what was holy. There is no need of stressing his feeling of happiness. The mention of the morning star is not accidental. Not only was it one of the most important of the old Winnebago spirits but it also signified the termination of the night ceremony in the old rituals. Here it has been symbolically reinterpreted as ineffable light. The phrase *nothing would be invisible* is an old belief belonging to the Medicine Dance and to the shaman. It also occurs in practically all the peyote cults. His sudden television is, of course, simply an expansion of what we have just discussed. In the vision of his family we have a first mention of Rave's hostility to drunkenness and whiskey. His wife's decision to take one road in preference to the other so that she is not likely to meet anyone is old Winnebago etiquette. All the relatives he mentions are those against whom his hatred was originally directed.

In the third prayer only the peyote is mentioned and declared holy. To Rave, of course, both God and the Son of God were really incidental. In speaking of the peyote here, he uses a conservative and old religious terminology. Externally, this prayer, therefore, contains practically no Christian elements except the final *I give myself up to you.* But even here the implications are only mildly Christian. Yet the transformation into a prayer utterly different from the old prayers is complete. Where in the old prayers a man would have said *Grandfather, this is a holy thing we are doing,* here we have *You are holy;* where he would have said *We have thought ourselves in connection with life,* here we have *All that is connected with you I would like to know;* where he would have said *We desire that you give us life,* here we have a completely new note, *I give myself up to you.* In short, an individual is no longer a free agent asking for the specific goods of life in return for offerings and worship, but a groping weakling, putting himself completely in the hands of the peyote, of God, and of the Son of God. All will be well if he renounces his past and his faith.

Before proceeding to a discussion of the second part of this document, let us pause and see whether the form and content can throw any light on its possible history. If we knew nothing about Rave or the specific history of the cult, we might feel inclined to pay little attention to the differences between the three prayers and indulge in meaningless remarks upon the dynamics of conversion or the adjustment of a new rite to the older cultural patterns, etc.[5] Naturally, such an attempt is fraught with pitfalls. I am well aware of this.

It is my feeling, for instance, that, in spite of its coming last, the third prayer was formulated much earlier than most of the second, and that the second prayer had been greatly transformed, probably not long before Rave gave me the foregoing account. Not all of it, for the first two sentences represent an old formula and could easily have followed the first prayer. Indeed, it would be reasonable to expect that it did, for it would fit in most admirably with the old vision type.

As I indicated before, the first three spirits to appear in the old puberty vision were always impostors. In the first prayer, we assumed that the peyote could be taken as constituting the fourth spirit. But naturally, to a Winnebago, even a poorly adjusted one like Rave, this was not on a par with the three others. The vision of Earthmaker—God—in the middle of the night would, however, have made the old vision requirement complete. The God whom Rave sees, we may definitely surmise then, was not the Christian God, but the old Winnebago supreme deity Earthmaker. Indeed, it is fairly transparent that

[5] I myself was guilty of this in the paper on the Peyote cult previously quoted.

what Rave must have had in mind here originally was a very well-known vision experience wherein a famous Winnebago of former times attempts to obtain a blessing from Earthmaker.[6] He is represented as succeeding only after a fashion. Rave, on the other hand, represents himself as succeeding completely. By thus recognizing the power of the divine herb and attaining to a completed puberty vision, even if a belated one, Rave obtains a double conversion—a conversion to the new religion and an adjustment to the old—and this, coming at the time it did, must have had all the implication and power of a sudden and immediate revelation. Subsequently the rest of this second prayer was added, and the first part received its definitely Christian imprint.

In making this last statement, I do not wish it to be inferred that I am simply indulging in casual speculation. On the contrary, I have some specific facts in mind. I know that practically all the overt Christian dogmas were introduced between 1905 and 1910 by an Indian named Albert Hensley who had been brought up in a devout Episcopal family, that Rave was very tolerant to Hensley's innovations—the bodily introduction of the Bible, so that it became one of the sacred objects in the cult, the reading of the Bible, the Christian exegesis,

[6] See my *Crashing Thunder*, pp. 20–23, 1927.

etc. To Rave all this was of no moment as long as the peyote remained supreme and the ritualistic procedure which he had originated was not questioned. When Hensley questioned the latter, Rave took issue with him. Hensley thereupon seceded and his personal influence stopped. Nevertheless, Rave retained Hensley's additions, and it is the equation of the peyote with the Christian God, and the incorporation of the dogma of the trinity, that became the full creed of the peyote, not the simple transformation of the old prayer formula as exemplified by the first and third prayers.

Let us now turn to the second part of the document. It runs as follows:

Many years ago I had been sick and it looked as if this illness were going to kill me. I tried all the Indian doctors and then I tried all of the white man's medicines, but they were of no avail. "I am doomed. I wonder whether I will be alive next year." Such were the thoughts that came to me. As soon as I ate the peyote, however, I got over my sickness. After that I was not sick again. My wife had suffered from the same disease, and I told her that if she ate this medicine it would surely cure her. But she was afraid, although she had never seen it before. She knew that I used it, but nevertheless she was afraid of it. Her sickness was getting worse and worse and one day I said to her, "You are sick. It is going to be very difficult, but try this medicine anyhow. It will ease you." Finally she ate it. I had told her to eat it and then to wash herself and comb her hair and she would get well, and now she is well. Then I painted her face and took my gourd and began singing very much. Then I stopped. "Indeed you are right," she said, "for now I am well." From that day on to the present time she has been well. Now she is very happy.

Black Waterspirit at about that time was having a hemorrhage and I wanted him to eat the peyote. "Well, I am not going to live anyhow," he said. "Well, eat this medicine soon then and you will get cured." Consumptives never were cured before this and now for the first time one was cured. Black Waterspirit is living today and is very well.

There was a man named Walking-Priest and he was very fond of whiskey; he chewed and he smoked and he gambled. He was very fond of women. He did everything that was bad. Then I gave him some of the peyote and he ate it and he gave up all the bad things he was doing. He had had a very dangerous disease and had even had murder in his heart. But to-day he is living a good life. That is his desire.

Whoever has any bad thoughts, if he will eat this peyote he will abandon all his bad habits. It is a cure for everything bad.

To-day the Indians say that only God is holy. One of the Winnebagoes has told me, "Really, the life that I led was a very bad one. Never again will I do it. This medicine is good and I will always use it." John Harrison and Squeak-Wings were prominent members of the Medicine Dance; they thought much of themselves as did all the members of the Medicine Dance. Both of them were gamblers and were rich because they had won very much in gambling. Their parents had acquired great possessions by giving medicines to the people. They were rich and they believed that they had a right to be selfish with their possessions. Then they ate peyote and ever since that time they have been followers of this medicine. They were really very ill and now they have been cured of it. Now if there are any men that might be taken as examples of the peyote, it is these three. Even if a man were blind and only heard about them he would realize that if any medicine were good, it is this medicine. It is a cure for all evil. Before, I had thought that I knew something but I really knew nothing. It is only now that I have real knowledge. In my former life I was like one blind and deaf. My heart ached when I thought of what I had been doing. Never again will I do it. This medicine alone is holy and has made me good and has rid me of all evil. The one whom they call God has given me this. That I know positively. Let them all come here; men and women; let them bring with them all that they desire; let them bring with them their diseases. If they come here they will get well. This is all true; it is all true. Bring whatever desires you possess along with you and then come and eat or drink this medicine. This is life, the only life. Then you will learn something about yourself, so come. Even if you are not told anything about yourself, nevertheless you will learn something of yourself. Come with your disease, for this medicine will cure it. Whatever you have, come and eat this medicine and you will have true knowledge once and for all. Learn of this medicine yourself through actual experience.

Here we have a detailed account of Rave's proselytizing zeal and the testimonial as to the peyote's curative power. We must first ask ourselves how this proselytizing zeal is to be explained. To say that it lies in the very nature of a prophet and a convert to a new religion to seek proselytes is neither adequate nor very illuminating. The psychologizing and speculation into which one is inevitably led in order to explain this desire of Rave's for converts are admittedly dangerous. But these speculations have their value, and they are immeasurably nearer the truth than the general discussions on the dynamics of culture or on generalized processes and events, with their impressionistic evaluations that have no body. I can personally attest that Rave's craving for proselytes was almost an obsession, and I am inclined to explain it as follows. He had failed to make the two fundamental adjustments to the old life, the attainment of a successful puberty vision and membership in the Medicine Dance. I do not know enough about his personality to give any adequate reasons for this failure. I know from what he himself and others told me that his parents were devoted adherents of the old culture, that his father had received a blessing from the spirits at puberty, and that he transmitted much that was transmissible in a direct personal manner to his son. I also know that Rave attempted to secure a vision at puberty and failed, that as he grew up he participated in many of the important rites of the tribe. But I am reasonably convinced that for an individual not to have been blessed by the spirits at puberty and not to have been a member of the

Medicine Dance meant that he was debarred from ever having any great influence in his tribe. I infer further from his specific hatred of the Medicine Dance that he felt his disadvantage deeply. I also infer from what I knew of him that he probably was that type of individual who insists upon a real subjective thrill before he will accept the truth of a religious belief. It was the custom for Winnebago parents practically to tell their young children what they were to expect during their puberty fast. Only those who were peculiarly nonsusceptible to such parental direction and who looked for a personal revelation could possibly have failed. Rave apparently belonged to this group. I take it then that, when at the Peyote meeting he received this personal revelation, he felt that he had at last attained full equality with the normal members of his tribe. But more than that, he could now become the founder of a new society, rivaling that of the Medicine Dance. Originally, I imagine, such must have been his main purpose, as the conversion of his wife seems to imply. This normal proselytizing zeal was subsequently strengthened and transformed far beyond what one might have ordinarily expected, by the implications of the cult which he had taken over and the economic and social conditions of the Winnebago. All these factors changed him from being simply the founder of a new cult—nothing by any means uncommon in Winnebago history—to a prophet who was to enable the Winnebago to survive. Winnebago history is full of such prophets. The net result was that proselytizing came to be for him an end in itself.

The transformation of Rave from being the founder of a cult to that of the preacher of a new gospel meant that he was forced to take a definite stand toward the fundamental question of what ailed Winnebago society. Was it merely that the numbers and firearms of the whites had treacherously and unfairly overwhelmed it, or was there something fundamentally wrong with the old life? He accepted the second alternative. Why, I do not know. It was clearly one of the possible interpretations and had been taken by Winnebago prophets before him. It meant defining precisely what was wrong and insisting upon his fellow men renouncing these evil customs and habits. To judge from this document, he asked the Winnebago to give up everything connected with the old background. That this was not his original thought the description of the conversion of his wife proves. At what time he arrived at it I do not know. No members of the other tribes who adopted the peyote cult gave up their old beliefs, for to them it was simply another ceremony to be added to those they already possessed. It never was synchronous with the negation of the entire old background. That was a specific Winnebago development to be ascribed to the influence of John Rave.

It is simple enough to find an hypothesis that will explain this in terms of Rave's personality, but such an explanation would be entirely subjective. I think the facts could have been ascertained at the time—at least Rave's version of what had happened. But this information was unfortunately not obtained. Let me, however, suggest an explanation. Rave, from my observation, was an extremely logical and ruthless thinker and very loyal where his feelings were aroused. He had experienced no thrill in the old Winnebago fasts and received no revelations. He was vouchsafed both by the semi-Christian peyote directly, without the intermediation of any offerings. It seemed to him that his tormented soul attained to this ineffable peace as soon as he ceased to struggle externally and internally. Translated into the old Winnebago formula, this inward acceptance can be regarded as having taken the place of the visible and objective offerings of tobacco, eagle feathers, moccasins, etc. An inward acceptance, a "concentration of the mind," as they put it, had likewise been part of the old Winnebago requirements, but not the exclusive requirement, for success. Here in the peyote it was the exclusive one, and that did away with the whole sacramental system. This insistence upon inward acceptance brought with it the idea of inward purification. Outward purification was well known to Rave, for it was an essential ingredient in the old religion. Inward purification, however, meant a purging of evil thoughts, desires, and compulsions. Rave may be dramatizing the extent of his demoralization and the degree to which he was dominated by murderous thoughts, but demoralization unquestionably did mean in his case, as in that of many of his contemporaries, a compulsive emergence of desires and impulses that in his calmer moments must have overwhelmed him with horror. The compulsive desire to kill his brother and sister was just such a one. When the euphoria that followed upon his partaking of the peyote, so admirably described—"Thus I sat, very quiet. And then I beheld the morning star and it was good to look upon. The light was good to look upon"—came upon him, in his exalted state he argued that it had been the inward evil which had caused his outward viciousness. Thereupon he turned all his efforts to stressing this inward evil. Evil desires became disease. The outward manifestations of a disease and its inward causation were unimportant. "Bring whatever desires [i.e., evil ones] you possess along with you, and then come and eat this medicine," he states. Naturally he never attained consistency in this doctrine of inward evil. It is not difficult, then, to see how he could claim that all the feelings and beliefs connected with the old religion were evil and how in this fashion the whole old background was completely negated.

In some such way do I picture the evolution of Rave's antagonism to the old background and it is because of this tremendous insistence upon the inward purification to be obtained only by direct eating of the peyote and experiencing its effects that he was so urgent about prospective adherents trying the peyote themselves and not being content with merely hearing about it.

It is, of course, impossible to discuss Rave's document in all its various phases here and I shall accordingly limit the remainder of my remarks to two points: how large do the pagan elements loom in the accounts of other adherents of the cult, and how are we to account for this? Finally, we shall briefly touch upon the attempt that was made to give the new cult its proper historical setting.[7]

The first document is that of Oliver Lamere. It was obtained in 1908. He there describes the importance of the family to which Rave belonged,

---

[7] The pertinent documents are all published in my monograph on the Winnebago before alluded to, and it is from these that I am quoting.

Rave's participation in all the old Winnebago ceremonies except the Medicine Dance, his immoral life and his uneasiness, and his demoralization, typified by his continuous wandering. He gives 1901 instead of 1893 as the date of Rave's conversion. The details of his conversion are not stressed. I am certain, however, both from my personal knowledge and from passages in Lamere's account, that Rave had already "codified" his description and that all the important adherents must have heard it. Lamere may not have, for he was not, at that time, a person of prominence in the ceremony. He states emphatically that Rave had very few converts at first, and that in the beginning there was very little religion connected with the new ceremony, people eating the peyote because of its peculiar effects upon them. He adds, "Nevertheless these peyote people preached good things and gradually lost all desire for intoxicating drinks or for participating in the old Winnebago ceremonies. Then Rave began to do away with the old Indian customs." Drunkenness and participation in the old Indian life are here coupled together. In 1905–1906, according to Lamere, the Bible was introduced by Hensley. Hensley is pictured in the same terms as Rave, as a reformed drunkard and wanderer. It is as a follower of Hensley, when Hensley's influence was at its highest, and just before his break with Rave, that Lamere speaks. Yet although this account is shot through with references and quotations from the Bible, the details of the ritual and all the cardinal doctrines are those Rave formulated, even if the phraseology is no longer his. It should be recollected that both Hensley and Lamere had gone to Carlisle and were one-quarter white.

According to Lamere, Rave begins with a prayer called "Turning oneself over to the care of the Trinity." This is simply a rendering of Rave's phrase, "I give myself up to you entirely," reinterpreted probably by Hensley. The ceremonial unit is that characteristic of all the old Winnebago rituals. The baptism Lamere mentions was certainly not introduced by Rave. He has no reference to it. Yet in 1908 and in 1912 he was definitely practicing it.[8] I should like to hazard the suggestion that he accepted it so readily because it was essentially merely an expansion of the typical Winnebago procedure which he had followed in the conversion of his wife. The formula of baptism as given by Lamere is that which Rave actually used, except that it should read, "God, his Son, and

---

[8] "John Rave baptizes by dipping his hand into a diluted fusion of peyote and rubbing it across the forehead of a new member, saying, 'I baptize thee in the name of God, the Son, and the Holy Ghost, which is called God's holiness.' "—*Ibid.*, p. 395.

his Holiness." There is no attempt at rendering Holy Ghost. I think the difficulty was, first, that a ghost could not be thought of as holy, and, second, that a deity, according to Winnebago conceptions, could never die and therefore could have no "ghost." Rave and Hensley could easily have surmounted this difficulty had they fallen back upon the widespread Winnebago belief in reincarnation. But this belonged to the old background and accordingly was taboo. The meetings were always begun at night, an old Winnebago practice, but Hensley found Biblical authority for it.

We did, however, find evidence that He [Christ] had been out all night in prayer. As it is our desire to follow as closely as we can in the footsteps of Christ, we hold our meetings at night. Then, too, when we pray, we wish to get away as far as possible from earthly things, and the night is the best time, for then we are not likely to be bothered by anything.[9]

The cardinal doctrine, the interpretation of what constitutes acceptance of the peyote, is manifestly Rave's, although the phraseology is patently Hensley's. For instance, Lamere says,

If a person who is truly repentant eats peyote for the first time, he does not suffer at all from its effects. But if an individual is bull-headed, does not believe in its virtue, he is likely to suffer a good deal. . . . If a person eats peyote and does not repent openly, he has a guilty conscience

[9] *Ibid.*, p. 396.

which leaves him as soon as the public repentance has been made.[10]

So, too, is his interesting attempt to prove the divinity of the peyote. "We claim," he insists, "that some earthly things can have the virtue of God, for instance the Bible, which is entirely made up of earthly material—the ink, the paper, the cover—yet it has survived the ages."[11] The next document is that of Albert Hensley. In it Rave's name is not even mentioned. It was obtained after Hensley had broken with Rave and I presume that the complete silence about the founder of the cult was the reflection of this very recent antagonism. According to all informants, there had been no ill will between them until then. Hensley's extreme susceptibility to suggestion, upon which he himself comments, would indicate that he had, at one time, been a loyal adherent of Rave and that, like all the other peyote people, he had been dominated by Rave's personality. He felt himself, however, an innovator and prophet in his own right and he had ample justification for regarding himself as the former.

What his life had been like as a young man the following quotation will indicate.

[10] *Ibid.*, p. 395.
[11] *Ibid.*, p. 396.

I am 37 years old. It was 37 years ago that my mother gave birth to me in an old-fashioned reed lodge. When I was a year old she died and my grandmother took care of me. I had come into the world a healthy child, but bad luck was apparently to pursue me, for when I was 7 years old my grandmother died. Then my father took care of me. At that time he began to be a bad man; he was a drunkard and a horse thief. He would frequently get into trouble and run away, always taking me along with him, however. On one occasion we fled to Wisconsin, and there we stayed two years. We got along pretty well, and there my father married again. By his second wife he had three children.

After a while he got into trouble again, and misfortune followed misfortune. People were killing each other, and I was left alone. If at any time of my life I was in trouble it was then. I was never happy. Once I did not have anything to eat for four days. We had fled to the wilderness, and it was raining continually. The country was flooded with high water, and we sat on the top of a tree. It was impossible to sleep, for if we went to sleep we would fall off into the water, which was very deep. The shore was quite far away. As we were prominent people, we soon heard that my father had been freed. We were very happy, and went back to our people.

At that time a young man named Young-Bear was starting for Nebraska, and he said that he would take me along. I was very happy. So in that manner I was brought to this country. Here I have had only happy days. When my father got married every one disliked me. When I worked I was working for my father, and all the money I earned I had to give to him.

After a while I went to school, and although I liked it I ran away and then went to school at Carlisle. I wanted to lead a good life. At school I knew that they would take care of me and love me. I was very shy and lacked a strong character at that time. If a person told me to do anything I would always obey immediately. Everybody loved me. I stayed there six months. I was also taught Christianity there. When I came back to my country the Episcopalian people told me that they wanted me to be diligent in religious matters and never to forsake the religion of the Son of God. I also desired to do that. I entered the church that we had in our country and I stayed with them six years.

At that time the Winnebago with whom I associated were heavy drinkers, and after a while they induced me to drink also. I became as wicked as they. I learned how to gamble and I worked for the devil all the time. I even taught the Winnebago how to be bad.

After a while they began eating peyote, and as I was in the habit of doing everything I saw, I thought I would do it, too. I asked them whether I could join, and they permitted me. At that time I had a position at the county commissioner's office. I ate the peyote and liked it very much. Then the authorities tried to stop the Indians from eating peyote, and I was supposed to see that the law was enforced. I continued eating peyote and enjoying it. All the evil that was in me I forgot. From that time to the present my actions have been quite different from what they used to be. I am only working for what is good; not that I mean to say that I am good.

After that I married and now I have three children, and it would not have been right for me to continue in my wickedness. I resolved that thereafter I would behave as a grown-up man ought to behave. I resolved never to be idle again and to work so that I could supply my wife and children with food and necessities, that I would be ready to help them whenever they were in need. Here in my own country would I remain till I died. This [Peyote] religion was good. All the evil is gone and hereafter I will choose my path carefully.[12]

Apparently Hensley had become a good Christian, and it is both interesting and illuminating to realize that the man who was fundamentally to transform the Peyote cult and to overwhelm it with Christian elements was essentially a Christian convert to the Peyote, not an adherent of the old Winnebago background or a Peyote worshipper who was secondarily introducing Christian elements. Indeed, it is because he was a convert to the Peyote from Christianity that his hostility was directed not toward the old background but toward the official Christian churches. For Hensley the Peyote was a personal katharsis that made him a good man in the accepted American sense of the term, something which his adoption of Christianity had not done.

I do not think it possible to overestimate the fact that Hensley was really a Christian who had adopted the Peyote religion, for this is the key to the ease with which he was enabled to introduce the Bible, the specifically Christian use of the Bible, the specifically Christian interpretations and exegesis. Neither Rave nor any other member

[12] *Ibid.*, pp. 397–398.

of the peyote group could have had the slightest
objection to so ardent a believer and so staunch a
defender of the sacred object, the peyote, introducing anything. Not even Rave had succeeded in
putting the case for the Peyote so well as this:

It is a true religion. The peyote is fulfilling the work of
God and the Son of God. When the Son of God came to the
earth he was poor, yet people spoke against him; he was
abused. It is the same now with the peyote. The plant
itself is not much of a growth, yet the people are talking
about it a good deal; they are abusing it, they are trying to
stop its use. When the Son of God came to earth the preach-
ers of that time were called Pharisees and Scribes. They
doubted what the Son of God said and claimed that he was
an ordinary man. So it is to-day with the Christian Church;
they are the Pharisees and Scribes, they are the doubters.
They say that this is merely a plant, that it is the work of
the devil. They are trying to stop its use and they are calling
it an intoxicant. But this is a lie. If they will but come and
see this ceremony they will realize this.[13]

Hensley, following Rave, insisted upon the necessity of a complete inward purification. Indeed, so
rigorously did he insist upon this point that he
went far beyond Rave's demands and contended
that no matter how completely a man had accepted
the truth of the Peyote religion, if his outward life
was evil, he had no right to membership in the
cult. It was precisely because he objected to a

[13] *Ibid.*, p. 400.

particular individual's being entrusted with a prominent position in the ceremonial that he and Rave parted company, Rave contending that it was the position that was sacred and the official's personal life, for the time being, immaterial, a characteristically old Winnebago conception. Hensley's objection represented an equally old and integral part of the Winnebago religious theory, for without the proper "concentration of the mind" no success was theoretically supposed to attend upon man's supplication to the spirits.

It is because he introduced so many Christian elements that it is all the more difficult to understand other aspects of Hensley's document. Why, for instance, did this ostensibly Christian convert to the Peyote find it necessary to elaborate and introduce what, to all intents and purposes, is an old-fashioned origin myth? Let me quote it:

Once in the south, an Indian belonging to the tribe called Mescallero Apache was roaming in the country called Mexico, and went hunting in the high hills and got lost. For three days he went without water and without food. He was about to die of thirst but he continued until he reached the foot of a certain hill, on top of which he could find shade under a tree that was growing there. There he desired to die. It was with the greatest difficulty that he reached the place and when he got there, he fell over on his back and lay thus, with his body stretched toward the south, his head pillowed against something. He extended his right arm to the west and his left arm to the east, and as he did this, he felt something cool touch his hands. "What is it?" he thought to himself. So he took the one that was close to his right hand and brought it to his mouth and ate it. There was water in it, although it also contained food. Then he took the one close to his left hand and brought it to his mouth and ate it. Then as he lay on the ground a holy spirit entered him and taking the spirit of the Indian carried it away to the regions above. There he saw a man who spoke to him. "I have caused you to go through all this suffering, for had I not done it, you would never have heard of the proper [religion]. It was for that reason that I placed holiness in what you have eaten. My father gave it to me and I was permitted to place it on the earth. I was also permitted to take it back again and give it to some other Indians.

"At present this religion exists in the south but now I wish to have it extended to the north. You Indians are now fighting one another, and it is for the purpose of stopping this, that you might shake hands and partake of food together, that I am giving you this peyote. Now you should love one another. Earthmaker is my father. Long ago I sent this gospel across the ocean but you did not know of it. Now I am going to teach you to understand it." Then he led him into a lodge where they were eating peyote. There he taught him the songs and all that belonged to this ceremony. Then he said to him, "Now go to your people in the north and teach them. I have placed my holiness in this that you eat. What my father gave me, that I have placed therein."[14]

[14] *Ibid.*, pp. 398–399.

Although this experience is attributed to a Mescallero Apache, it is really a very typical Winnebago myth. There are innumerable parallels for the theme of a man seeking death or even being accidentally lost and about to die in precisely such a fashion. The first part of the sentence beginning *It was with the greatest difficulty, etc.*, is lifted out bodily from an old myth. The latter part of the same sentence and the next few sentences, barring certain details, are merely a paraphrase of the opening of the most sacred of all Winnebago myths, the Origin Myth of the World and of the Medicine Dance, as told in the Medicine Dance. Such a phrase as *A holy spirit entered him* is, of course, not Winnebago in intent, although it would be possible to explain it in terms of the old Winnebago religious concepts. But what is amazingly old is the manner in which Christ appears to the Indian, the phraseology of his speech, and the equation of the peyote (*i.e.*, the object which the dying man has found) with tobacco in its old sacramental sense. Such phrases as *I have caused you to go through all this suffering* and *My Father [Earthmaker] gave it to me and I was permitted to place it upon the earth* can be found in any typical fasting experience. Similarly, it could be shown that the whole of what is contained in the first paragraph of this myth, with the exception of the last few lines, is but a transparent paraphrasing and condensation of certain episodes in the origin myth of the Medicine Dance referred to above. The finding of the peyote is again merely a substitute for the "sign" that, in the older fasting experiences, a spirit was supposed to leave as a visible indication of his presence and his blessing.

The symbolic interpretation of the whole incident might be taken to be either old or new. I am inclined to regard it as new because, although a marked tendency toward symbolism is found in many old Winnebago rituals, it is there fairly stereotyped, whereas it is a well-known ingredient of the Peyote cult wherever encountered.

Following the origin myth, Hensley attempts to explain what is manifestly an historical fact: the readoption by the Mescallero of a custom they had presumably once had and given up. The syncretism here is exceedingly interesting. We must bear in mind that this Mescallero Apache is, of course, really a Winnebago seeking blessings for the greatest of all Winnebago passions, success on the warpath. The phrase *They really ate too much of it* receives its full significance only when taken in conjunction with other phrases, such as *The leader began to think the medicine might harm them* and *The man did not know even at that time that a big war party was coming upon them.* It is then that we realize that we are here dealing with the customary tragedy which, according to the old Winnebago doctrine, overtakes all those who have fasted too long. From the perusal of this origin myth we are thus compelled to conclude that Hensley's knowledge of the old pagan background must have been much more extensive than he was willing to admit or than I had any reason at the time to suspect, and the question inevitably arises whether it is not legitimate to assume that, unwittingly, and despite all the Christian embellishments for which he is responsible, his conversion to the Peyote cult did essentially mean for him what it meant, in a much larger measure, for Rave—a return to the old culture.

The third document, that of John Baptiste, obtained in 1909, is that of a very lukewarm adherent. John Baptiste was a full-blood Winnebago of unusual intelligence who had received an excellent English education, which had not, however, in the least affected the hold which the old Winnebago background continued to have upon him. He was, unfortunately, a confirmed cynic and drunkard. Let me quote the short account that he gave me:

Among the Winnebago there is a man named Little-Red-Bird, and when he reached middle age he began to travel round the world and learn different Indian languages. He used to travel inland a good deal. Once he joined a circus and crossed the ocean. He felt so ill while crossing that he wanted to die. Suddenly a wind came up and he got very frightened. He did not know what to do. Then he prayed to Earthmaker. When he came to the other side of the ocean there he saw a big island and a big city [London], and in this last place they held their circus. The chief of that country [the king] he met there.

When he came back to his own people he told them that on the other side of the ocean the Thunderbirds did not thunder. All they did was to drizzle. There was no lightning either. As he crossed the ocean on his return it thundered and lightened.

When he came home he was very glad to see his relatives and he offered tobacco in thanksgiving.

Shortly after this he traveled again and came to a band of Indians who were eating peyote. It was his custom to try everything when he went visiting. He did not realize what he was doing when he ate this medicine, but he did it anyhow. After a while he began to think of his manner of life, and he felt that he was doing wrong. All the evil he had done he remembered. Then he prayed to God. Suddenly it occurred to him, "Perhaps I am the only one doing this." Then he looked around and watched the others, and he saw them praying in the same manner.

Not long after that he came home, taking with him some of the medicine. He knew it was holy. At home he offered tobacco to it and kept on eating it. Soon it cured him of a disease he had. He tried to induce some of the others to try it, but they refused. After a while a few tried it, and the peyote movement began to spread. All the old customs that they had been accustomed to observe they abandoned.

They gave up the Medicine Dance and the ceremonies connected with the clans. For that reason, therefore, the conservative people hated them, their own brothers and sisters hated them, for they had abandoned what were considered holy ceremonies.[15]

In the last paragraph of the foregoing document we are given some insight into the evolution of Rave's point of view. Baptiste tells that at first he offered tobacco to the Peyote and that it cured him of a disease. There is a simple statement to the effect that, after the movement began to spread, the old customs were abandoned, particularly the Medicine Dance and the clan ceremonies. As one might have expected from John Baptiste, he stresses the hatred that the conservatives felt for the new cult and the disruption introduced into family life.

As a final contribution to our understanding of the Rave document, I should like to discuss briefly three further statements, all of them exceedingly articulate as to what was implied in becoming a convert to the new cult. The first comes from a convert who could not have joined the cult much later than 1906. According to him, the belief in the Peyote implied the following:[16]

[15] *Ibid.*, pp. 396–397.
[16] RADIN, PAUL, "Autobiography of a Winnebago Indian," *University of California Publications in American Archaeology and Ethnology,* vol. 16, pp. 431–432, 1920.

What we do amounts to nothing, but we stop drinking.

Sick people get well.

We, your mother and I, became well after joining it, and we joined it because we were told it would do this for us.

We offer prayers to Earthmaker [God].

We cry when we feel happy.

We throw away all our medicines.

We give up all the blessings we have received in fasting and the belief in all the spirits who had appeared to us then.

We stop smoking and chewing tobacco.

We stop giving feasts.

We stop making offerings of tobacco.

We burn up our holy things.

We burn up our war bundles.

We burn up the medicine bags, even cut up the otter-skin bags.

We give up the Medicine Dance.

We claim that there is nothing holy except Earthmaker [God].

We claim that all the things that we are stopping are those of the bad spirit, that the bad spirit has deceived us.

We claim that there are no spirits who can bless except Earthmaker [God].

Here the whole Winnebago background has been given up by an old man who up to the time of his conversion was one of the pillars of the old order of things.

The second statement comes from a convert in 1909. To him the specific Peyote beliefs, etc., were all submerged in the new mission with which he had identified himself, *viz.*, to give me a complete account of the Medicine Dance.

That week there were four meetings, and I went to all of them and ate very much peyote. The fourth meeting was at the usual place, John Rave's house. I sat with Sam as usual. At night I became filled with peyote. All at once I heard a voice saying, "You are the one who is to tell of the Medicine Dance." And I thought that Sam was speaking to me, so I turned around and looked at him, but he hadn't said a word. Soon I realized that nobody near me had said anything, and I began to think, "Why should it be I? Why not one of the others?" I rather pushed the idea from me; but no sooner had I done so than I began to have a tired and depressed sensation. This passed all over me. I knew that if I got up with the sincere purpose of giving in to the power that was wanting me to speak of the Medicine Dance I should be relieved. However, for some reason, I know not why, I felt like resisting.

The next morning I asked to be baptized, and said that I would thereafter have nothing more to do with offerings to the spirits; that I would not give any more feasts; and that I would not have any more to do with the Medicine Dance. From that day on I quit all my old beliefs. I did not feel like saying all this, for indeed my heart was turned just the other way, but I couldn't help it, for I was filled with the peyote.

From that time on, at every meeting that I attended, I could not rid myself of the idea that I must tell of the Medicine Dance. At all such times a feeling of heaviness would come over me. There I would be with but one thing on my mind; should I, or should I not, tell of it? I did not want to, and thought of all sorts of excuses—that I was not a member of the Nebraska division, etc.

I was in this frame of mind while living with John Walker. There I received word that I would be wanted to tell of the Medicine Dance. From that moment I could not rest easy. I went to the barn and prayed and wept, asking that God might direct me. I went about but could not sit quiet. My wife stayed around me crying. As I stood there, someone drove up with a white team. Then I thought of all the unhappiness I would cause to members of the Medicine Dance if I told the secrets of the Medicine Dance; and I asked myself if it really would not be a sin to cause so much misery. The man who was driving the white team was John Baptiste, and he told me that I was wanted to tell of the Medicine Dance. I got ready and entered the buggy. I was still crying and praying. Then it occurred to me that I would like to see John Rave. No sooner had I thought of this than John Rave appeared in the road. I got out and shook hands with him and told him where I was going and for what purpose, and asked him what he thought of the matter. He began to thank me for the work I was going to do and said, "This is what we should try to do, to help one another and to work for our Creator." Then he thanked me again. Perfect happiness now came over me and I went to Sioux City and got married legally. From now on I was entirely filled with the desire to tell all that I knew about the Medicine Dance. "This must be the work assigned to me by the Creator," I thought; and yet I have rejected the idea all the time.

On Paul's last trip, although I had not finished the translation, I didn't care to have any more to do with it, and said that somebody else should finish the work, my excuse being that I was busy. So, as soon as I heard that Paul had come,

I packed up and hurried out west as quickly as possible, for I knew that he would bother the life out of me if he found me. However, no sooner had I reached the home of my friend than I was seized with an attack of rheumatism, with which I had never been afflicted before, and the next morning Paul appeared with a wagon to take me back to Winnebago. Now I know that the telling and the translation of the Medicine Dance is my mission in life, and I am willing to tell all to the full extent of my knowledge.[17]

Apparently with this man his conversion to the peyote was not complete until he had rid himself of his one consuming evil, his unwillingness to divulge the secrets of the Medicine Dance. The foregoing quotation demonstrates how beautifully and skillfully he had dramatized the whole event.

The third statement comes from a convert in 1906. To him, as to John Rave, it meant a true psychical integration and the peace that passeth understanding. To what kind of amazing speculation it could lead even in the hands of a person who knew practically no English, as in his case, the following will indicate:

Once we had a meeting at the home of a member who was sick. The sick would always get well when a meeting was held in their home, and that is why we did it. At that meeting I got into the "shaking" condition again. My body told [us] how our religion [Peyote] was an affair of Earthmaker's [God's] and even if one knew only a portion of it,

17 *Ibid.*, pp. 413–414.

one could still see [partake of] Earthmaker's [God's] religion.

Thus it went on talking. "Earthmaker [God], His Son [Christ] and His Holiness [the Holy Ghost], these are the three ways of saying it. Even if you know one [of these three], it means all. Every one of you has the means of opening [the road] to Earthmaker [God]. It is given to you. With that [your belief] you can open [the door to God]. You can not open it with knowledge [alone]. How many letters are there to the key [the road to God]? Three. What are they?" There were many educated people [there], but none of them said anything. "The first [letter] must be a K, so if a person said K, that would be the whole of it. But let me look in the book [the Bible] and see what that means," said the body. Then it [the body] took the Bible and began to turn the leaves. The body did not know where it was itself, for it was not learned in books. Finally, in Matthew, chapter 16, it stopped. There it speaks about it. "Peter did not give himself up" [it says]. "For a long time he could not give up his own knowledge. There [in that passage] it says Key." That is the work of Earthmaker [God]. At least so I understand it. He made use of my body and acted in this manner, in the case of the peyote.[18]

Let us now turn to the attempts made to give the new cult an historical perspective. In Hensley's account we saw how he used an old origin-myth formula in order to naturalize the ceremony more specifically among his people, and how he traced its history before the Winnebago received it from

[18] *Ibid.*, pp. 411–412.

the Oto. It was not the possession of an unusually well-developed feeling for history that guided him in this matter, but the theory that the Winnebago were, in a fashion, the elect of God, to whom had been entrusted the true meaning of the Peyote and the duty of spreading it among other people. Assuredly both these doctrines had emanated from Rave.

The desire to develop a pedigree was, however, very strong, and as a result older prophecies were reinterpreted to fit into the Peyote revelation. This was particularly true of what, according to tradition, the famous Shawnee prophet had taught the Winnebago. What purports to be the account of his teaching is really a hodge-podge, including reminiscences from all the contacts which the Winnebago had had with the whites for the last two hundred years.[19] I suspect that this document looked quite different before it had been subjected to reinterpretation by some member of the Peyote. As it now stands, some of the resemblances to the Hensley document are startling. As in the case of the Peyote, a powerful herb that had belonged to a number of famous Winnebago was lost in the hills. Although the account I received is somewhat confused on this point,

[19] *Ibid.*, pp. 69–74.

I think the inference is plain enough, that the peyote is this lost medicine. According to this document, the lost herb had once belonged to a well-known Winnebago named Dog-Head, and he had received it from an even more famous Winnebago named Large-Walker. Dog-Head gave it to his son Small-Snake, presenting it to him with a speech which is an excellent blend of the old and the new:

> Then Dog-Head blessed them with a powerful medicine that he possessed. "My son [he was addressing Small-Snake], if I were to induce you to join the Medicine Dance, why that honor would perish with your death. Now they say that a man named Large-Walker had a vision in which he was blessed by a loon. The loon blessed him, saying, 'Large-Walker, I also bless you with this [medicine]. When I work for the chief and when I sweep his lodge, I sweep all the bad things outside. It will be the same with this medicine. If a person partakes of something bad, he will not die, no matter how bad it is, but, on the contrary, he will live. Now when you wish to use this medicine, pour some tobacco for me and I will smoke it.' Then he looked at the loon and the loon had something growing out of his back. That is what he was referring to. Then the loon said again, 'When you want to dig it, don't dig it right away [*i.e.*, without performing the proper rites]. You must offer a white feather, a white deerskin, red feathers, and tobacco. Then you can dig it. If you make these offerings, you will never fail in anything. With this I bless you [this herb], and no one else in the world will know it.'"

This is what Dog-Head told Small-Snake: "As long as your posterity lasts, so long can you use this medicine. If I had given you clothes, when they were worn out, that would be the end of them. Your father spoke to me in your behalf and that is why I am giving you this medicine." Dog-Head told the truth, for even to the present day this medicine is being used. It is a purgative and a valuable medicine.

When the Winnebago returned, the possessor of the medicine was careless and placed it in a hole in a cliff. When he came back for it it could not be found. He looked all over for it but it was apparently gone. Then they said, "We should not have done this. We should look before acting." Indeed, nowhere did they ever find it afterwards.[20]

The Shawnee prophet's injunction: "Let the people give up the customs they are now observing and I will give them new ones," might almost have been uttered by Rave.[21] That such appeals struck on sympathetic ears is evidenced by the statement that some of the Winnebago threw away their war bundles. But this is not what the prophet had meant, the author of our document somewhat lamely adds. The figure of the Shawnee prophet, in this document, is, in fact, somewhat of a composite picture of the four great culture heroes of the Winnebago. For instance, he forgets his mission completely the first time, is recalled by the creator,

[20] *Ibid.*, pp. 72–73.
[21] *Ibid.*, p. 69.

reprimanded, and sent back again. On his first appearance, when he had been completely misled by the devil, the Winnebago accepted his distorted teachings immediately. On his second appearance, however, when he told the truth and when, as the author says, "He came to tell the mysteries," no one would believe him. "He was just getting crazier all the time," the document states. He is credited, however, with giving the doubters a number of evidences of the truth of his contentions so that they accepted him. There is an interesting passage to the following effect:

One day they told him that the whites were coming. After a short time they said, "They are still coming. There are very many of them." The lookouts were always watching and they saw them coming. Then the prophet said, "When they come, listen to them, and when they sleep we will attend to them." Now the whites had come; they had to cut through the roads to come. When they were near, one of their number came over to ask where they could camp and they were told to camp right there. In the night, when they were asleep, they shot at them. They were half asleep and they ran away without their weapons. A tribe of Indians was just then going down the stream and these shot at the whites, too. Then they turned back and the commander had the bugle blow and called them to themselves. Then they took their guns and fought. Many Indians were killed. The one who had led the Winnebago over was killed in this battle.[22]

[22] *Ibid.*, p. 72.

Our Peyote revisionist wishes us apparently to draw two inferences from the foregoing incident: first, that the Shawnee prophet instead of teaching the true mysteries allowed his egotism to triumph, and, second, that the whites could not be ejected. Rave assumed this as an axiom. For him the problem was simply, "How can we adjust ourselves to the white man's ways and still exist?" That had been a burning problem for at least two hundred years and there had always been at least two parties, the die-hards and the compromisers. Rave sided with the compromisers. Not so very long before his advent there had been a prophet named Noise-Thunder who had taken precisely the other side, and who had warned his fellow Winnebago that an evil thing had come upon them that would make them forget their own ways. He had specifically cautioned his fellow Winnebago against adopting the life of the white man, lest they die. To this our Peyote commentator adds:

Now, he was mistaken in that. "The Creator has given two plates and they are getting empty. He gave the men a plate for them to fill and the women a plate for them to fill. The women's plate is empty." He meant that the Creator had made men to hunt and the women to dig the soil and raise vegetables and that the latter were not doing it. That is what he meant by saying that their plates were empty. Noise-Thunder insisted that this was the white man's fault; he thought that we were being weakened by the white man's food. Quite a number of people believed him. "The birds eat what was provided for them to eat, game and vegetables, and the whites eat what was provided for them. Why should we not eat what was provided for us?" He was right, but then the Creator also created the food that the whites are eating. We are now getting accustomed to it and are getting strong on this food.[23]

This die-hard attitude was admirably put by another conservative, a contemporary of Rave, as follows:

This medicine is one of the four spirits from below, and for that reason it is a bad thing. These spirits have always longed for human beings and now they are getting hold of them. Those who use this medicine claim that when they die they will only be going on a long journey. But that is not the truth, for when they eat peyote they destroy their spirits, and death to them will mean extermination. If I spit upon the floor, the sputum will soon dry up and nothing will remain of it. So death will be for them. I might go out and preach against this doctrine, but it would be of no avail, for I certainly would not be able to draw more than one or two people away from this spirit. Many will be taken in by this medicine; they will not be able to help themselves in any way. The bad spirit will certainly seize them.[24]

It would seem, then, that both the Peyote worshippers and the defenders of the older cults strove valiantly to view the new religion in its

[23] *Ibid.*, p. 74.
[24] *Ibid.*, p. 426.

proper perspective and place it in its proper setting. I hope I have made clear by this commentary and exegesis how illuminating a document may become, how specific and how vivid are the multiple interrelations between an old culture and a newly introduced cult, and what reality some of the intangible and unformalized aspects of culture assume when seen through the mirror of an actual man's heart and brain and not through the artificial heart and brain of the marionettes with which Boas and Sapir and Kroeber operate. And surely, even if all I have contended proves to be completely unacceptable, there still remains the document for them to interpret better and more profoundly.

II. The Interpretation of the Myth: The Chief's Daughter and the Orphan[25]

In the necessarily short analysis of the myth which I shall give here, I shall attempt to indicate how much of the present cultural background is reflected, how much is omitted, and how the deviations are to be interpreted. Our first task must be to characterize the myth stylistically and to place it. That is comparatively easy, for it belongs to a fairly widespread type, which I shall designate

[25] RADIN, PAUL, "Literary Aspects of Winnebago Mythology," *Journal of American Folklore*, 1926, pp. 27-33.

as the village-origin myth. A hero, either disguised as an orphan or exhibiting strange and unusual traits, saves the village from threatening disaster. How old this type of myth is, it would be difficult to say. The presumption must be, however, that it antedates the Winnebago contact with the whites, for it obviously belongs to a period when the Winnebago were living in distinct and well-delimited villages. The stylistic deviations of our particular myth from this general type are considerable. There is only the slightest suggestion that the hero has come on his usual mission of succoring a village in distress, and the test theme so prominent in all village-origin myths is subordinated to a marked and persistent romantic *motif*. Such a *motif* occurs among the Winnebago in only one other myth or group of myths, those referring to the attempts of a bereaved husband to recover his dead wife from spirit land. Both in content and in stylistic elaboration, we may then surmise that this story has been greatly influenced by the former. This we may safely predicate, even if, as in our myth, there is no actual journey to the spirit land.

I base my assumption that we are here dealing with a village-origin myth on the following passage:

One day the man said to his wife, "Only for a number of years does my father expect me to stay here, and I am going home now. But I will not die as human beings die. I will simply go away." Thus the young man spoke. His wife cried so much that he told her, "Go and ask your old folks whether they will permit you to leave them. If they think they will be able to endure your absence and that they will not miss you, then you may come along with me. Go over and ask them." Then the woman went to her parents and asked them. "My daughter! my daughter! We have hardly seen you again, and you want to go away so soon. We shall feel very bad again."—"Father, you will always be able to see me and I shall be able to help you at all times." The old folks thanked her and they said again, "Daughter, as it is your wish, you may go with our son-in-law. We were very glad to see you again but nevertheless you may go with him. Your son, when he grows up will surely be like his father; he will kill plenty of game and he will go on many warpaths. If it should go hard with him, you will surely come and help him."

That same night, when the people were all asleep, a wolf howled in the east and shortly after a wolf howled from the direction of the spring, and another wolf howled in the west and still another howled in the south. Thus it was. The man went out and the woman followed him. She could not help it. The people in the village knew of it but they did not follow them. The orphan and his wife were wolves. Earthmaker had made a wolf and he was the father of this boy. Now he was going home. They are under the earth. When the people fast, the wolves underneath the earth bless them. [They are the orphan and his wife.] Thus it is said.[26]

The transformation from the accepted ending of a village-origin myth has been great. Such a pas-

[26] *Ibid.*, p. 33.

sage as *Only for a number of years does my father expect me to stay here and I am going home now* would have read something like this: *But now I must return. I was sent to help you against your enemies.* It would not have been necessary for the hero to say *I will not die as human beings die. I will simply go away,* or to motivate his wife's leaving with him. The same holds for other details, and we are thus forced to the conclusion that the original purpose which such an origin myth was supposed to fulfill has either been forgotten or that the myth has been consciously reinterpreted. I incline definitely to the latter hypothesis because I think it could be reasonably well demonstrated that the character and the events in the myth have been altered almost beyond recognition: that the chief's daughter was not originally a benevolent and kind figure, that her people did not leave the village in charge of the orphan for the reasons given, and, finally, that the tests to which the hero submits were not originally endured for the very romantic purpose stated, *viz.,* of rescuing the girl from spirit land, but to destroy her evil powers and to conquer her. We must, however, leave this proof for another occasion. Let us instead ask ourselves what explanation is to be offered for this change from a typical village-origin myth to a bourgeois idyll. In the absence of actual historical documents we are admittedly skating on thin ice in suggesting even a tentative explanation. That myths are specifically reinterpreted we know, but, apart from innocuous generalizations, little attempt has ever been made, here in America, to inquire into the specific factors that may be involved in such change and reinterpretation. I myself was content for a long time to ascribe such change and reinterpretation almost exclusively to literary and artistic considerations. That would, however, account only for part of the transformation. It has been pointed out above that documents barely a hundred years old can be fundamentally altered in the interests of a new dominant movement. There is, likewise, ample evidence to prove that old and sacred mythological figures like the Earth deity and the culture hero Hare have among the Winnebago been definitely reinterpreted and revaluated from the viewpoint of the adherents of the Medicine Dance. Nor is there any reason for believing that this has been recent, that, in fact, it may not have occurred as long as three hundred years ago. Now can we draw any inferences as to what causes may have led to the radical alteration of the myth under consideration?

From the point of view of recent Winnebago culture there are some strange facts in this myth. We have the daughter of the tribal chief falling in love with an orphan, and seriously playing with the idea of asking him to marry her. We have her dying of a broken heart, and the chief actually leaving the village in which his lodge is situated, *i.e.*, the semisacred lodge of the tribe, because he cannot bear to be reminded of his loss. Ghosts seem to have no terror for the living. What should take place in the land of the dead, in the ghost village, takes place in the land of the living. Assuredly all this is not simply a reflection of a time when women courted men, when a village was abandoned because a death had occurred in it, and when ghosts were not feared. The stressing of facts so contrary to present Winnebago thought and custom rather suggests that the author-raconteur wished to create a completely ideal and unreal world, a kind of Land of Cocaigne where there was no breath of that all-consuming passion of the Winnebago, war, and where, as he puts it, people lived in peace without troubles. Surely one lives in peace without troubles in the spirit land. But our poet wished to visualize such a world here on this earth. So he created this romantic idyll, transferred as much of the current conception of the spirit land as would fit into his picture to a mundane reality, robbed ghosts of their maliciousness and creepiness, and preached the gospel that romantic affection had a right to be heard. All this is at direct variance with accepted Winnebago life and theory. Just as the old Winnebago background, however, could be mercilessly pilloried in such satires as the Trickster cycle, so it could be challenged by a picture of what life would look like, if a woman could marry the man of her own choice without the intermediation of her parents or her older brothers, if parents could give expression to their natural feelings without having to clothe them in set forms, and if there were no war. And it is just because Winnebago society could not tolerate such a direct challenge that myths of this type, it may be surmised, were not officially popular, and that few of them survive.

Such is my explanation of the stylistic peculiarities of this interesting myth. What diverse ingredients have gone into its making is a chapter by itself and does not belong here.

So much, then, for its pertinent literary aspects. The stylistic analysis has also answered the question of why certain fundamental traits of Winnebago culture have found no reflection in the myth. The question that still remains to be answered, however, is the significance of certain customs mentioned therein. We have a marked intimation of the existence of a stratified society—a special term even being applied to the chief's daughter—an unusual mode of burial, etc. Whether such details are of any value in dating the myth or not, they manifestly belong to a stratum of Winnebago customs that no longer exists and which, from the evidence of other documents and of archaeology, we know is extremely old. Even then, if we refuse to commit ourselves as to the age of the document, in whole or in part, we have a right to conclude that the author was well aware of the fact that the Winnebago had at one time possessed customs since lost. And it is really of subsidiary importance, as far as the facts themselves are concerned, whether they have been injected here because of an archaizing tendency or not.

III. Interpretation of the Legend: How the Winnebago First Came into Contact with the French[27]

This legend purports to be primarily an account of the first discovery of the Winnebago by the whites, to which a secondary theme has been added, viz., the origin of a specific half-breed family, the Decoras. It is manifestly a medley of the most varied elements. In its present form I suspect it is not very old—possibly not more than a hundred years, if that. The first part may even have been formulated within the last two generations. It falls naturally into four parts, an impro-

[27] The Winnebago . . . . , pp. 65–69.

vised description of the salient traits of Winnebago
culture, a mythical account of the origin of tobacco,
the first appearance of the French and the manner
in which they were welcomed, and, finally, a very
short passage bringing the descendants of one of
these Frenchmen into relation with the Decora
family. The first part runs as follows:

The Winnebago originated at a place called Red Banks,
Green Bay, Wisconsin. They had no tools to work with at
that time. All they had were bows and arrows and a fire-
starter. They had no iron, and if they saw a stone that was
naturally sharpened in any way it was considered sacred
and they offered tobacco to it. They had tobacco from the
beginning. It was their most valued possession.

They fasted and became holy. The greatest honor was to
be a brave man, and for that reason they did nothing but
go to war. They were prepared for war at all times. They
tried to obtain war honors. They wished to go to war all
the time and kill many enemies. If a person fasted and went
without food for a long time, gave offerings of tobacco
often, and was then blessed by the spirits, then it would be
very hard to kill such a person in battle. The people knew
that such powers could be obtained, and that is why they
did these things all the time.

They gave many feasts. When a person gives a feast,
then he offers the spirits tobacco and asks in return that
their weapons be sharper than those of their enemies [*i.e.*,
that he kill an enemy and escape unharmed]. That is why
they used to give so many feasts, that they might be vic-
torious in war. They make offerings to the war spirits, and

if these then bless them they will become great warriors. They desired greatly to obtain these blessings.[28]

The simplicity of the material culture this passage would imply is borne out by many other documents, just as is the rôle played by war, fasting, and tobacco. That war should be so tremendously glorified at the expense of everything else needs some explanation, I feel. Warfare was unquestionably the dominant ideal of the old Winnebago culture. Its glorification at the expense of other dominant trends of their civilization is, however, to be ascribed to two tendencies: first, the natural desire of the modern Winnebago, living in a degenerate time, to unduly exalt the military prowess of his ancestors, and, second, to the directly opposite desire, that of comparing the endless strife of the old days with the calm and peace of white civilization. The concluding paragraph shows very clearly that our document voices the point of view of those Winnebago who insisted that the old culture must be given up. "The ways of the white man are the best," we are told.

The second part of the document contains the accepted Winnebago theory of the sacramental significance of tobacco. This is the account:

[28] *Ibid.*, pp. 65–66.

Tobacco is the greatest possession they have. After Earthmaker created all things he created man. Man was the last of the created objects. Those created before were spirits, and he put them all in charge of something. Even the smallest insects are able to foresee things four days ahead. The human beings were the least of all Earthmaker's creations. They were put in charge of nothing, and they could not even foresee one day ahead. They were the last created and they were the poorest. Then Earthmaker created a weed with a pleasant odor and all the spirits wanted it. Some were almost certain that it would be given to them. They would each think to themselves, "I am going to be put in charge of that, for I am one of the greatest spirits in the world." Then the Creator said, "To all of you [spirits] I have given something valuable. Now you all like this weed and I myself like it. Now this is the way it is going to be used." Then he took one of the leaves and mashed it up. Then making a pipe he smoked it and the odor was pleasant to smell. All of the spirits longed for it. Then he gave each one of them a puff. "Now, whatever [the human beings] ask from me and for which they offer tobacco, I will not be able to refuse it. I myself will not be in control of this weed. If they give me a pipeful of this and make a request I will not be able to refuse it. This weed will be called tobacco. The human beings are the only ones of my creation who are poor. I did not give them anything, so therefore this will be their foremost possession and from them we will have to obtain it. If a human being gives a pipeful and makes a request we will always grant it." Thus spoke Earthmaker.[29]

This account of how human beings came into control of tobacco is clearly a secondary rational-

[29] *Ibid.*, p. 66.

istic interpretation: the enunciation of a religious doctrine in a mythical dress. In the old myths the episode is described in an entirely different manner. We have, then, both here and in the first part, an attempt made by Winnebago to assess their past culture and to look at it objectively. Whether such objectivity would have been possible when the culture was fully functioning and the threat of annihilation not constantly present, it is difficult to answer. But the native evaluation given here, taken together with that found during the last generation in the various documents relating to the Peyote cult, and that implied in the Trickster cycle, proves conclusively that a critique of the native background was by no means uncommon and that it naturally found more articulate and fuller expression during tribal crises.

The historical portion of this legend represents events that can be fairly well controlled. The French discovered the Winnebago in 1634, and there is no reason to call seriously into question the description given of the first ship the Winnebago saw, the manner in which they greeted the French, etc.

The Frenchman referred to in the document was a Sieur De Cora, and his Indian wife's name was Glory-of-the-Morning. It is to the rôle she exercised as daughter of a chief and wife of a distinguished white man which so impressed itself upon the minds of visitors that Jonathan Carver could state in his account of his travels that the Winnebago were governed by a woman. The accuracy of the chronology of the events described here is quite surprising. We know that the younger son of De Cora— Tcaposgaga—was a mature man in 1729, and the hero of the Winnebago in their war with the Foxes. If we assume his birth to have taken place between 1670 and 1680, this would fit in perfectly well with the actual facts, for Sieur De Cora must have come to the Winnebago between 1650 and 1665. It is thus apparent that the Winnebago have retained an accurate memory of events for the last two hundred and fifty years, an assumption that most American ethnologists are inclined to deny categorically.

A number of very interesting consequences for Winnebago history flowed from the marriage of De Cora with Glory-of-the-Morning. To begin with, since the Winnebago reckon descent in the paternal line, what would be the status of the children? We know that the Decoras today belong to the Thunderbird clan, and from this we must infer that the children of Glory-of-the-Morning were placed in her clan, thus contravening one of the fundamental principles of Winnebago social organization. After this temporary irregularity, however, descent must have become patrilineal again. I do not have to point out what effect it must have had upon the older structure of Winnebago society to have two of its great heroes of the eighteenth century, Tclaposgaga and his older brother, with an equivocal status and yet in direct contact with the new ideas. Both sons of Glory-of-the-Morning, no matter how conservative their education might have been, would most naturally take sides with the compromisers in the internal struggle that now began as to the attitude to be taken toward the whites. Our account reflects very accurately the importance of having white blood. "A person with French blood has always been the chief. Only they could accomplish anything among the whites . . . His descendants are the most intelligent of all the people and they are becoming more intelligent all the time. What they did was the best that could be done."[30] So says the author of this document. But it was not only as intermediaries between the Winnebago and the whites, of course, that the early Decoras exercised so tremendous an influence. They must have introduced many white beliefs and customs or, at least, stimulated a new reading of the old ones. It is therefore of more than casual significance to our understanding of recent Winnebago culture to be

[30] *Ibid.*, pp. 68–69.

told that the older of Sieur de Cora's sons introduced a ceremony in honor of Earthmaker, devoted to the interests of peace as opposed to war. I obtained no information whatsoever about this specific ceremony. But since the Winnebago form of the Medicine Dance is so largely concerned with peace, and since Earthmaker plays so prominent a rôle in it, one naturally ponders over the possible influence Christian conceptions may have had in molding the ceremony into its present form. We could, however, go on interminably, with such an exegesis. All that I desire to emphasize here, as in the case of the other documents discussed, is the very great advantage that accrues to our understanding of a native culture when it is studied in this specific manner. I need not again stress its two great dangers: first, that it is easy for an ethnologist, lord as he must feel himself of all he surveys, to persuade himself that he knows more about a given culture than he actually does, and, second, that of falling into speculation for its own sake.

Chapter VIII
Theoretical Ethnology

Ethnology in the narrower sense of the term owes its origin to those studies of the customs and beliefs of mankind that began in the seventeenth century and received their clearest expression in the eighteenth, in the writings of Montesquieu and Rousseau. Ethnological theory was cultivated long before it ever dawned upon students that each primitive group had a very specific culture and a very specific history. For Bachhofen, McLennan, Morgan, and even Tylor, primitive peoples were only pawns in a much larger game. To the English amateur ethnologists and to Boas is due the credit for emphasizing the specific nature of primitive civilizations. Indeed, it was Boas who first attempted to stem the tide of those speculations on the history of mankind which had received a renewed impetus from the works of Tylor and the French sociologists. As a result, here in the United States, there has perhaps been an exaggerated distrust of theories of whatsoever description.

Indeed, this went so far at one time that history itself was in large measure regarded as a theory. The danger inherent in such an attitude toward theoretical speculations lies in the fact that, unless we have carefully analyzed the reasons for this abhorrence, *i.e.*, if it remains essentially on an emotional plane, we ourselves are apt to fall into such speculations without realizing it. The writings of Boas, Wissler, Kroeber, Sapir, Benedict, Mead are full of them, as I have tried to show in the previous chapters. Perhaps Kroeber is the only one of these ethnologists who recognizes, even if somewhat dimly, their existence. I do not wish to imply that Boas or Wissler or Sapir has not been aware of the problems that arise in all inquiries into human society. That would manifestly be incorrect. But I do mean to imply that they have not adequately recognized the premises underlying these problems, and that this failure or lack of interest of theirs is to be directly accredited to their somewhat emotional antagonism to what they term theoretical speculations for their own sake. For had they really made such an examination, they would have been forced to the conclusion that, in the main, there is no such gulf separating them from the theorists of England, France, or Germany as they fondly imagine. They will not have it so, however. Even Kroeber, who has indulged in general speculations on the superorganic and the significance—more precisely the lack of significance—of the individual in society, is inclined to be very indignant when the French sociologists hail him as one of their own. Thus whether they wish it or not, the students of primitive cultures have found it difficult to refrain from theorizing. Of late, indeed, there has been an increasing tendency, particularly in England, to relegate ethnographic descriptions, as such, to a secondary position. Malinowski, in the preface to a recent study by Fortune, pokes fun at the "fact-worshipping, theory-dreading, curio-hunting anthropologist" who would criticize Fortune for constantly mixing abstract descriptions of a theoretical nature with a statement of solid fact. Malinowski insists that it is the duty of the anthropologist "constantly to make inductive generalizations . . . to construct theories and draw up the charters of native institutions. In short, he has constantly to theorize in the field, theorize on what he sees, hears, and experiences."[1] Radcliffe-Brown would divide anthropology into two distinct planes, descriptive ethnology and comparative sociology, of which the latter is by far the more important. Mauss informs us that the writings of Malinowski demonstrate clearly

[1] FORTUNE, R., "Introduction," *The Sorcerers of Dobu*, p. xxiv, 1932.

the superiority of an observation when it is made by a real sociologist—a sociologist apparently being an individual who will rush in where an ethnologist fears to tread.[2] But why, may I be permitted to ask, does the study of ethnology always lead to sociological speculation? Is it inherent in the facts brought to light from primitive cultures? If ethnology is merely a general term which we apply to the study of primitive cultures, is the sociological or comparative approach more justified there than in descriptions of the great European or Asiatic civilizations? The evolutionists and the sociologists are in this respect far more consistent than many of the American ethnologists. They frankly state that primitive peoples are not on a par intellectually and culturally with civilized nations and that group tendencies and activities, present everywhere, can best be studied among them. We have pointed out in the previous chapters that the majority of the American ethnologists, although in theory they deny this contention, actually treat the data as though this were really the case. In fact, ethnological data would seem to have no theoretical significance unless we were disposed to grant the premise that the gulf between all aboriginal civilizations and any of the major

[2] *Essai sur le don.* . . . , p. 76, note 2.

European or Asiatic civilizations is of a fundamentally different nature from that which separates any of these major civilizations from one another. It is, of course, my contention that in ethnology we merely have descriptions of specific cultures, possessing no more and no other implications than the descriptions of Spanish or English or German cultures. Possibly many American ethnologists would in the main agree. But whereas I see no necessity for proving that culture is culture, they apparently feel that it is incumbent upon them to laboriously demonstrate that, among primitive people, we are dealing with human beings who think as we do, feel as we do, and act as we do.

Many of the problems with which the ethnological theorists and sociologists of the nineteenth century and early twentieth century dealt were thus those that developed from their original premise of a difference in the forms culture assumed among ourselves and aboriginal peoples, and in the differences of the type of mentality. By civilization, however, they understood predominatingly the culture of that small group of individuals who, for the last five to six thousand years, have been literate and to whom we must ascribe the great achievements in philosophy, mathematics, and the sciences. Depending in large measure upon their individual interests, these scholars attempted to account for the inequality in achievement between aboriginal peoples and this special class, either by assuming fundamental differences in the economic and social structure or by the extent and nature of the accumulated knowledge. Only Lévy-Bruhl predicated an inherent difference in mentality that was not dependent upon other causes. Unfortunately, so many of the older dogmas of the evolutionary hypothesis, disguised or undisguised, were included in their views that they have never adequately visualized or stressed those cardinal components of our culture that no aboriginal peoples possessed, *viz.*, a system of writing, and machines. Nor did they ever seriously inquire into the fundamental question of whether implicit human nature was expressed more clearly and simply in aboriginal cultures than in our own. Dogmatic and definite answers were frequently enough given to this last question. They did not, however, flow from an intensive study of the pertinent facts and situations but from preconceived premises and bias. Yet I feel very strongly that, fascinating as is the appeal of the developmental schemes that have figured so largely in ethnological theory, they are at best futile, and that, even if they possessed greater validity than I am disposed to give them, they would be built on sand, unless the questions

I have just mentioned have first been carefully and adequately investigated.

I propose, therefore, to omit from consideration here all those problems connected with the nature of the relation of the group to the individual, acculturation, etc., and to devote the remaining part of this chapter to some remarks on the inferences which a cursory study of the significance of the invention and use of writing and the invention of machines may have had upon the growth and direction of aboriginal cultures and mentality. Before doing so, however, it might be well to attempt some explanation for the unanimity with which the vast majority of ethnologists throughout the world and all sociologists agree that the individual has had no perceptible influence on the course of events. Upon the nature of the metaphysical elements involved in this argument I shall make no comment. It is one of the possible positions that can be taken, and, if consistently adhered to, it is irrefutable. But the proponents of this theory should then be willing to admit its metaphysical character and treat the inferences flowing from it simply as illustrations of a viewpoint. Strictly speaking, their task must be confined to a rigorous presentation of how society looks when regarded from this angle. They cannot, however, have it both ways. They cannot by assumption eliminate the problems that arise when the individual is allowed a definite but undetermined influence upon the course of events and yet discuss culture as though there existed a dichotomy between the individual and the group. Now the contention of the modern French sociologists Durkheim, Mauss, *et alii*, is that the individual is an abstraction, and, while it may be of practical advantage to operate with these abstractions, it is only society that really exists. I should have no quarrel with this viewpoint if it were consistently kept on a metaphysical plane. But this is not the case. For, to do so, the theorists would have scrupulously to refrain from ever being historical. The history of society would then have to be the unfolding of a prearranged plan. We have only to cast a cursory glance at Durkheim's famous book *Les formes élémentaires de la vie réligieuse* to realize that they have not really done so. Yet the concept that an integrated societal unit conditions another integrated societal unit is tacitly given up, unless each one is regarded as coming about by some fiat. A doctrine of change is impossible, for to introduce increments of growth implies either that the series of such increments is unlimited and unpredictable—and this must as a corollary introduce a real individual—or that these increments are artificially delimited, and this would take us back to the hypothesis of preformation and deprive chance of any intelligible meaning. Unfortunately, in culture the genetic problem always obtrudes itself. In the end the proponents of such theories are forced to operate with individuals as if they really existed. A large part of their presentation of cultural data, in fact, is concerned with an economic conditioning of this artificially hypothesized individual in order to show that he cannot significantly function as an individual. I cannot help feeling therefore that these scholars have attempted to apply to culture a type of reasoning that has applicability only in a theory of knowledge, that they have secondarily individualized a *synthesis a priori.*

What holds for Durkheim and Mauss holds to a far more pronounced degree for less rigorous logicians, such as Malinowski, Radcliffe-Brown, Lévy-Bruhl, and Kroeber. The attitude of Boas and so many of his school with regard to societal conditioning is so variable that it cannot be regarded as really embodying a consistent theory, a fact that has had fortunate consequences for ethnological field work.

Let us now return to the question of the invention of writing. What its practical significance was is clear enough. It enabled the past, or some mirror of the past, to survive into the present. Instead of

each generation's being constrained to expend
most of its energies and time in preserving the
memory of the deeds and words of their own and
the preceding generation, it gave those intellectually qualified an opportunity for more rationally
and artistically organizing the past achievements
of their people. As the mass of facts and knowledge
multiplied, it taught each generation due humility
and, at the same time, allowed large increments of
growth. As Goethe has so wisely and profoundly
remarked:

> Was du erebt von deinen Vätern hast
> Erwirb es um es zu besitzen.

Growth is possible, however, only when we have
intelligently and actively absorbed the past. For
this there is no opportunity, if each generation can
preserve this heritage only by bodily and mechanically repeating it lest it be forgotten. The invention
of writing freed us from the necessity of doing
only this. How concerned nonliterate man is that
the past of his fathers and his grandfathers should
not be forgotten, everyone who has had any contact with aboriginal peoples can testify. Faced with
the alternative of preserving this or embarking
upon something new, he has quite sensibly chosen
the former. It is thus erroneous to imagine that
he is innately any more conservative than civilized

man. He is simply more insistent upon preserving the continuity of his culture under unfavorable circumstances, in the only fashion possible. Where there is a written record, continuity, of course, exists without man's intervention. It is then an increased freedom and leisure that the introduction of writing bestowed upon man. That many, probably the vast majority of, thinkers, even after the introduction of writing, confined themselves to repeating the past is obvious. But they did not do so under constraint, and therein lies the fundamental difference. We cannot here pause to comment upon the nature of this difference and its possible effect on the direction and the growth of specific cultures. Instead, I would like to point out what it must have meant to those few thinkers and writers who were not content even with a conscious and artistic restatement of the past. Where there is no written record, personal views and personal interpretations tend very naturally to be lost in a corporate anonymity. But individualism and subjectivism are the very breath of creative expression and this individualism and subjectivism are quite definitely thwarted and stunted by the threat of impermanency and the absence of an audience. To have great thinkers and artists, there must be large audiences, or at least the possibility of large audiences. This holds as rigidly for the great as for the small thinkers and artists. If to the prospect of permanency and the larger audience we add the opportunity for privacy which the written medium allows, then all the conditions for an astounding increase in the technique of thought are given, an increase undreamed of before. But more than that. Where the records of previous thinkers and poets are permanently preserved, their successors can start where they left off. Philosophies do not have to be rethought in each generation or new analyses reattempted.

It is, however, not only in its effects upon this forward thrust that the importance of the invention of writing lies, but in its effects on the nature of man's mentality. Through it another reality developed, a written reality that was destined to be of incalculable significance for good and for evil, for growth and for retardation. As I have stated elsewhere,[3] the whole tendency of writing has been to elevate thought and thinking to the rank of the exclusive proof of the verities, to differentiate the subjective from the objective in a fashion unknown until then, and, since this was necessarily accomplished by a small group of individuals, the new world of the literate man became set off against that of the illiterate and

[3] *Primitive Man as Philosopher*, pp. 59–61, 1927.

that of the man of action. New conflicts and new
stresses arose, new disagreements and agreements,
adjustments and maladjustments. Problems of far-
reaching importance are contained herein which
the ethnologist, sociologist, and psychologist have
hitherto barely touched, and whose investigation,
I cannot help feeling, would yield a far richer
harvest of results than has been reaped from those
hitherto explored. It is here where the psychoanalysts have been illuminating, although it is
difficult to escape the conviction that, with the
possible exception of Jung, they have blundered
upon this field rather than come upon it properly,
with a true realization of what it contains.

Just as writing thus opened up a new realm by
increasing the sphere of man's activities, enlarging
his ego, and reconditioning and reaffirming the
past in a different manner, so, too, was a new path
revealed to him by the invention of the machine.
A machine, in its narrowest and truest sense, is a
mechanism devised by man which sets into action
another mechanism, either devised by man or
existing in nature. It is consequently to be carefully
distinguished both from those mechanisms that
are set into action by natural phenomena and those
transformations from one static condition to
another static condition that are brought about
by other mechanisms devised by man, *i.e.*, by

tools. The essential characteristic of a machine is that its end result be removed by more than one stage from its maker, and that the secondary activity engendered be of considerable duration. An illusion of self-acting is thus produced—of autonomous creativeness. This is completely foreign to aboriginal cultures. Indeed, the machine in this sense, as opposed to a mere tool or a mechanical device, was fairly foreign to all civilizations until the sixteenth century.

Much of what I have said about the effect of writing applies likewise to the effect of a machine upon cultural growth. It, too, added a new, if illusionary, reality, although the never-forgotten connection with its maker and its relative impermanence have prevented it from ever becoming as independent and as fixed as the thoughts translated into the written word. Its influence on the enlargement of the ego has been just as great, and on that of the enlargement of the external world far greater. Its multiple implications have been so frequently stressed that I can pass them by here and simply ask the student of culture to visualize what the world must have looked like when not even the most elementary machine existed and where, with the exception of the sail, no attempt had even been made to harness the ever-present forces of nature. And the difference between aboriginal cultures and our own is not merely that the former were barred from the consequences that flowed from the possession of a written language and machines, but that they were barred from the consequences that flowed from having both of them together.

Before concluding, let me refer briefly and superficially to what is perhaps the core of all investigations of culture: can we ever arrive at any satisfactory knowledge of what constitutes human nature? To say with Boas and so many ethnologists and sociologists that the cultural pattern hides this knowledge from us forever is a counsel of despair. Some significant light can surely be obtained, even if today the technique for this type of investigation has not as yet been perfected. Here again, I feel, that a psychoanalyst like Jung is on the correct trail. I doubt whether the picture of essential human nature that eventually emerges will be flattering to our understanding, although possibly there may be some solace in the fact that the history of civilization is largely the history of the diminution of the rôle played by our compulsive activities, the record of the enlargement of the sphere of awareness of the nature of our actions.

POSTSCRIPT

Ideological Themes in American Anthropology*

ARTHUR J. VIDICH

An underlying assumption of the approaches in vogue in American social anthropology in the years just before, during, and immediately after World War II was that the societies studied by anthropologists were qualitatively different from the advanced industrial societies to which they were frequently compared. Moreover, because of these qualitative differences, it was necessary for anthropology to develop approaches, methods, and concepts appropriate to the study of the primitive, tribal, and preindustrial world. Anthropologists were preoccupied with such themes as the concept of culture (Kroeber, White), the relationships between culture and personality (Linton, Kardiner, DuBois), cultural patterns and configurations (Benedict, Kluckhohn), the essential ingredients of folk culture (Redfield), and the rational

*Reprinted with permission of the editors of *Social Research*.

administrative application of anthropological knowledge to the governing of men (Leighton).

Neither Marx nor Weber in their work assumed the dichotomization of industrial, urban, Western society *and* primitive, preindustrial, and feudal societies. Their views focused on the growth and spread of industrial civilization, which destroyed the historical territorial limitations placed on culture and exposed all areas of the world to its central tendencies. These tendencies included not only bureaucratization, mass communications, political, military, and economic penetration, but also the exportation of science and its techniques and agents. Anthropology, like Christianity, was one of these tendencies and a part of the process of Western cultural hegemony and political penetration. This perspective is one that has not been utilized by American anthropologists, who have continued to see their subject matter as distinct from the central trends and tendencies of industrial civilization.[1]

[1]This, however, has not interfered with the field's self-definition as an all-embracing and universal science. Anthropology is defined as "the science of man," in time and in space. Space refers to the entire surface of the globe, and time refers to man from his prehominid past to the present. Thus anthropology is defined as including the cultural and physical history of man from his earliest beginnings to the present time. Physical anthropology involves the entire sweep of man's physical history and is linked to paleontology, biology, evolution, geology, and the other natural sciences. Archeology, as another branch of anthropology, includes the entire prehistoric record of mankind and is anthropology's connecting link to the philo-

In this chapter I wish to reverse the perspective usually employed by the anthropologist. I will not assume a dichotomy between the primitive, preindustrial world and the industrial world in which anthropology itself has developed. Instead, I will examine the ideological, intellectual, and historical factors that have governed the anthropologist's relationship with his own society and with the primitive world which as his subject matter. I will assume that modernizing tendencies have eroded many of anthropology's basic assumptions about itself and its subject matter, and I will try to indicate some implications that follow for the future of the craft. In order to set the stage for this discussion, let me sketch how anthropology's role within the United States has been influenced by its relationship to public policy since World War II.

sophical, social, and cultural sciences. Cultural history includes both the archeological and written history of mankind and embraces mankind's entire cultural legacy, including language, science, the arts, society, and everything else relating to man and his works. Social anthropology deals with the living cultural traditions and societies of the world in the full scope of their cultural legacy and social organization. In spite of, and perhaps because of, the vastness of the territory claimed, anthropologists have devoted little attention to the direct study of modern industrial society. This essay is limited to an evaluation of American social anthropology.

It may be argued that Marxist anthropology has not observed such distinctions, but as I will point out later, Marxism in American anthropology has been highly selective in its uses of Marx.

I wish to thank Joseph Bensman, Stanford Lyman, and Jay Mullen, whose helpful comments I have incorporated into this chapter.

Beginning with World War II, the concepts of culture, folk culture patterns of culture, modal personality, and administration were applied to the study not only of traditional primitive society but also of the modern nation-state. Ruth Benedict's book *Patterns of Culture,* which dealt with four primitive societies, was used as a model for her study of wartime Japan, as reported in her book *The Chrysanthemum and the Sword.* Margaret Mead studied New Guinea islanders in addition to Samoans in order to inform Americans of their own sexual biases and values. Clyde Kluckhohn combined administrative and research skills gained among the Navajo to establish the cold war Russian Research Center at Harvard University.[2] The conclusions of his book *Navajo Witchcraft* were thought to be applicable to an understanding of the social psychology of the populations of the nation-state. The modal personalities of such diverse peoples as the Alorese of Indonesia, American Plains Indians, and Americans of Plainsville, were cross-compared by Kardiner's psychological measurements. Yucatan and Tepotzlan places studied by Robert Redfield were defined as models of folk societies that retained their preindustrial fla-

---

[2]See Walter W. Taylor and others, *Culture and Life: Essays in Memory of Clyde Kluckhohn* (Carbondale: Southern Illinois Press, 1973), especially Talcott Parson's essay, "Clyde Kluckhohn and the Integration of Social Science," pp. 30–57.

vor and remained free of the negative features of modernization. Alexander Leighton's book, *The Governing of Men,* described the administration of "interned" Japanese Americans during World War II and suggested the feasibility of humane and rational application of anthropological knowledge for governance. These workers argued from the proposition that solutions to the problems of industrial society and the modern nation-state could be found by studying the primitives.

World War II and the cold war placed the United States at the center of the world stage at a time when anthropology was in a favored position among the academic disciplines to claim special knowledge of the cultures of the world, and consequently the demand for anthropological expertise rose rapidly. Job opportunities for anthropologists became available in the C.I.A., the State Department, the Operations Research Office, foreign area studies programs, centers for international studies, Russian research centers, language schools and institutes, and in academic departments designed to reproduce the trained corps of anthropologists necessary to fill the new positions. The economic support in depth for the new corps of anthropologists was supplied by acceptance of the belief that anthropological knowledge could be applied usefully and that anthropologists had a unique role to play in furtherance of national policy goals.

Cold war policies resulted in a great expansion in the volume of support at all levels of the profession. As a result the public image of anthropology was reinforced not only in the United States but in all the countries and provinces where overseas research was being conducted. Frequently in overseas territories, sociologists and political scientists were mistakenly thought to be anthropologists. This source of unexpected reinforcement of the anthropologists' image gave him the appearance of ubiquity.

When, beginning in the early sixties and with greater intensity throughout the decade, world public opinion was informed of the role of American social scientists in the covert activities of American intelligence agencies—Project Camelot, counter-insurgency research, and Vietnam—anthropologists were given undue credit as agents of American capitalism, imperialism, and big business. Because of their entrenched image as researchers in distant countries, anthropologists absorbed the weight of the world's negative opinion more than other scholars, and became more acutely aware of the reactions of their respondents.

Up to the time of the exposures that linked social science and intelligence agencies, anthropologists, unlike sociologists who primarily studied groups within their own society, had never had to be concerned with their subjects' reactions to their work because these subjects were not the constituency to which the profession addressed itself. Even the American Indians who lived within the borders of the United States were not thought of as an intellectual constituency by the anthropologists. While the Indians, as wards of the Federal government, were frequently assisted by anthropologists in their efforts to influence the policies of the Bureau of Indian Affairs, this political support defined the Indians as a welfare constituency in relation to the Federal bureaucracy. Historically, anthropology had addressed itself to its Western audiences and, because worldwide communications networks did not exist, was free to use the primitive world as a mine of information. In spite of the worldwide scope of anthropological researches, the profession prior to Camelot and Vietnam was not inclined to examine its own role in world affairs, and the issues of the ethics, morals, and values of "science as a vocation" were seriously raised some fifty years after Weber had written his essay.

Even before American anthropology was able to digest the consequences which stemmed from the recognition given to it by its new worldwide audiences, it was attacked from within by younger (and some older) radical students and professors who thought that anthropology should be an instrument for social change and revolution within the United States. These radical contingents within the ranks of academic anthropology were similar to those in other academic departments except for the fact that anthropological radicalism had become linked to Third World radicalism and domestic black nationalism. The term "internal colonialism" was used by Third World and black students to accuse the profession of occupational and intellectual discrimination. Blacks, Latin Americans, Africans, Pakistanis, American Indians, and others who previously had been seen as objects of research suddenly emerged as a political and intellectual force within the discipline itself. American anthropology suffered under this development because its effective leaders were not prepared to use science as an open political instrument within the political life of American society.

Events within the metropolitan country had broken the protective shield that anthropology had historically enjoyed by reason of the distance between its objects of study and the audiences to which it addressed itself within the metropolis. Societies that had previously seemed far removed were now part of big-power alignments or objects in international political struggles. The distance between aboriginal and metropolitan societies was almost erased.

The Breakdown of Ethnocentrism

Historically, the older primitive, tribal, folk, and peasant societies developed their central characteristics because they were spatially isolated and small. Their separation from other societies—supported by their own ideologies of ethnocentrism—and the density of their internal social (particularly kinship) relations allowed them to develop distinctive cultures that were supported and reinforced by the isolation and the ethnocentrism. It is perhaps true also that in the early stages of outside penetration the ethnocentrism of the primitive, tribal, and folk societies was enhanced as a defensive psychological reaction against an inability to absorb the initial shock of the penetration.

From the studies of earlier anthropologists, ethnocentrism was seen as a central element of social organization and a major psychological prop supporting the self-confidence of the tribesman and the primitive in their own institutions and in their own world views.

It is relatively easy to understand why the earlier anthropologists accepted the concept of the isolated society and utilized the idea of ethnocentrism to supply coherence and integration to the psychological and social structures of the societies they studied. However, acceptance of these concepts and ideas had far-reaching consequences because they also served as props to support the justifying ideology of the profession in the metropolis. So long as anthropology's data were thought to be the institutions and cultures of primitive societies, it became necessary to preserve an image of primitive society in spite of the penetration of the world by the industrial nations.

An image of primitive society thus became a key element in the professional ideology of anthropologists.[3] Some of the forms in which anthropologists stated this ideology are as follows:

1. Because primitives and aborigines live in simple societies, their study would reveal the paradigms of social life more easily than the study of complex societies, which could not easily be studied in their totality.

2. Primitives should be studied in order to discover the full range of solutions to problems of social life that mankind had invented.

3. The study of simple societies could provide us with insights into our own society and its values, thus enabling us to solve our own problems more readily. Primitive men live closer to the human condition than do the alienated men of capitalist, industrial society. Hence, the study of the primitive is no less than Western man's quest for his own original identity.

4. The world is a ready-made laboratory for the comparative study of cultures. The existence of primitive cultures makes possible comparative studies

[3] I have examined some consequences that this ideology has had for the work of anthropologists in my introduction to this book.

of child rearing, music, pharmacology, social roles, political institutions, and so forth and contributes to the building of a truly universal comparative science of man.

5. Primitives and aborigines should be studied now, before their extinction makes it impossible to preserve the record of world cultures.

6. Greater knowledge of the cultures of the world would make possible rational policies for bringing the developing countries and societies into the modern world while allowing them to retain their own distinctiveness and authenticity. If industrialization is to be brought to the preindustrial world, it should be brought without the negative features of eighteenth- and nineteenth-century industrialization in the West.

The image of the primitive included exotic customs, irrationality, and enchantment with the world. Methodical work, discipline, and the routinization of daily life were not part of the schemes of life in the worlds of primitives depicted by anthropological reporters. Primitives, tribesmen, and peasants knew their statuses and roles, passed through well-defined life stages marked by rites of passage, and lived simple and unharried lives compared to ours. This image of preindustrial society offered a striking contrast to industrial society. The negative features of industrialization and modernization were absent and primitive man was not yet alienated. Acceptance of the convention of the isolated ethnocentric society shaped the profile of anthropological researches more than any other single theoretical perspective. So long as anthropology could conceive of the world as a vast laboratory for the science of man, the anthropologist himself did not have to identify either with his own national ideologies or with the processes of Western conquest and penetration of the primitive and tribal world. The ideology of the universal science served as the cornerstone for upholding both the anthropologist's self-image as a disinterested scientist and the image of primitive and tribal society as an entity that could be studied in terms of itself alone. It was thus relatively easy to preserve the model of primitive society as a self-contained social organism in spite of the world historic and unrelenting penetration of industrial society and its institutions into all remote areas of the globe.

Within anthropology there are two lines of thought, Marxism and culture contact studies, that might have threatened the dominant model. For different reasons, neither did so. The anthropological Marxists such as V. Gordon Childe, Leslie White, and Julian Steward were more interested in the history of civilization than in the institutional tendencies of the eighteenth to twentieth centuries. Childe's Marxism was expressed in his archeological studies of the origins of civilization in the Middle East, where he attempted to show the origins of class structure and the invention of ideologies by ruling groups. His project was designed to support established Marxist theories by research on the evolution of early political institutions. Leslie White, following Morgan and Marx, wished to prove linearity in the evolution of world culture, and he finally focused on energy production as a universal index for the measurement of cultural evolution from low to higher stages. White's energy index went from hand labor to atomic power, and is primarily a theory of technological advance. Thus he shared with Marx a belief in progress.

Julian Steward's basic ideas were formulated in his study *Basin Plateau Aboriginal Socio-Political Groups,* where he tried to relate forms of sociopolitical groupings to ecological habitat, a theme which he also continued in his book *The People of Puerto Rico,* which tried to relate type of commodity production (sugar, coffee) to forms of social organization. The latter study also includes an investigation of the San Juan upper class, but failed in its effort to relate class, political administration, and production. Steward's work focused on production, and in this respect he was closest to Marx, but because he thought of himself as an anthropologist, he dealt with agricultural and not industrial production, in spite of the fact that Puerto Rico was already embarked on an industrialization program at the time of his study.

He and his colleagues did not attempt to relate the two forms of production to each other, as did Marx. Steward's Marxist orientation was restricted to preindustrial societies, and in this respect it was not equipped to examine the effects of the penetration of capitalism into the areas he studied. Marxist-oriented anthropologists did not focus on Marx's more obvious notion of the international division of labor and did not use this concept as the link between the industrial and preindustrial worlds. They did not do so because, as anthropologists, they did not think of themselves as students of the industrial world.

Students of culture contact, especially since Herskovits's use of the term "acculturation," tended to think of the contacts between the anthropological world and the industrial world as a mutual exchange of cultural artifacts, usages, traits, and occasionally personnel. Great emphasis was placed on the weight of tradition as a source of resistance to those elements of Western culture not suited to the context of primitive life and institutions. Students of acculturation pointed to the American reservation Indians as an illustration of the resilience of native culture under the impact of the dominant society surrounding it. It is only more recently, with some prodding from the Indians themselves, that American anthropologists have begun to see Indians as a minority group, impoverished and frequently bypassed by the larger society. In any case, the concept of acculturation deemphasized political and economic factors, so that when it was used, it tended to reduce the contact to a melange of cultural factors. Neither the culture contact nor the Marxist perspective challenged prevailing models employed by field investigators. As a result, dichotomization remained as a theoretical perspective long after its utility had been exhausted by the events of the twentieth century.

Some Effects of Anthropology on Aboriginal Society

Beginning in the early twentieth century, anthropology itself became one of the export commodities of the industrial nations. Aborigines trained in mission schools began to study anthropology in the metropolitan countries. Jomo Kenyatta of Kenya, Busia of Ghana, and Peter Buck of the Maori are early and better known examples of aborigines who became anthropologists. However, they were only forerunners of a trend that eventually included students from almost all areas of the world. During the cold-war period, aboriginal students were systematically recruited under programs organized by universities and foundations. The indigenous anthropologist became a new expert audience for the works of nonindigenous anthropologists.

The worldwide literacy movement and the growth of universities in all parts of the world have brought the anthropological monograph within reach of some members of the educated classes in most societies. It has been my observation, however, that higher education is not a necessary prerequisite for the stimulation of indigenous interest in the anthropological report. When I interviewed Palauans in the South Pacific in 1948 about their traditional institutions, I was referred to the ethnographic works of Japanese anthropologists who had studied Palau during the earlier Japanese occupation of these islands. Wherever anthropologists studied nonliterate societies, the local population placed great value on the monograph or book because it was an historical record which the society otherwise lacked.

As the rate of production of anthropological monographs increased and as the world literacy movement spread, anthropological publications became part of the public life and cultural heritage of the societies that were studied. It is widely known that the Indians of the Southwest, especially the Zuni and Navajo, not only stock ethnographic monographs about themselves in their tourist stores, but use these monographs as reference works concerning their own history and cultural practices. Studies of the mental health of the Nova Scotians or the Nigerians, based on Western-oriented measures of mental pathology, have been known to arouse the ire of both public officials and subjects. Where studies of the entire political structure of new or old nations have been published, as for example on Ethiopia and Ghana, or Steward's book on Puerto Rico, such books enter the mainstream of public debate and discussion. Oscar Lewis's work on the Sanchez family in Mexico City and his book *La Vida,* on slum dwellers in Puerto Rico, were regarded by political leaders and middle classes in both places as an affront to the national dignity, and productive of bad public relations for the American middle classes who were the readers of these books and potential future tourists.

To complete the spectrum of possibilities, Lawrence Wylie's book *Village in the Vaucluse,* about a town in southern France, was widely read by Americans before their summer trips to France. When in France these readers visited the village in such large numbers that tourism became a new industry in the town. Thus this ancient town, like Yucatan and Tepotzlan, was brought into the modern world by the ethnographer's book. His later study of the village of Chanzeaux in Anjou was carried out over a period of some ten years with the aid of several generations of Harvard students. The influence of this research

team on the town has been reported by Dr. William
Beer:

Off and on since 1958 Americans have been residing in Chanzeaux to do field work. They published a book on the village
which has been translated into French, a copy of which can
be found in nearly every home in the commune. A television
show was made that had Chanzeaux as its topic as a result
of the Americans, and an article, published in *Réalités* and
read by many Chanzeans, made some comments on the
Americans' favoring the Jolivet team (the new political elite)
and their style of politics. . . . The favor of the Americans
in general for Mayor Jolivet, Batardiere, Martineau, Cher-
bonnier, Bedouin, and Belliard has been well known for a
long time in the village and though some of the researchers
were friendly with Aubert and Charbonnier, it was clear that
they, specimens of a modernized world themselves, supported the new political elite. How influential they have been
cannot be quantitatively established, but it is certainly a factor. Hence the criterion "friend of Americans." In gathering
this information it was made quite clear that this meant
people who were generally known as friends of the Americans, not that those not listed so were necessarily hostile. In
this sense it was similar to a political badge of modernity.[4]

The ethnographic monograph has long since lost
its status as a document addressed only to scientific
and educated lay audiences in the metropolitan coun-

[4]William Beer, "Chanzeaux in Transition: Modernization in a Village of
Anjou," Ph.D. dissertation, Graduate Faculty, New School for Social Research, 1974, p. 264.

try. Now the field worker must reckon with his subjects as part of his audience, and this change is a symptom of the altered status of the subject. For present purposes we may illustrate the substance of this changed relationship with examples from American Indians and African Pygmies. American reservation Indians have been among the most intensively studied natives in the world. Generations of American graduate students have written dissertations on them, and many anthropologists have maintained lifelong relations with Indians on a particular reservation. For their part, the Indians were ghettoized reservation inhabitants whose main connections to the outside world were anthropologists and the Bureau of Indian Affairs. The caste relation of the Indians vis-à-vis the dominant society was legally supported by the Bureau, so that the anthropologist, in studying the Indian, also willy-nilly supported the caste structure of which he was a part. Yet as the following account shows, the Indians were hardly in a position to assert any rights to refuse to be studied:

We can mark the beginning of deteriorating relationships between Indians and anthropologists when, about twenty years ago, a joke came out of the Southwest which had already become a mecca for a great many anthropologists. The average Navajo family, it was said, consisted of father, mother, three children, and an anthropologist. In the last few years the joke has been repeated by Indians all over the country to describe an average Indian family. Furthermore, while more anthropologists have sometimes begun to mean more money for the Indian community, they do not necessarily mean more fun and sometimes they are no fun at all but a source of hurt. They are not so easily gotten rid of today as in the past as there are always fresh reinforcements from our growing ranks. A lone stranger can be dealt with but when the ratio approached 1:100 as I am told it does in some places, e.g., Hopi and Pine Ridge in the summer of 1969, Indians are hard put to decide what to do about such an invasion. It is also hard to just withdraw when working for the anthropologist helps put bread on the table.[5]

Clearly, this is an extreme example since there are no other cases except perhaps the Vicos project in Peru where the research funds of anthropologists have become a prop in the native economy. Yet the illustration makes the point that the Indian as a result of his caste position is relatively defenseless against the attention of the investigators. Not even the Bureau of Indian Affairs seems to be able to regulate this form of Indian hunting.

From the Indian's point of view, the presence of large numbers of anthropologists increases the market value of his information. In addition, his knowledge of native lore and culture becomes a valuable commodity which he must market selectively so as

[5]Nancy Oestreich Lurie, "As Others See Us," *New University Thought,* VII (Spring 1971), 4.

not to devalue it. One can imagine that such a situation might also stimulate the creative inventiveness of informants whose stock in trade has been exhausted. This possibility is difficult to document because the anthropologist himself may have a vested interest in the informant's inventiveness. I know of only one case where I suspect the natives played into the field investigator's conception of himself as an anthropologist by supplying him with data he wished to have. In his book *The Forest People,* Colin Turnbull reports how he was initiated into the secrets of the sacred tribal symbol of the Pygmies. He was told that the symbol could be viewed only at night and at a propitious time. One night he was awakened and led through the dead of night over treacherous forest trails. Eventually the group reached the place where the sacred symbol was located and Turnbull was allowed to see it. It turned out that the sacred object was a piece of sewer pipe, dug up and discarded by a construction crew that had built a road through the area. Turnbull took the Pygmies' sacred object at face value, and presents the astonished reader with his lucky discovery. I am inclined to believe that Turnbull wished it to be true and that the Pygmies thought of it as a joke. Of course, it is impossible to know how frequently such instances occur, but they can only occur if the anthropologist is insensitive to the natives' reaction to his position of dominance and superiority. The "put-on" is the standard defense of the lower caste.

In practical terms, I believe that the "natives" have become worldly, sophisticated, defensive with respect to their own traditions, and conscious of their inferior status in relation to the anthropologist and the society he is thought to represent. Acceptance of the superiority of advanced industrial society results in a sense of status inferiority in relation to the representatives of the dominant industrial nations. It also produces a psychology of the underdog or the outcast who must learn to live by his wits in a world where the dominant caste accepts its position of dominance without conscious reflection. The social psychology of the "native" is in part a product of both the anthropologist and the institutions of the society he represents.

The Defeat of Tradition and the Substitution of Goals

By now it is understood that the older and simpler forms of ethnocentrism based on attitudes of the superiority of one's own culture have been deeply shattered for most of the small and some of the large-scale societies of the world. This has resulted not only from the breakdown of the spatial and territorial isolation of all but a few of the world's communities, but also because the dominant tendencies of world drift have been felt almost everywhere. For example: 1. The rates and intensity of penetration of industrialization and resource exploitation has accelerated and has reached all previously remote areas. 2. The scope of corporate organization is worldwide. Bureaucracy as an instrument of organization and policy execution has become in its policy consequences a feature of all the world's communities. 3. Worldwide organization and distribution of mass media and its byproducts make available alternative information, patterns of conduct, and images of life styles to audiences everywhere on the globe.

If the field-worker anthropologist continues to operate on the assumption that he is studying a self-contained society whose relationship with the dominant industrial countries is not central to its internal existence, he is making an assumption that is not shared by his subjects and informants. The latter, as residents and inhabitants of new nations, small countries, and penetrated areas, have been subject to the policies of the dominant industrial countries and their agencies long enough to understand that their societies do not possess internal autonomy.

Fluctuations in world prices for basic commodities may mean feast or famine for a particular production area. Competition between industrial powers for control in a given part of the world may accidentally increase the importance of one and decrease the importance of another place. Agreements on spheres of influence between dominant powers may destroy the bargaining position of one country and increase the strategic value of another. A war between industrial nations may make battle fields of what were once thought to be remote and isolated areas of the earth. It is difficult for members of smaller nations and penetrated territories to maintain any illusions of ethnocentric superiority because the overwhelming weight of the dominant industrial countries has been felt everywhere.

The very conception of the Third World, so called, was given its definition in relation to the other worlds and could not exist except in relation to them, as has been shown by the Third World disarray created by the Nixon-Brezhnev-Mao policy of détente. Nonetheless, the failure to develop a unified Third World attitude in no way reduces the importance of the dominant nations in the lives of Third World inhabitants. Even in disarray, the Third World remains committed to industrialization and to an emulation of the social institutions of Western industrial nations. This social-psychological orientation to the world centers of industry and political power now underlies the cultural situation of almost all societies studied by anthropologists.

No areas of the world have been left untouched, though rates and intensities of penetration may vary from region to region. Thus some areas distant from metropolitan centers may be influenced in greater depth than those nearby. Similarly, areas within industrialized nations may remain untouched while remote areas may undergo intensive modernization. Small town, rural, and remote areas within dominant countries may be culturally and economically isolated in the same way that tribal and peasant societies once were. The logic of penetration has been governed, not by distance or by national or societal boundaries, but by available sources of labor, raw materials, and other economic and political opportunities.

The challenge to older forms of ethnocentrism has been worldwide and the communities and the societies of the world have absorbed in varying measure the social effects of the spread of industrial civilization. In some cases, aboriginal societies have been destroyed by policies of genocide and, in other cases, their populations have survived while their cultures have disappeared. In still other cases—for example, Russian ethnic groups under Stalin's nationality policies—populations have been politically and economically integrated while retaining language and cultural customs. The latter has commonly occurred in many other parts of the world as well. Everywhere, traditional cultural and social forms have been on the defensive and nowhere have revivalistic and messianic movements succeeded in reversing the process of modernization, industrialization, and urbanization.

By and large, the populations of the primitive, tribal, and peasant societies have accepted the values and goals of industrialized civilization. They have been willing to abandon their cultural traditions and their creeds (though they have less willingly accepted the idea of disciplined, methodical work for low wages) for the promise of a way of life that would eliminate the drudgery and monotony of their own way of life and allow them to participate in modern life-styles and in the excitement and anonymity of city life. They have replaced tradition with a commitment to the future and a hope for a share of the fruits of industrialization.

The traditional societies of the world have exchanged their past for a future that has not yet arrived, but which it is hoped will soon appear. Since industrialization's full impact has yet to be felt in these societies, its negative features have not yet been fully experienced, and commitment to industrialization remains a primary societal goal. The result is a sense of optimism about the future even though there is relatively little about their objective situation to warrant the hope or the optimism.

The source of hope and optimism in the developing world is derived from the expectation that it will achieve what it now sees only as a distant reality in the main centers of industrial civilization. Such hopes for other and better worlds have frequently been identified with religious ideologies and we may, perhaps, regard these newer ideologies as substitutes for the traditional ones that have been forgotten or abandoned. Insofar as this is the case, it would be incorrect to say that the industrialized nations have been wholly exploitative in their relations with the underdeveloped world. In exchange for material exploitation, they have supplied an image of a future for the other parts of the world. Their example provides a substitute in the form of hope for the abandoned spiritual values of traditional society.

The dialectic in the relations between the two worlds would be incomplete without an examination of other ideologies that have attempted to revive an image of primitive, tribal, and peasant society as superior to the urban industrial metropolis.

The Revival of Primitive and Tribal Values in the Metropolis

In the heart of industrial society, frequently in its most intensively urbanized centers, some groups of academic intellectuals, youth, particularly from the upper and middle classes, and some members of the economically successful middle classes and upper classes have rejected, in the tradition of romanticism and Rousseauism, the dominant tendencies in their own society and have opted for primitive, communal, and tribal life and expression. In some instances these forms of expression include images of primitive communism, socialism, and romantic anarchism. In practice, this has meant the establishment of rural and urban communes, migration from the city to recently abandoned rural areas within the metropolitan countryside, or to villages, islands, towns and archipelagoes in what were until recently primitive, tribal, and peasant territories. It also has meant pilgrimages, especially to India and to Mecca, to the ancient citadels of newly found religions, and other forms of withdrawal from participation in a society whose values are found to be unacceptable. Underlying these intellectual and geographical migrations is an effort to rediscover the lost world of preindustrial society which, for those sectors of the population engaged in the pursuit, never before existed as part of their personal experience. Theirs is a reaction to images of other ways of life whose sources lie in ideologies that have romanticized communal, agricultural, and primitive life-styles as being free from the problems of advanced industrial society.

The groups who have recently turned to these ideologies have been the college educated or their sons and daughters, and some have been exposed to these ideologies in their collegiate courses in anthropology and in the popularized anthropological reports on primitive and tribal societies. To some extent, academic anthropology has played the role within the metropolis of being the carrier of ideologies of primitivism and of preindustrial ways of life. Thus tendencies within anthropology have found a means of broader expression within the metropolis.

Within its own ranks, academic anthropology was affected by these same tendencies which, as we have indicated, were expressed in the ideologies of the internal integrity of primitive society and in the use of primitive societies as a point of departure for the criticism of capitalist industrial society. When efforts were made to practice these ideologies within the academic ranks, the result was an attempt on the part of some groups to think of the profession itself as a tribal grouping. The annual meeting of the association was likened to a gathering of the clans, and special efforts were made to give representatives of aboriginal groups a place on the program to exhibit their arts and crafts.[6] The practice of anthropology, which heretofore only preserved primitive artifacts

[6]The tradition of live specimens in anthropology goes back to the early explorers who returned to Europe with American Indians, Africans, and Pacific Islanders. In the United States, in the early part of this century, African blacks were exhibited as a matter of course as part of the freak shows connected with state fairs. In 1911 the last surviving member of the Yahi tribe, Ishi, was brought by Alfred Kroeber to the museum of anthropology at the University of California, Berkeley, where he was employed as part specimen and part maintenance worker until he died; see Theodora Kroeber, *Ishi in Two Worlds* (Berkeley: University of California Press, 1962).

in museums, has begun to include measures for the preservation of traditions which are disappearing in their original habitats.

Thus groups within the metropolitan centers are in the anomalous position of being unwilling to sustain ethnocentric attitudes with reference to their own society, but uphold as ideologies the ethnocentric values of past societies which are no longer the carriers of those same values on which their own original ethnocentrism was based.

Furthermore, this means that to the extent that primitive and preindustrial cultures are used as source materials for these newer ideologies, to that extent those who so use them have added a newer psychological level to the exploitation of primitive and preindustrial societies. This psychological form of exploitation is added to the older forms of exploitation such as colonialism, missionary proselytization, and direct economic exploitation.

The analysis can be carried one step further. Within the metropolis, romantic ideologies of the primitive and the preindustrial serve as a counterfoil for the disenchantment with one's own world of meaningless, repetitive, competitive work and the all but complete secularization of older religious ideologies. The preservation of the idea that there exists somewhere simpler, more comprehensible and authentic ways of life to which the individual can relate directly and meaningfully may be a source of hope and an avenue of escape for the disenchanted sectors of the middle and upper-middle classes.

Many parts of the world, such as the beaches of the Caribbean, Africa, the South Pacific, fishing and big-game hunting areas everywhere, and the surviving primitive and peasant cultures in many areas previously known only to anthropologists, missionaries, and businessmen have now become part of the established tourist world. The tourist appeal exists in spite of the fact that these same areas are being modernized and developed economically. The tourist industry is itself part of this economic development, but since it stresses the charm, exoticism, and primitive authenticity of the area, some elements of aboriginal culture are consciously preserved for the benefit of the tourists. This form of mummification of aboriginal culture requires natives as actors to assure their audiences that disenchantment is not universal. The entire performance is made possible by the application of rationality to the production of etiquette, courtesy, deference, and naive charm. The techniques of industry may preserve some dimensions of aboriginal cultures as part of an industrialization process which is capable of training natives to act like natives in social and ceremonial settings designed to recreate authentic cultures of the past.

Anthropology as an Applied Science

The above discussion points to some of the implications for anthropology if the assumption is made that the primitive, peasant, preindustrial, and excolonial societies are no longer to be treated as isolated or as polar dichotomies of the industrial world. To some extent, the governing ideology of anthropology has now changed and gives some recognition to the intensified rates of worldwide penetration and industrialization over the past thirty years. Many of the elements in anthropology's older creed have disappeared from the literature and have been replaced by themes developed during the cold war, the Vietnam War, and the university upheavals. Some of these newer themes are:

1. The study of culture enables us to assess a specific culture's potential for economic development. Rational planning for economic development is not possible without a consideration of cultural variables.

2. Analogues to Western cultural values that facilitate economic development—especially the Protestant ethic and ideologies of entrepreneurship—should be looked for and supported in the developing countries.

3. The discovery of the national values of new na-

tions can contribute to the process of nation building. Newly emerging nations would lack cultural cohesiveness unless they stressed their dominant integrating values.

4. The anthropologist has a critical role to play as consultant in the formation of aid programs and political strategies for the underdeveloped world.

5. Peasants and peasant cultures are major forces for social and revolutionary change in underdeveloped countries. Peasants such as those in Cuba, Mexico, Vietnam, and China are a source of energy in revolutionary independence movements against the dominant colonial powers. The domination of dominant powers can be checked by the internal resistance of rural peasant masses. Capitalist and big-power domination will be checked by Third World movements.

6. The research skills of the anthropologist, especially his ability to live with the people and to observe while participating, are ideally suited to the study in the metropolis of the lower and working classes, slums, classrooms, educational institutions, and communes. Urban anthropology, anthropology and education, anthropology and utopian communities, and revolutionary and countercultural movements in the metropolis are not only legitimate subject matter for anthropology, but are central sources for stimulating opposition to the domination of capitalist institutions.

These newer ideological themes record the split within anthropology of those who supported cold-war goals and those who opposed capitalism and big-power domination in general. The latter group (represented by those who see peasants and urban masses as revolutionaries) hope to link the peasants of the underdeveloped world and the workers, students, and urban masses of the developed world into a new revolutionary world force that would contribute to the downfall of, especially, capitalism. However, in spite of these ideological differences, the newer themes shared with the older ideologies a vision of a dichotomized world. The dichotomy was now expressed in such terms as developed and underdeveloped, advanced and developing, industrialized and industrializing, exploiters and exploited, alienated and unalienated, capitalist-communist and Third World. The older imagery of small-scale primitive societies and communities was replaced by images of larger groupings and entities, but the opposition between the groupings and entities was retained.[7]

[7]Today, use of such terms as "primitive," "preliterate," "nonliterate," and "aborigine" is a source of embarassment to both the anthropologist and his subjects. Moreover, the invention of such terms as "underdeveloped" and "developing" has done little to assuage those who are so designated, because they imply a continuous state of backwardness as well as the self-defined superiority of the designators. For the time being, the terms "industrializing" and "modernizing" seem to be in vogue, but they too imply the invidious comparison. The failure to find acceptable terms to refer to the exprimitives is simply a linguistic symptom of the fact that the problem so defined lacks a solution.

302 The Method and Theory of Ethnology

While the world scope of the industrial powers' influence was recognized in theory, the newer ideologies expressed a commitment to social engineering for economic development and political modernization, and to activist participation in creating social change and revolution. Both left and right are prepared to assist their subjects to achieve the goals which they have defined for them.

The newer ideology points to a belief that anthropology as a science can, through its "researches," produce the means for transforming the world and making it amenable to the reason of either industrialization or revolution. In either case, anthropology is conceived of as an instrumental science governed by ideals which are higher and beyond those of science itself. This is a newer form of applied anthropology which goes beyond that of the anthropologist as adviser to the colonial administrator or resident director of the Indian reservation. This desire to apply anthropological knowledge to the solution of the world's problems is part of a tradition that goes back to the original idea of the philosopher-king, but which, in its newer application, takes the whole world as its arena for action.

Yet today it is understood that public and private agencies have an interest in using anthropology for their own purposes. These agencies include foundations with high-minded social objectives, intelligence organizations with covert objectives, revolutionaries who would overthrow capitalism, exaborigines in pursuit of their self-interests, and governments of both large and small nations. The desire of others to use anthropology is a general phenomenon. American anthropologists, like sociologists, psychologists, and economists before them, have had to discover that the sponsors of anthropological research do not forfeit their right to exercise direct or indirect control over those whom they sponsor.

Anthropology sits astride the horns of a dilemma. As a policy science dedicated to transforming the world by peaceful or revolutionary means, it is necessarily committed to the goals and objectives of its sponsors, whether these sponsors are modern governments, heroic nineteenth-century revolutionaries, or both, as is frequently the case. As a science of man, it is dedicated to the discovery of universal truths in a world which it has not made and which changes even faster than the capacity of received theory to comprehend it. Seen in this light, even claims to instrumentality may be voided by the march of events, so that abrupt changes in policy—for example, the shift from cold war to détente—may require additional modifications in ideologies of instrumentalism. The same world-historic forces which gave anthropology an opportunity to claim itself the science of man have also broken the boundaries of parochial ethnocentrism on which the claim was partly based.

The long-term, worldwide drift toward industrialization and urbanization, and the application of rationality to the solution of man's material and spiritual requirements is not likely to abate. With time, all but isolated areas will have come within the reach of the central tendencies of modern civilization. When this occurs, the traditions of primitive, tribal, and peasant societies will have ceased to exist.

However, as older traditions disappear, newer traditions will appear, but these newer traditions, simply because they are new, do not possess legitimacy based on acceptance. The former bearers of the older traditions may begin to view their own pasts with feelings of nostalgia in the same sense that images of those same traditions have served inhabitants of advanced industrial societies with counterimages that have enabled them to reject their own societies. When industrial and urban civilization becomes the dominant tradition of the world, almost all populations will be able to share in the rejection of it and in a longing for simpler, more primitive and pastoral forms of existence that no longer exist except as they are recreated by the process of industrialization. If and when this happens, the images of primitive, tribal, and peasant life supplied by anthropology will be a source of raw materials for the creation of myths and life-styles that allow the inhabitants of industrial civilization to reject their world while living in it. In this sense, anthropology may yet achieve its objective of becoming an applied science.

But the role of the anthropologist as myth-maker for the industrialized, alienated world of the present and future is likely to be effective only if anthropologists communicate in forms of language and vocabularies that are directly comprehensible to their domestic and international audiences. If, however, the anthropologist, in his efforts to be scientific, stresses technical vocabularies and specialized modes of communication (like mathematical models which are based on codes intelligible only to other professionals), anthropology is not even likely to be able to fulfill a mission as a supplier of raw materials for the creation of myths and new combinations of life-styles.

Another role available to anthropology as an applied science is to become producer and distributor of old and new radical political ideologies. As the penetrated provinces and countries of the world absorb more fully the full effects of penetration, resentment and hostility against the penetrators is likely to increase. Moreover, just as in the advanced industrial countries where it is industrialism that is resented, the locus of this resentment is likely to be the educated middle and upper-middle classes, in-

cluding in some instances former natives who have
become professional anthropologists. These classes,
having arrived and now possessing vested interests
of their own, are likely to express their interests in
ideologies designed to preserve the historic traditions
of their own society. In so doing, they will renew and
revitalize, to suit their own needs, the earlier Rousseauism and romanticism of American anthropology.
In their case, however, it will be with respect to their
own past as this past was given or brought to them
by Western anthropology. Anthropology's historic
romance with primitivism and tradition will be given
a new lease on life by those whom anthropologists
in the metropolis would regard as exprimitives.

The modern anthropologist in the metropolis who
clings to his romance with primitiveness is more likely
to identify with ideologies that promise the salvation
of mankind and the restitution of men to their original
humanity. At a political level, Marxism and Maoism
are obviously possible choices and have been chosen
by those whose inclinations are revolutionary. When
this choice is made, however, the revolutionary project is planned less for the metropolis and more for
those areas of the world that have not yet reached
the levels of decadence said to exist in the advanced
industrial nations. Mankind, it is hoped, will be saved
by those who still retain some elements of primitiv-
istic purity, or failing the availability of such a con-

stituency, by the toiling peasantry of the world whose
direct connections to natural man are still retained
by virtue of working the soil. These anthropologists,
as self-proclaimed missionaries to the Third World,
have replaced the older missionaries and have combined with the newer radical Christian missionaries,
especially of the Catholic Church, who have also
elected to enact their politics in overseas areas. Thus,
the "New Left missionaries" to the penetrated areas
of the world, like the multinational corporations, are
part of the overall process of penetration, and carry
out their mission whether invited or not.

The revival of Marxism in the metropolis by these
same anthropologists has taken a new form. The earlier Marxists' connections to Marx through the concept of evolution via Morgan, White, and Steward
are deemphasized. Now it is Marx himself who is
emphasized. Apparently the prohibition on the use
of Marx's name which went into effect in 1948–50
under McCarthyism has been rescinded. Under détente and the termination of the cold war, these anthropologists have found it convenient to rehabilitate
Marx and have done so without opposition from the
political establishment. In his new persona as an anthropologist, Marx has been assigned a conventional
role as an academic commodity. In this role Marxism
is likely to generate still another set of secondary and
tertiary investment sectors in the curricula and pub-

lications industries, and should supply anthropology with additional materials for exegetical analysis. If these teachings of Marx by the New Left anthropology are to be used, it is less likely that they will be applied in the metropolis than in the Third World by Third World students trained in the metropolis. Revolutionary activity would thus become another form of anthropological field work. In addition to its other problems, such as industrialization, poverty and starvation, the Third World will have the privilege of conducting social experiments designed to bridge the gap between theory and practice.

Author and Title Index

A

American Museum of Natural History, 110
Ankermann, R., 75, 76
Année sociologique, L', 256n.
Anthropology, 44n.
Argonauts of the Western Pacific, The, 115n.

B

Bachofen, J. J., 253
Balfour, H., 67f.
Bastian, A., 72, 75, 77
Benedict, R., criticism, 42f., 141, 179f.
method and theory, 42f., 141, 179–180, 254
writings, 42n., 51n.
Bernheim, E., 80n.
Bernice Pauahi Bishop Museum, 70n.
Best, E., 70n.
Birket-Smith, K., 83n.
Blagden, C. O., 67
Bloomfield, L., 161
Boas, F., criticism, 5ff., 19f., 39f., 64f., 157, 160, 238

Boas, F., method and theory, xii, 4–19, 24–29, 39f., 49f., 52ff., 60, 80, 91ff., 101, 105, 114, 116n., 117, 131–134, 138, 142, 168, 176, 253f., 261, 267
writings, 8, 13, 19, 50n., 55n., 64, 110, 114
Bogoras, W., 84
Brinton, D., 97
Brown (*see* Radcliffe-Brown)
Bureau of American Ethnology, 88n., 110
Buschan, G., 74n.

C

Callaway, H., 62, 64f., 67
Castren, M. A., 83
Chief's Daughter and the Orphan, The, 186, 238ff.
Children of the Sun, The, 162n.
Codrington, R. H., 62, 66f., 118
Coming of Age in Samoa, 26
Comte, A., 84
Concept of the Guardian Spirit in North America, The, 51n.
Configurations of Culture in North America, 180n.
Crantz, H., 83n.
Crashing Thunder, 202n.
Culture, 54, 174n.

Norden, E., 186n.
Nordenskiöld, E. von, 85–86, 127

O

Oral Tradition in History, 50n.
Origin and Growth of Religion, The, 78
Origin of Totemism, The, 13*

P

Pallas, M. P., 83
Parsons, E. C., 20n.
Patwin and their Neighbors, The, 45
Perry, W. J., 24, 133, 160f., 163
Peschuel, Loesche, E., 76n., 118
Peyote Cult of the Winnebago Indians, The, 189n.
Polynesian Society, The, 70n.
Powell, J. H., 90ff., 97
Present Position of Anthropological Studies, The, 20n.
Preuss, K. T., xii, 75f.
Primitive Culture, 3
Psychologie des Primitiven Denkens, 181n.

Q

Queries, 163n.

R

Radcliffe-Brown, A., criticism, 170ff., 182
   method and theory, xii, 20, 24f., 52, 119, 171–173, 182, 255, 261
   writings, 20n.

Radin, P., criticism, 139ff.
   method and theory, xiii, 32–39, 68, 139–142, 186–252, 257
   writings, 32n., 50n., 135
Radloff, W., 83
Rasmussen, K., 83n., 96n.
Ratray, R. S., 67, 118f.
Ratzel, F., 72, 75
Reichsmuseums, Katalog des Ethnographischen, 82n.
Religion of the Kwakiutl, The, 64
Religious System of the Ama-Zulu, The, 62n.
Reports of Fifth Thule Expedition, The, 83n.
Reports of the Jesup Expedition, The, 110
Reports of the Torres Straits Expedition, The, 66
Rice, S., 16n., 128n.
Rink, H., 83n.
Ritual and Significance of Winnebago Medicine Dance, The, 135f.
Rivers, W. H. R., criticism, 118, 157ff.
   method and theory, xii, 10, 61, 68–69, 78, 118, 133, 157–166
   writings, 10, 69n., 118
Robertson-Smith, W., 14, 62
Roscoe, J., 67, 118
Rousseau, J. J., writings of, 253

S

Sahagun, B. de, 65, 105
Sapir, E., criticism, 17, 42, 56f., 238
   method and theory, xiii, 16f., 29, 51, 55–60, 92, 146, 254

Subject Index

A

Acculturation, study of, 15, 26, 51f., 120ff., 186ff.
Adhesions, theory of, 133ff.
Africa, cultures of, 61f., 75n., 77
Antiquarianism, 88f.
Arapaho, 50n., 111f., 146ff., 152, 154
Areas, culture, theory of, 21ff., 29ff., 53
Association, frequency of, principle of, 58
Australia, cultures of, 137, 159

B

Baptiste, J., 24ff.
Bible, peyote interpretation of, 188, 202f., 215, 218f., 231
Blackfoot, 110ff., 152, 154
British Columbia, cultures of, 137

C

Centers, culture, 21ff., 142
Cheyenne, 111, 146f.
Combination, principle of, 77ff.
Configurations, cultural, 16, 42ff., 141, 169, 179f.
Content and form, problem of, 141
Convergence, theory of, 77, 138, 142

Criteria, cultural, establishment of, 5ff., 16, 39ff., 55ff., 68f., 77ff., 131ff., 157ff., 163ff., 180f.
Crow, 110f.
Culture, origin of, multiple, 11, 175f.
  primitive, interpretations of,
    analytical-psychological method, 5ff., 29, 39ff., 50f., 111ff., 136ff.
    culture-historical method, 6, 10f., 13f., 20, 31ff., 40f., 63, 82f., 169, 184
    evolutionary method, 3ff., 14, 24, 61ff., 68, 131–133, 170ff., 173ff.
    functionalist method, 24, 115, 169, 171ff., 177ff., 255
    quantitative-distributional method, 6, 21, 24, 29, 50ff., 59f., 99, 129–167, 169, 183
    reconstruction from internal evidence, 32ff., 68, 139ff., 180–252
    statistical method, 61ff., 131–133
    typological method, 85f., 127
Cultures, aboriginal, definition and nature of, 5ff., 22f., 26ff., 29ff., 41ff., 44ff., 56f., 61ff., 70, 71ff., 81ff., 90, 94ff., 98ff., 120ff., 169ff., 184

315

Other Books of Interest from *Bergin & Garvey*

APPLIED ANTHROPOLOGY
An Introduction
JOHN VAN WILLIGEN
288 Pages   Photos

AGING & CULTURAL DIVERSITY
New Directions & Annotated Bibliography
HEATHER STRANGE & MICHELE TEITELBAUM
352 Pages

QUEST FOR THE REAL SAMOA
The Mead/Freeman Controversy & Beyond
LOWELL D. HOLMES
256 Pages

IN SEARCH OF EVE
Transsexual Rites of Passage
ANNE BOLIN
160 Pages

AFRO-CARIBBEAN FOLK MEDICINE
The Reproduction & Practice of Healing
MICHEL S. LAGUERRE
256 Pages

COLONIALISM & AFTER
An Algerian Jewish Community
ELIZABETH FRIEDMAN
288 Pages

DEVELOPMENT AND DECLINE
The Evolution of Sociopolitical Organization
HENRI J.M. CLAESSEN, PIETER VAN DE VELDE, M. ESTELLIE SMITH &
CONTRIBUTORS
384 Pages

NEW METHODS FOR OLD-AGE RESEARCH
CHRISTINE L. FRY, JENNIE KEITH & CONTRIBUTORS
320 Pages   Illustrations

MEAD'S OTHER MANUS
Phenomenology of the Encounter
LOLA ROMANUCCI-ROSS
256 Pages   Illustrations

WOMEN'S WORK
Development & the Division of Labor by Gender
ELEANOR LEACOCK, HELEN I. SAFA & CONTRIBUTORS
320 Pages   Illustrations

WOMEN & CHANGE IN LATIN AMERICA
JUNE NASH, HELEN I. SAFA, & CONTRIBUTORS
384 Pages   Illustrations

POLITICAL ANTHROPOLOGY
An Introduction
TED C. LEWELLEN
Foreword by Victor Turner
160 Pages   Illustrations

THE ANTHROPOLOGY OF MEDICINE
From Culture to Method
LOLA ROMANUCCI-ROSS, DANIEL MOERMAN, LAURENCE R. TANCREDI & CONTRIBUTORS
416 Pages   Illustrations

TRIBES ON THE HILL
The United States Congress — Rituals & Realities
J. McIVER WEATHERFORD
320 Pages

THE STRUGGLE FOR RURAL MEXICO
GUSTAVO ESTEVA
320 Pages

SEX & CLASS IN LATIN AMERICA
JUNE NASH, HELEN SAFA & CONTRIBUTORS
352 Pages   Illustrations

WOMEN AND COLONIZATION
MONA ETIENNE, ELEANOR LEACOCK & CONTRIBUTORS
352 Pages   Illustrations

THE NICARAGUAN REVOLUTION IN HEALTH
From Somoza to the Sandinistas
JOHN DONAHUE
188 Pages   Illustrations

SPIRITUALIST HEALERS IN MEXICO
KAJA FINKLER
Foreword by Arthur Kleinman
272 Pages

WOMEN & NUTRITION IN THIRD WORLD COUNTRIES
SAHNI HAMILTON & CONTRIBUTORS
160 Pages

TRANSNATIONALS & THE THIRD WORLD
The Struggle for Culture
ARMAND MATTELART
192 Pages

IN HER PRIME
A New View of Middle-Aged Women
JUDITH BROWN, VIRGINIA KERNS & CONTRIBUTORS
240 Pages   Illustrations

PEOPLE IN POWER
Forging a Grassroots Democracy in Nicaragua
GARY RUCHWARGER
320 Pages   Illustrations

THE CONTRAS
Interviews with Anti-Sandinistas
DIETER EICH & CARLOS RINCÓN
208 Pages   Photographs

NICARAGUA — *THE PEOPLE SPEAK*
ALVIN LEVIE
Introduction by Richard Streb
224 Pages   Illustrations

CRISIS IN THE PHILIPPINES
The Making of a Revolution
E. SAN JUAN
288 Pages   Illustrations

U.S. LABOR & LATIN AMERICA
A History of Workers' Response to Intervention
PHILIP S. FONER
320 Pages

RECALLING THE GOOD FIGHT
An Autobiography of the Spanish Civil War
JOHN TISA
265 Pages   Illustrations

THE POLITICS OF EDUCATION
Culture, Power & Liberation
PAULO FREIRE
240 Pages   Illustrations

LITERACY
Reading the Word & the World
PAULO FREIRE & DONALDO MACEDO
192 Pages   Photos

EDUCATION UNDER SIEGE
The Conservative, Liberal and Radical Debate Over Schooling
STANLEY ARONOWITZ & HENRY A. GIROUX
256 Pages

AMERICAN SOCIETY
The Welfare State & Beyond (Revised)
JOSEPH BENSMAN & ARTHUR J. VIDICH
416 Pages

ACADEMIC WOMEN
Working Towards Equality
ANGELA SIMEONE
176 Pages

MARCUS
Critical Theory & the Promise of Utopia
ROBERT PIPPIN, ANDREW FEENBERG, CHARLES P. WEBEL & CONTRIBUTORS
352 Pages

BEYOND REVOLUTION
A New Theory of Social Movements
DANIEL FOSS & RALPH LARKIN
Introduction by Stanley Aronowitz
256 Pages

BERGIN & GARVEY PUBLISHERS
670 Amherst Road
South Hadley, Mass 01075
(413) 467-3113